NATIONAL PASTIMES

NATIONAL PASTIMES

Cinema, Sports, and Nation

KATHARINA BONZEL

UNIVERSITY OF NEBRASKA PRESS | LINCOLN

Portions of chapters 1 and 4 were
previously published in "Reviving
the American Dream: The World
of Sports," in *Learning from Mickey,
Donald and Walt: Essays on Disney's
Edutainment Films*, ed. A. Bowdoin
Van Riper (Jefferson NC: McFarland,
2014), 201–8. © 2011. Used with
permission of McFarland & Company,
Inc., Box 611, Jefferson NC 28640.
www.mcfarlandbooks.com.

An early version of chapter 2 was published
as "Soccer to the Rescue: How *The Miracle
of Bern* Gave Germans Their Identity
Back—Twice," *Sporting Traditions* 22, no.
2 (2006): 1–12. Used with permission of
the Australian Society for Sports History.

Portions of chapter 5 were previously
published as "*A League of Their Own*:
The Impossibility of the Female Sports
Hero," *Screening the Past* 37 (2013): n.p.

∞

Library of Congress
Cataloging-in-Publication Data
Names: Bonzel, Katharina, author.
Title: National pastimes: cinema, sports,
and nation / Katharina Bonzel.
Description: Lincoln: University
of Nebraska Press, [2020] | Series:
Sports, media, and society | Includes
bibliographical references and index.
Identifiers: LCCN 2019007288
ISBN 9781496215529 (cloth: alk. paper)
ISBN 9781496218247 (epub)
ISBN 9781496218254 (mobi)
ISBN 9781496218261 (pdf)
Subjects: LCSH: Sports films—History. |
Nationalism in motion pictures. | National
characteristics in motion pictures.
Classification: LCC PN1995.9.S67 B66
2020 | DDC 791.43/6579—dc23
LC record available at https://
lccn.loc.gov/2019007288

Set in Adobe Garamond by
Mikala R. Kolander.
Designed by N. Putens.

For Katie

CONTENTS

ILLUSTRATIONS

ACKNOWLEDGMENTS

Sometimes writing this book has felt like going thirteen rounds in the ring with Rocky; but thanks to the enduring support and cheer from family, friends, and colleagues, it has also at times felt like running up those stairs at the Philadelphia Museum of Art. This project would not have been possible without those who encouraged and supported me along the way. I am grateful to my colleagues at both the University of Melbourne and the Australian National University, and for the financial and in-kind support I received from both institutions and their libraries; this project was also generously supported by an Australian government scholarship. In particular, I would like to thank Jeanette Hoorn, Barbara Creed, Wendy Haslem, Nicholas Chare, Will Christie, Leslie Barnes, Kate Flaherty, Monique Rooney, Catherine Travis, Kate Mitchell, and Julieanne Lamond.

Friends near and far have commiserated and cheered in equal measures through this project, and I am grateful for their support, in particular Susy MacQueen, Rohan Chandran, Ishita Palit, Shae Parker McCashen, Isolde Lueckenhausen, Suntje Schmidt, and Sarah Cutfield.

My sincere thanks to the anonymous reviewers at the University of Nebraska Press, who pushed the manuscript in new and improved directions, and editors Alicia Christensen and Abigail Stryker, who have made the process of publishing as painless as possible; I am especially grateful to Alicia for her enduring enthusiasm and support for this project, and series editor Aaron Baker for supporting this publication from the start. Many thanks also to Sara Springsteen and Jane M. Curran and the rest of the production and design team at UNP for their keen eye for detail and the wonderful cover design.

My family both near and far has also been a wonderful source of support: Helen and Tassilo, Maria and Udo, Judy and Kevin, Kandida and Jürgen, Roman and Susanne, and all my fabulous nieces, nephews, and fairy godchildren! Lastly, none of this would have happened without my partner, Katie, to whom I'd like to say: "Yo, Adrian, I did it!"

NATIONAL PASTIMES

INTRODUCTION

> The name on the front is a hell of a lot more important
> than the one on the back!
>
> Herb Brooks in *Miracle* (2004)

The "name on the front" of the team jersey in the epigraph above is, of course, that of the United States of America. In *Miracle* (O'Connor, 2014), which celebrates the momentous win of the American national ice hockey team over the much-favored Soviet Union at the 1980 Winter Olympics in Lake Placid, Coach Herb Brooks (Kurt Russell) works hard to forge a team from a group of college players heavily invested in their existing college rivalries: to his oft-repeated demand "Who do you play for?" he receives answers such as "University of North Dakota" or "UMD Bulldogs." It is only after the captain of the team, Mike Eruzione (Patrick O'Brien Demsey), finally answers "I play for the United States of America" that the team's fortunes slowly begin to change: the seeds of success are sown in this patriotic declaration of national identity.

The "Miracle on Ice" depicted in this film demonstrates how closely ideas of nation and sports are intertwined. Remembering the event thirty years on, *New York Times* veteran sports reporter Gerald Eskenazi wrote that Coach Brooks "spoke passionately of creating an American style of hockey, a form of sport making use of capitalistic ideals—competition, exuberance, youth."[1] This crucial match came at the height of the Cold War, and in the dramatic historical context of the hostage crisis in Iran and the Soviet invasion in Afghanistan, it was widely received as a battle between West and East. This match, like many of the contests examined in this book, whether played out on ice, the football field, the athletics track, the baseball diamond, or on the basketball court, shows how sport so often transcends being merely a "game" that people play. It is intimately connected to a society's cultural, social, and national values and ideas. Sports films reflect and expand on these ideas and, most importantly, bring them to life in an emotionally engaging viewing experience. Film engages the spectator through sight and sound; it can persuade or deter, make the audience cry, laugh, or shiver with fear: it has the power to inspire emotions, values, and ideas. The sports film multiplies the affective potential of film with that of the sports contest to great effect, creating an emotionally charged experience that can help turn any number of social, political, and cultural issues into a persuasive narrative.

This book examines how sports films work to tell stories about national identity and belonging. It argues that ideas about the nation are often represented in culture in unexpected ways, intersecting with social identities such as those grounded in ethnicity, race, class, and gender. Popular cultural forms such as the sports film can provide a powerful point of identification for individuals; a locus of perceived national unity and community. At the same time, these films reflect the ways in which ideas about the nation and national belonging change over time and are always implicated in larger historical developments. From the Cold War paranoia of postwar America to the changing class dynamics in 1980s Thatcherite Britain, or the fragmented sense of nation in post-unification Germany, the sports films under scrutiny in *National Pastimes: Cinema, Sports, and Nation* provide a means for renegotiating understandings of the nation in an accessible, emotionally engaging form and take an active part in the maintenance and construction of national identity. The popularity of these films maximizes their ideological reach across social, cultural, and class boundaries, as they work to create new myths and strengthen old myths of the nation. With its focus on heroic deeds and mythic narrative form, the sports film is particularly suited to constructing and supporting myths of past and present national unity. In particular, this book explores how such films work to establish a sense of "emotional authenticity" in their representations of national identity through sport and actively renegotiate the individual's place within the nation, often with the help of what I call "hero Others."

These films frequently reach across boundaries of nation and genre. My aim is not to provide a comprehensive account of sports films around the world but rather to highlight, through the close analysis of a diverse group of iconic cinematic texts, the value and insights that can accrue from studying the multiple ways in which national identity is represented and at times contested by other social identities. I cover a time frame that begins in the mid-1970s, with what would later become one of the biggest sports film franchises in the history of cinema, if not *the* biggest: the *Rocky* series (1976–2018). While this book focuses on Western sports films, it challenges the dominance of Hollywood within existing research by examining films from other national contexts, in particular from Great Britain and Germany, countries with comparable cinematic traditions to the United States, but with very distinct ideas about, and expressions of, national identity. The continuing cultural currency of the main case studies of this study, from *Chariots of Fire* (Hudson, 1981) to *The Miracle of Bern* (Wortmann, 2004), and from the *Rocky* films to *Hoosiers* (Anspaugh, 1986), *Bend It Like Beckham* (Chadha, 2002) and *A League of Their Own* (Marshall, 1992), is demonstrated by their enduring presence in public life. For example, with the exception of *Hoosiers*, all of these films have been resurrected as musicals in Germany, the United Kingdom, and the United States. Both the *Miracle of Bern* and *Chariots of Fire* continue to serve as motivational reminders for athletes and their audiences every four years before the soccer World Cup championship (*Bern*) or Olympic Summer Games (*Chariots*). In Philadelphia every day, tourists and Philadelphians alike run up the seventy-two steps of the Philadelphia Museum of Art, reenacting the famous training sequence from the *Rocky* films. All of these films have captured the hearts and minds of their audiences both domestically and internationally, making them prime examples to investigate their role in discourses of the nation. *National Pastimes* brings theories of nation and national cinema together with methods of visual film analysis to provide the first in-depth study of how sports films cultivate spectators' engagement to construct and maintain national identity.

Sports Films: History and Genre

Since the early days of cinema, sports have featured fairly consistently in film, as is evidenced by the 612-page filmography by Harvey Marc Zucker and Lawrence J. Babich, *Sports Films: A Complete Reference*.[2] In the beginning, topical films about boxing matches or rowing regattas dominated the field, as this 1896 excerpt from the *Photographic Journal* illustrates: "Mr Birt Acres gave a demonstration of an apparatus which he called the Kinetic Lantern. The object of this was to throw a number of pictures upon the screen in such rapid succession as to reproduce the motion of life. . . . The subjects shown included men boxing, a review of the German Emperor, Epsom Downs, and the Derby race, serpentine dancing, and the sea breaking against an embankment."[3] These kinds of films eventually moved to television and would nowadays be considered "sports coverage"—the reporting of live sporting events as they happen. The sports documentary presents another, more investigative form of sports reportage and includes films about sports history or social commentary films, such as the critically acclaimed documentary *Hoop Dreams* (James, 1994), which follows two young basketball players as they try to make it to the NBA.

Yet sports films understood as narrative feature films were also an important and dynamic aspect of early cinema. "It was the beginning of sport as a worldwide popular phenomenon," as Luke McKernan observes, "something that went hand in hand with the rise of film through the twentieth century . . . we see the birth of twins: motion pictures and mass appeal sport."[4] Taking into account larger debates surrounding cinematic genres and sports as a cultural phenomenon, I argue that it is not only legitimate but indeed analytically productive to view the sports film as constituting a genre in itself. Although Seán Crosson notes that, historically, sports films were often identified "in terms of individual sports rather than sports as a whole,"[5] the sports film as a genre—or at least as a distinguishable film category—has long been accepted by cinema audiences and film critics alike. Scholarly acceptance, in contrast, has developed more slowly, with Deborah V. Tudor's *Hollywood's Vision of Team Sports: Heroes, Race, and Gender* from 1997 the first academic monograph on sports films, followed by a handful of significant studies, focusing particularly on Hollywood productions, by scholars such as Crosson, Aaron Baker, Nicholas Chare, and Bruce Babington.[6] These exceptions notwithstanding, the relative neglect of the sports film as a genre in its own right and as an object of cinematic analysis warrants closer examination and a more precise definition.

In their milestone work on film art David Bordwell and Kristin Thompson concede that a "genre is easier to recognize than to define" and conclude that "most scholars now agree that no genre can be defined in a single hard and fast way."[7] Genre definitions and their usefulness have long been contested within film theory.[8] While early studies sought to delineate the boundaries around certain genres—for example, what is a Western?—more recent scholarship emphasizes that genres are inherently flexible and multidimensional. In this context genre is commonly understood as multilayered, simultaneously representing "a particular mode of film production, often equated with the classic Hollywood studio system; a convenient consumer index, providing audiences with a sense of the kind of pleasures to be expected from a given film; and a critical concept, a tool for mapping out a taxonomy of popular film and for understanding the complex relationship between popular cinema and popular culture."[9]

Sports films often follow the model set by the classic Hollywood studio system and thus have a certain aesthetic style (for example, the fast editing and action replays of the sports contest), recurrent plot points (for example, the big game) and a familiar iconography in the mise-en-scène (for example, team jerseys, sporting paraphernalia, and the locker room). These characteristics are expected in turn by the audience that goes to see a "sports film." However, Jeffrey H. Wallenfeldt points out that "it isn't easy to define the difference between a sports film and a film with sports in it."[10] He argues that sports films must involve sporting contests of a competitive nature, and that the sports element needs to be of central importance to the narrative.

These two points are, I agree, crucial. For the purposes of this study, I define sports films as those that adhere to recognizable "patterns/forms/styles/structures which transcend individual films, and which supervise both their construction by the film-maker, and their reading by an audience."[11] These include the plot point of the "big game," a mise-en-scène filled with sports paraphernalia, and a visual style that seeks to re-create realistic sporting action; in these films competitive sports and, by extension, sports competitions are not only central to the narrative of the films but also propel it forward. These characteristics, however, are not seen as separate from but as integral to the sociocultural, political, and economic spheres and institutions in which the individual film is embedded. By this definition the popular film *Field of Dreams* (Robinson, 1989), about a man who turns the wheat field of his farm into a baseball field in order to reconnect with his past and reconcile with his father, is not a sports film. Neither are the Oscar nominated *Jerry Maguire* (Crowe, 1996) about a sports agent or Ivan Reitman's *Draft Day* (2014) about NFL drafting practices. Similarly, this definition excludes the 2015 film *Concussion* (Landesman), which tells the story of a forensic pathologist (Will Smith) trying to warn the NFL and its players of the dangers of repeated head injuries due to playing football. These films may well ask larger questions about the nature of sports having redemptive (or damaging) qualities, but since sports as a competitive contest is not a central part of the narrative, they remain, in my definition, films with sports in them rather than, per se, "sports films."

Genres are, after all, more than simply a set of features and expectations. They also work, as Christine Gledhill argues, as a "conceptual space" in which "issues of texts and aesthetics—the traditional concerns of film theory—intersect with those of industry and institution, history and society, culture and audiences—the central concerns of political economy, sociology, and cultural studies."[12] The sports film genre, with its myriad connections to a wide variety of social spheres through the diverse sporting cultures it references, offers a good example of such a conceptual space. Steve Neale argues, for example, that instead of being just fixed "bodies of work," genres are also "specific systems of expectation and hypothesis which spectators bring with them to the cinema and which interact with the films themselves during the course of the viewing process."[13] These "systems of expectation and hypothesis," in other words, necessarily influence the spectator's reading of the film. For instance, while the German soccer film *The Miracle of Bern*, examined in chapter 2, might be generally considered a classic sporting tale in the David versus Goliath vein, middle-aged German viewers familiar with the ensuing catchcry of "We are somebody again" might well feel reminded of their youth and the atmosphere of postwar change in 1950s Germany—a feeling that could in turn become the central aspect of their viewing experience.

This example points not only to the highly flexible boundaries of the sports film as a genre, which Bruce Babington describes as "a genre of considerable plasticity," but also introduces the notion of intertextuality, according to which texts—in this case films—can be, or indeed must be, read with awareness of their relation to other texts.[14] An increasing emphasis on the degree of intertextuality embedded in the cinematic text is, as Jim Collins observes, "at cross-purposes with the traditional notion of genre as a stable, integrated set of narrative and stable conventions."[15] While non-cinematic influences have softened the once seemingly stable boundaries of filmic genres, this is further complicated in the case of the sports film by uncertainty surrounding the very definition of sport itself: for example, does chess qualify? Anthropologists J. M. Roberts, M. J. Arth, and R. R. Bush have argued that games—and therefore, by extension, sports—are "a recreational activity characterized by (1) organized play (2) competition (3) two or more sides (4) criteria for determining the winner (5) agreed upon rules."[16] This definition of games and sports aligns with the definition of sports films I am developing here. The difficulty, however, involved in fixing the generic boundaries of the sports film are best illustrated by examining films that sit at the borders of this genre. Taking the example of chess, which easily fulfills the criteria set by Roberts, Arth, and Bush, the 1992 film *Knight Moves* (Schenkel) is about a series of murders during a chess tournament, as the chess grandmaster is pulled into a "deadly game" with the killer. If one considers chess a sport, understood as a competitive form of play, this still leaves open the question of just how important the sporting aspect of chess is to the film. Alternatively, this might be better categorized as what Wallenfeldt calls a "film with sports,"[17] for while chess is a part of the narrative, it is not the central focus of the film, as the attention is not so much directed toward the sport of chess, but rather to the chasing of the killer. Indeed, Robert Perinbanayagam has convincingly argued that sports and games are constructed as narratives into which human agents can inject themselves: "They [games] enable agents to engage with each other and develop ongoing dramas of the self with performances and presentations. And because each of these games presents a series of moves that are sequentially and causally related to each other with an agent (or a set of agents) as protagonists, they also enable him or her to narrate a self and obtain a sense of agency and control."[18]

The narratives of sports and games, with which human agents identify or in which they participate, are similar to narratives of film, defined by a narrative arc with a beginning, middle, and end. Sports films often align the narrative arc of the sport depicted with that of the film, albeit more often than not they use the longer narrative arc of a season rather than a single match. For example, *Hoosiers* follows the winning season of the Hickory Huskers, where each game mimics the narrative arc of the film, culminating in the final, championship-winning game. This last game is a mirror of the struggles and triumphs of the preceding season as well as of the narrative arc of the coach and his team beyond the court.

Sports Films and National Identity

The oft-predicted death of the nation at the hands of globalization—and with it the seeming permeability of national borders—has failed to materialize, and as Sabina Mihelj asserts, "far from being an obstacle to globalization, nationhood constitutes one of its fundamental premises."[19] Indeed, rather than the demise of the nation, the last twenty-five years have seen a rise of nationalism and right-wing populism, from the break-up of Yugoslavia to the resurgence of right-wing populist parties, such as the UK Independence Party (UKIP, strong supporters of Brexit), the Front National in France, or more recently the rise of the Alternative für Deutschland party (AFD) in Germany and the election of Donald Trump in the United States on the back of an increasing frustration with the political establishment's handling of the challenges of globalization. Trump's campaign slogan, "Make America Great Again," his populist nationalism, and his protectionist policies recall a time before globalization and reach out to the so-called globalization losers—the predominantly white working class.[20] The ideals of the nation-state these parties champion are rooted less in theories and critiques of globalization than in theories of nation from the last century.[21] In the face of globalization, the relationship between the local and the global is, as Wimal Dissanayake puts it, "convoluted and complex," making an investigation of the many ways in which popular culture reflects the discourses of nationalism all the more pertinent.[22] Arguably, sports films from the 1970s and 1980s were produced before the increasing onslaught of globalization on the nation-state, allowing for much clearer visions for the role of nations and national identity than the late 1990s and early 2000s afforded with the rapidly increasing interconnectedness of the world. Yet even in very recent films, this study argues, nationalism and national identity are not only far from extinguished but keep intervening in how audiences understand their national belongings, and thus remain productive research frameworks.

Representations of sports in films are intricately connected to the larger "imagined community" of the nation, with all its constructed ideologies and mythologies.[23] Indeed Perinbanayagam argues (using "games" and "sports" in an interchangeable sense) that "games are, in fact, mimeses of the interactional life of human agents who live in organized societies," or, to put it differently, games and sports are effectively society writ small. They function as an "as if" space allowing us to perform our self in different ways—testing our emotions, expressing our values, and challenging our relationships to others.[24] Similarly, David Rowe points out that "it is clear that they [mythologies and ideologies of sports] share a profound attachment to the idea that sports constitute a subsystem of signs that can be scrutinized for their capacity to reveal or represent 'truths'—direct or indirect, literal or metaphorical—about the social world."[25]

Thus sports are an intricate part, not only of everyday life but also of the larger community of the nation. Sports in film can then function as a virtual "sandbox," a safe space in which those same values, emotions, and challenges expressed in sports with which the audience is familiar from their everyday life can be negotiated, challenged, or affirmed. It is in this space, this book argues, that we can see interconnection between everyday life and the maintenance and construction of the nation and national identity.

While my aim here is not to reproduce the extensive existing debates around national cinemas, it is important to note the difference between national cinemas, in the sense of a cinema attached to a particular nation-state (e.g., German Cinema), and the representation of national identity in film (e.g., Germanness in *The Miracle of Bern*). In exploring the relationship between sports films and national identity, this book builds upon investigations of nationalism and national cinemas by scholars such as Benedict Anderson, Michael Billig, Susan Hayward, and Mette Hjort. I focus particularly on the *idea* of national identity: how the nation and national identity are represented both in film generally, within the genre of the sports film, and, specifically, in the individual film examined in this book. While classic studies of nationalism, such those by Ernest Gellner and Anthony Smith, tend to concentrate on notions of official, traditional "high cultures," studies such as Billig's and Hjort's point to the frequently overlooked role of "popular" and everyday cultures in forming and maintaining nationalisms, nations, and identities.[26]

Michael Billig's notion of "banal nationalism" provides a particularly fruitful point of entry for this study for the way it examines nationalism as everyday occurrences—signaled by "a continual 'flagging,' or reminding, of nationhood"—with the implication that nations are maintained rather than created.[27] This maintenance of ideas about the nation and nationhood he terms banal, but not benign: far from being something extreme and on the periphery, nationalism is common and continuous: "In so many little ways, the citizenry are daily reminded of their national place in a world of nations. However, this reminding is so familiar, so continual, that it is not consciously registered as reminding. The metonymic image of banal nationalism is not a flag which is being consciously waved with fervent passion; it is the flag hanging unnoticed on the public building."[28]

National identity in sports films "works," I argue, through similar mechanisms; these are largely unconscious, yet at the same time omnipresent, constructing and maintaining national identity by a continual subtle flagging: from children dressed in lederhosen in *The Miracle of Bern* to the classic styling of the American football team jacket.

Susan Hayward, on the other hand, argues that the nation replaces the lost premodern realities of kinship and family; it is an ideological construct that aims to form a relationship between a defined cultural group and the nation-state. Referring to Anderson, Hayward points out that the imagined communities that form nations are often considered natural entities, although they are in fact discursively constructed. She concludes that national identity is equally unnatural and constructed: "each concept masquerades as a grounded reality, disguising the fact that, as such, these are imagined abstractions"; cultural artefacts such as films are produced to represent these "imagined abstractions."[29] Sports films, as this book shows, often reaffirm and strengthen these "imagined abstractions," often favoring older ideals of the nation, with Hollywood films such as *Hoosiers* harking back to a mythical "Golden Age" that never was. The nature of sports competitions with their clear heroes and antagonists represent stable social orders and geographical borders ("us versus them"), thus helping to delineate social and geopolitical boundaries. Hollywood sports films in particular make use of these clear-cut boundaries, more often than not affirming conservative race, class, and gender ideals. This trend has continued to shape post-9/11 sports films, such as the working-class hero in *The Fighter* (Russell, 2010) embarking on his search for the American dream, or the "white savior" narrative inherent in films such as *The Blind Side* (Hancock, 2009) and *McFarland, USA* (Caro, 2015).

Yet sports films can also work differently, as I show in my analyses of *Chariots of Fire*, *The Miracle of Bern*, and *Bend It Like Beckham*. Sport, as Crosson observes, "has also on occasion provided a means for filmmakers to contest hegemonic constructions of the nation."[30] Hayward suggests that an ideal national cinema should expose—consciously or otherwise—the structures of power and knowledge that constitute the nation. "By exposing its masquerade of unity," she argues, the ideal national cinema would lay bare the scattered fragments of a national culture that is commonly believed to be homogenous.[31] *National Pastimes* argues that sports films, perhaps surprisingly, can be prime examples of the kinds of cultural artifacts that contain less cohesive or "nationalistic" narratives and subtexts, in turn exposing the instability of the concept of national identity itself. The German film *The Miracle of Bern*, for example, imaginatively reclaims a decidedly West German founding myth to redefine a sense of belonging for a reunified nation, thus broadening conceptions of who belongs to this new imagined community. Similarly *Bend It Like Beckham* explicitly expands the boundaries of what it means to be part of a modern Great Britain. Yet close analysis of more mainstream sports films, such as *Chariots of Fire* or the *Rocky* franchise, shows that these, too, while seemingly affirming hegemonic ideals of national identity, often unwittingly reveal resistances to these very ideals and present far less stable visions of national unity than has often been assumed.

Building on Billig's and Hayward's studies, the central argument of this book is that national identity, far for being a natural or fixed entity, is constantly produced and reproduced, or, to put it differently, is maintained through everyday culture, of which sports films are a part. *National Pastimes* examines the specific conditions of the relationship between sports, film, and the nation across a range of national contexts to highlight the ways in which national specificity is reflected and to show that national identity is actively reproduced and maintained through the sports film. Specifically this book is concerned with charting how these processes function in the sports film—a genre that is particularly suitable for such an analysis due to the strong links between sports and the nation and also because of its high level of mainstream popularity, which ensures that these maintenance processes reach into all corners of the population. I examine these maintenance processes by combining close textual and visual analysis with the analysis of larger historical contexts, from Cold War to post-9/11 America, and from the changing class dynamics in 1980s Thatcherite Britain to Cool Britannia or the fragmentation of post-unification Germany, bringing together considerations of film production and cultural, political, and economic history. Films such as the 1981 *Chariots of Fire* or the 1976 *Rocky* are defined by radically different social, cultural, and political environments than, for example, post-9/11 films such as the latest offshoots of the *Rocky* saga, *Creed* (Coogler, 2015) and *Creed II* (Caple Jr., 2018). Yet as I argue in chapter 3, which for the first time charts the development of the American dream throughout the entire history of the *Rocky* franchise, the films demonstrate both a remarkable flexibility in their definition of the dream, while somewhat paradoxically propagating a consistently conservative view of what it means to be American.

Representing Authenticity

Since the early days of sports films, as Scott A. G. M. Crawford observes, "fact was leavened with fiction and reality tempered by liberal doses of illusion, myth and personal fable."[32] From Harold Lloyd's entirely fictional account of college football in *The Freshman* (Newmayer/Taylor, 1925) through to the attempt to incorporate World Heavy Weight Champion Max Schmeling as both an actor and himself in the early German boxing film *Liebe im Ring* (*Love in the Boxing Ring*, Schünzel, 1930), and on to *Knute Rockne—All American* (Bacon, 1940), a biopic about the legendary Notre Dame football coach, sports films have engaged in a complex relationship with authenticity and realism. While some films claim to depict the sport in question as realistically as possible, others concentrate on authenticity of narrative and characters. A brief survey of post-2000 productions centered on sports narratives reveals this still to be the case: the multi-award-winning *Million Dollar Baby* (Eastwood, 2004) was entirely fictional, while the inclusion of professional soccer player Vinnie Jones added a realist bent to *Mean Machine* (Skolnick, 2001) in much the same way that the real life boxers did in the *Rocky* films.[33] A large number of successful sports films in this period also fit into the tradition of the biopic, such as *Invincible* (Core, 2006), *Invictus* (Eastwood, 2009), *The Fighter*, and *Foxcatcher* (Miller, 2014). Particularly popular in the early 2000s were "true story" accounts of U.S. college or high school football and basketball, such as *Remember the Titans* (Yakin, 2000), *Coach Carter* (Carter, 2005), *Friday Night Lights* (Berg, 2005), *Glory Road* (Gartner, 2006), *The Mighty Macs* (Chambers, 2009), and *McFarland, USA*, a number of which I examine in chapter 4. Yet regardless of the degree of fictionality, almost all sports films make at least some claims to authenticity: they are—or at least aim to be—true to the sport.

This focus on authenticity and truth to the sport is highlighted by Paul Kelso's comments in the *Guardian* on the prospects of the soccer film *Goal!* (Cannon, 2005), which tracks the rise to soccer stardom of Mexican immigrant Santiago Muñez (Kuno Becker) from the United States to the world of European soccer: "The most marked difference between *Goal!* and its predecessors is the support it has received from inside soccer. Where previous movies have been undermined by a lack of access, *Goal!* has been welcomed into the dressing rooms of some of the world's biggest clubs. The world and European governing bodies FIFA and UEFA, the English Premier League and clubs including Newcastle United, Real Madrid, Bayern Munich and AC Milan have all co-operated with producer Mike Jefferies and his team."[34]

As with many films before it, *Goal!*'s claim to authenticity builds on its proximity to the "real thing"—professional soccer and its top teams. The production team of *Glory Road*, which follows the events leading up to the 1966 NCAA basketball championship game, in which Coach Don Haskins (Josh Lucas) fields an all-black starting lineup for the first time in the championship's history, employed a basketball adviser who had been a protégé of the real-life Coach Haskins. The reason behind these claims is, as David Thompson observes, that the sports fan "can smell a fake,"[35] a point to which I return in my discussion of how authenticity is created and used in the sports film.

Film theory and practice has long grappled with the "problem" of realism in film, from the seamless continuity editing of classical Hollywood that seeks to disguise the cinematic illusion of reality, to the realist aesthetic of Italian neorealism or cinema verité, to what Roland Barthes has termed the "reality effect," where details not necessary for plot development are included purely to signify the sense that, in Barthes's words, "*we are the real*; it is the category of the real (and not its contingent contents), which is then signified."[36] Scholars of historical films have been particularly concerned with these issues and the necessity of looking beyond the facts. Robert A. Rosenstone, for example, works to rehabilitate historical films from the accusation of mangling historical facts to being part of "doing history": "History need not be done on the page. It can be a mode of thinking that utilizes elements other than the written word: sound, vision, feeling, montage."[37] My interest in authenticity extends Rosenstone's conception of historical films *doing* history to sports films *doing* authenticity in the present as well as the past.

Watching a film, like watching a sports contest, is not just an intellectual experience, but also an embodied and affective one. From Linda Williams's concept of "body genres" to Vivian Sobchack's suggestion that "her fingers knew" to Jennifer Barker's "tactile eye," cinema has come to be seen as an "immersive perceptual event," to use Thomas Elsaesser's phrase.[38] As Siegfried Kracauer argued in the 1960s, "Let us assume that, unlike the other types of pictures, film images affect primarily the spectator's senses, engaging him physiologically before he is in a position to respond intellectually."[39] This understanding is crucial to my argument about the representation of national identity in the sports film. National identities are "continually and collectively constructed in a complex process of discursive exchange," and sports films, as this book argues, are an important example of this circulation of discourses.[40] They are particularly well placed to engage in such exchanges because of the ways in which they foster what Nira Yuval-Davis calls the "emotive dimension of association," utilizing the dual affective potential of both sports and film.[41] An emotional connection with the audience, this book argues, is crucial to a film's potential for the construction and maintenance of visions of the nation, and this emotional connection relies in turn on establishing a sense of authenticity.

Much work has recently been done on the role of emotions in cinema, including the emotional aspects of spectatorship. These studies differ from the above-mentioned phenomenological studies by Sobchak, Marks, and others in that they are less concerned with embodied viewership and more with the affective experience of the movies and the emotional relationship of viewers with fictional characters.[42] This study builds on both of these approaches by developing the concept of "emotional authenticity" as a means of articulating the ways in which sports films create a *perception* of realness. My emphasis here is on a *sense* of authenticity rather than actual historical accuracy, and how this engages the audience emotionally but also allows for the depiction of significant historical *in*accuracies in the service of a particular vision of national identity. Emotional authenticity, I propose, prioritizes the senses and the emotions over intellectual engagement with the film, moving away from the fact-checking of film critics—an aspect of scholarship that has played a particularly prominent role in analyses of historical and biographical sports films. My concern is less with questions of historical accuracy and more with the processes by which filmmakers work to establish a *sense* that the film is true to the event by targeting the embodied, experiential, and emotional levels of viewership.

In addition, sports themselves offer an experiential quality that is translated onto the screen by sports films. Sports and games, Perinbanayagam argues, "give a sense of immediacy and presence, a feeling of getting one's hands and feet dirty, the body sweaty, the mind engaged, emotionally and cognitively. One can then conceive of games as narrative structures that represent the societal and the interactional and the temporal orders of a human life and provide opportunities for participants to enjoy a sense of power and control by casting themselves into the proceedings."[43]

It is, then, the narrative power and sensory involvement of sports that engage the players and allow them to inject themselves into the proceedings as well as derive enjoyment from it. Films build on this sensory experience of sports and magnify it through its own immersive, sensory, and experiential quality. Aligning the drama of the sport depicted, for example, with the narrative arc of the film thus taps into two different kinds of emotional engagement that ultimately strengthen each other.

Emotional authenticity appeals to our senses more than to our minds. Discussing the problematic relationship films have with history, Rosenstone further describes what he calls the "myth of facticity" as a common mode in Hollywood films. This myth, he argues, "is the mistaken notion that mimesis is all, that history is in fact no more than a 'period look,' that things themselves *are* history, rather than *become* history because of what they mean to a people of a particular time and place."[44]

Emotional authenticity evokes this "becoming history," as it is directly linked to the emotional impact of the past that is gained through the affective power of both cinema and sports. The sports film with its emphasis on physical exertion, on bodies at their limit, on pounding hearts and gasping breaths, is particularly suited to creating the sense of the spectatorial immersion described by Kracauer, Elsaesser, and more recently Luis Rocha Antunes, who argues that "a multisensory experience is the natural and common way for all of us to perceptually experience film."[45] The sports film speaks directly to the audience's senses through their own experiences of exertion—it literally "feels" with the protagonists.

In the depiction of the actual sports content, the following chapters argue, the makers of sports films face various unique problems. First, the style of the sports action must be historically and technically accurate, whether this concerns famous play-by-play reenactions or general playing style.[46] Secondly, this sporting action must be filmed, anachronistically, in a style that is interesting and engaging to a modern audience, which is accustomed to multiple camera perspectives and endless replays from contemporary sports television coverage. Thirdly, and crucially, the sports action has to be convincing in the sense of *feeling* like real sports action, that is, to avoid giving the impression that actors—rather than athletes— are playing a particular sport. If the film fails to convince on any of these levels, it will most likely be a failure, both commercially and critically. I argue, however, that what these attempts at authenticity ultimately achieve is a sense of *emotional authenticity*, which should not be confused with the idea of authentic emotions—whether or not emotions are "true" or "genuine," as is often discussed within the social sciences.[47]

Successful sports films achieve this emotional authenticity, I argue, by establishing a hypersaturated framework of technical verisimilitude and by engaging the emotional and sensory qualities of sports themselves. By overwhelming the audience with all manner of detail—flooding them with period details in the mise-en-scène or the minutiae of sports action, for example—the filmmakers create a framework in which technically or historically *in*authentic elements can easily be incorporated. As I show in the individual chapters, this framework is supported extra-textually by marketing campaigns citing vast historical research and, especially in recent years, "making-of" featurettes showcasing the painstaking efforts that go into the re-creation of the past and the sports action. Additionally, in invoking familiar sensory sports experiences of, for example, sweat and dirt on the baseball diamond or the emotional responses to defeat, sports films engage the audience's familiarity with sports. Emotional authenticity thus works by first overwhelming viewers with detailed verisimilitude in order to then envelope them in emotional and sensual engagement, prioritizing the senses and the emotions over the intellectual engagement with the film. When it comes to representing national identities, this means that sports films use emotional authenticity to construct visually and emotionally engaging visions of the nation and narrative belonging, while often taking quite considerable creative liberties with regards to "history."

Cinema, Sports, and Nation

Despite the popularity and global appeal of sports as a cultural and political phenomenon, sports films, until recently, have received little attention from film and media scholars, quite in contrast to the growing body of film studies scholarship focused on questions of nation and national cinema and the body of work concerning sports and the nation.[48] More often than not, studies on sports films are found in journals and anthologies rather than in monographs and are usually confined to one or two case studies. The approaches in these collections are diverse, although most preference narrative over visual analysis, and very few examine national identity in any detail.[49] Notable exceptions to this lack of scholarly engagement include the aforementioned studies by Tudor and Baker, both working exclusively within the realm of American film, and more recent works by Babington, Crosson, and Chare.[50] Tudor, a social scientist, uses a Marxist perspective to tackle the construction of the white, male athletic hero in her book *Hollywood's Vision of Team Sports*.[51] Aaron Baker's illuminating study *Contesting Identities: Sports in American Film* offers a more thoroughgoing analysis of the construction of social identities as an ideological battle within culture. By examining identity politics, in particular those of race, class, and gender, in Hollywood sports films, Baker critiques the worshipping of individual self-reliance and the perpetuating of this myth by sports films.[52] However, neither Baker nor Tudor investigates in depth the connection between the diverse social relations depicted within sports films and the broader context of national identity. *National Pastimes: Cinema, Sports, and Nation* sheds light on these larger connections. It bridges a gap in the scholarly discussion on film, sports, and the nation by arguing that it is the particular emotional and identificatory pull of the sports film that enables this genre to represent ideas and myths of the nation and national identity in powerful and popularly appealing ways and illustrates these arguments through a concerted focus on close visual analysis.

What unites the individual chapters, which are loosely grouped into three sections, is the question of how do sports films within different national and sporting cultures actively participate in the construction and maintenance of the respective national identity, and to what aim? The first two chapters of this book explore how sports films connect with their audiences by establishing the sense of emotional authenticity outlined above in order to help maintain particular visions of national unity in the service of the prevailing political climates. In chapter 1 I demonstrate how emotional authenticity helps create a foundation myth of British national identity out of two largely forgotten sporting heroes—Harold Abrahams and Eric Liddell, the two Olympic athletes at the center of the narrative in *Chariots of Fire*. To date, *Chariots of Fire* has been almost exclusively situated within the framework of the art-house genre of British Heritage Films, but not as being parts of a broader sports film genre.[53] I argue, however, that the representation of sports is crucial to the film's negotiation of national identity and British foundational myths. I show, moreover, that the creation of this myth is also formally disrupted at various points in the film, by employing Gilles Deleuze's concepts of the "time-image" and the "movement-image,"[54] which have been developed by David Martin-Jones to include what he describes as "films in-between," or "hybrid" films.[55] I argue that these disruptions at the level of subtext disturb the overall narrative tendency to create a vision of a unified British national identity, in a film that has as much to say about the fragmented national landscape of 1980s Thatcherite Great Britain as it does about that nation's athletic past. In the end, however, a discourse of national unity is the one that ultimately prevails in the film.

In chapter 2 I bring the concept of emotional authenticity into dialogue with Alison Landsberg's model of "prosthetic memory," in order to demonstrate how the film *Miracle of Bern* reappropriates an existing West

German foundation myth—the so-called Wunder von Bern.[56] It does so, I argue, in order to make this myth available to a pan-German audience following the reunification of Germany in 1989. By developing a sense of emotional authenticity, the film creates a basis for hyper-identification with the main protagonists, enabling the creation of a new prosthetic memory of this historically significant sporting event for contemporary audiences. The effect is a vision of renewed inner unity for a German population still negotiating the effects of the dramatic changes the nation has undergone since World War II.

The next two chapters address mainstream Hollywood cinema and the idea that shaped a nation—the American dream. This unstable ideological construct continues to fire up the imagination of Hollywood producers and works particularly well within the realm of sports, where fame and glory are just a few exceptional performances away. Tracing the *Rocky* series from the 1970s to the 2010s in chapter 3, I argue that the American dream not only is a key feature but is at the very heart of America's perception of itself. The *Rocky* series constitutes an exception to the scholarly neglect of the sports film outlined above—possibly, again, because of its focus on boxing. Scholarly interest waned, however, when *Rocky* developed into a formulaic blockbuster franchise.[57] I build on this existing *Rocky* scholarship to provide the first analysis of the entire series, including the first installment of the new *Creed* franchise, examining how the series engages with and intervenes in the changing sociocultural landscape of Cold War, Clinton-era, and post-9/11 America.[58] In these films the American dream is first defined and then defended against enemies from within and outside of the United States, in an ever-evolving sociopolitical and cultural climate. The films negotiate shifting perceptions of not only the American dream and its significance for national identity but also its interactions with changing ideals of masculinity, race, and gender relations.

In chapter 4 I continue with this approach to argue that the small town of the American heartland is constructed not only as the "real" America but also as the primary locus for the American dream, in a growing sub-genre of small-town sports films ranging from *Hoosiers* in 1986 to *The Final Season* (Evans) in 2007 and, most recently, *McFarland, USA* in 2015. These films foster a particular "small town-ness," characterized by a strong sense of place and community, but one that is not beyond modernization, and that can be successfully transposed and reappropriated to less traditional American landscapes in order to open up access to the American dream across boundaries of place and race. In films such as *Coach Carter*, I argue, the characteristics of small town-ness are decoupled from the actual small town and transferred to an inner-urban setting rife with social disadvantage. Through such transpositions, these films redefine the American dream and make it available for people other than the young white males of the original small-town films.

Most of the sports films examined in this book are peopled by heterosexual white male characters, a typical characteristic of the genre more broadly. While racial tension has long been an element in mainstream sports movies, as chapters 1, 3, and 4 examine, in more recent years a number of high-profile films with female or homosexual protagonists have also appeared, although they have seldom garnered significant popular or critical success. Paralleling the relative lack of scholarly interest in sports films generally, academic discussion in this area has "only . . . occurred in fits and starts."[59] In recent years the rise of the sports film heroine in films such as *A League of Their Own, Bend It Like Beckham,* and *Girlfight* (Kusama, 2000), has prompted a growing interest in analyzing sports films through the lens of gender.[60] Just as the appearance of the action heroine in the 1980s offered new insights into the broader construction of gendered identities in film at that time, so too does her closely related "cousin," the female sports heroine.[61] Nicholas Chare's work in particular, however, has done much to close the gap with his sophisticated phenomenological and psychoanalytic readings of how the figure of the sportswoman on screen offers a focus for intersectional analyses of bodies, gender, race, ability, and sexuality across various forms of athletic activity, from roller derby to climbing.[62] In chapter 5, I expand upon this scholarship by proposing the concept of "hero Others." These hero Others are female or homosexual athlete protagonists who threaten the conventional gender order by behaving outside of their assigned social roles and thus destabilize masculine norms. By extension, they present a threat to the perceived stability of the nation. Drawing on

George L. Mosse's theory of how the rise of nineteenth-century ideals of gender supported the stability of the nation during the rise of modernity, I examine the strategies developed by sports films such as *A League of Their Own* and *Bend It Like Beckham* in order to rein in the threat to national identity presented by such destabilizing hero Others.[63] By bringing ideas of the nation to bear on analyses of gender in sports films, I demonstrate how the female athlete forms a focal point through which hierarchical notions of national belonging and exclusion are negotiated.

CHAPTER I

"LET US PRAISE FAMOUS MEN"

Creating Myth and Memory in *Chariots of Fire*

> But in spite of all temptations to belong to other nations,
> He remains an Englishman! He remains an Englishman!
> Harold Abrahams in *Chariots of Fire* (1981)

> And thank you for reminding me that I am and will be
> whilst I breathe, a Scot.
> Eric Liddell in *Chariots of Fire* (1981)

Few sports films have enjoyed the critical and popular success of *Chariots of Fire*, the story about two rival runners competing at the 1924 Olympics that captured the British nation's imagination in 1981 and continues to do so. As with every Olympic Summer Games, the lead-up to the London 2012 Olympics (and subsequent analysis of the opening ceremony) provided ample opportunity to reanimate the sporting heroes of the 1924 Olympics made famous by the film. Occupying a central spot in the opening ceremony, a skit by comedian Rowan Atkinson not only brought back the iconic shots of the runners on the beach at Dover but did so with the help of Vangelis's famous score, and as the *Daily Mail* put it, "Bumbling Mr Bean brings down the house as he leads orchestra in hilarious rendition of *Chariots of Fire*."[1] One stage adaptation, *Chariots of Fire*, opened at London's Hampstead Theatre in May 2012 to rousing success, while the

British Film Institute, with the help of the Lottery Fund, re-released a digitally remastered version of the film in cinemas two weeks before the London Olympics.[2] More recently, in the lead-up to the Rio Olympics 2016 a new biography on Eric Liddell attracted some interest, while the University of Edinburgh, Liddell's alma mater, launched the "Eric Liddell High Performance Sports Scholarship" for elite student athletes.[3]

The two athletes at the center of the film, Jewish student Harold Abrahams and Scottish protestant missionary Eric Liddell, must overcome various obstacles—class and religious prejudice for Abrahams and shaky devotion to his faith for Liddell—to compete at the 1924 Olympic Games in Paris. Starting out as fierce rivals, they eventually compete together for the British Olympics team under the Union Jack. This chapter argues that the film lifts these runners out of historical obscurity and presents them retrospectively as mythic heroes, as part of a process of national identity transformation that was taking place in Britain during the early 1980s under Margaret Thatcher. In doing so, it creates a nation-building myth—indeed, the film itself became emblematic of the imminent (although ultimately unfulfilled) rise of the British film industry, epitomized by screen writer Colin Welland's assertion at the following year's Oscar ceremony: "The British are coming!" Yet despite the film's attempts to affirm a united British national identity, I argue that these attempts are only partially successful and that the film instead presents national identity as multifaceted and frayed—and in this heralds the tensions in British society at the cusp of the Thatcherite era.

In making this argument, I build on David Martin-Jones's application of Gilles Deleuze's concepts of the "time-image" and "movement-image" to the representation of national identity, to demonstrate how the film's aim to unify British national identity as a singular and monolithic formation is in fact formally disrupted at various points.[4] I argue that the purpose of such ruptures is to highlight—consciously or otherwise—the constructedness and complexity of national identity, even as at the level of narrative the film works to unite competing versions of British identity. I conclude that in this sports film, myths of national unity ultimately prevail over other motifs or structures that signify disunity.

The main frameworks to date for discussions of national identity in relation to *Chariots of Fire* have been Thatcherism and the heritage film debate, with the emphasis on the binary oppositions of progressive/conservative, and spectacle/history.[5] Heritage films, as Sheldon Hall argues in his analysis of the heritage debate, "ha[ve] come to signal not just a particular group, or cluster of interrelated groups, of films, but a particular *attitude* to those films, and indeed to the audiences presumed to enjoy them." They are often seen to be politically conservative (e.g., favoring Thatcherism), incorporate stunning visual displays of the past, and are often labeled "quality films," with the effect of being attractive to overseas audiences and film awards committees.[6] Within this context *Chariots of Fire* is considered to be the starting point of a new wave of heritage films, especially those of the 1980s and 1990s, which include a number of Merchant Ivory literary adaptations of authors such as Henry James and E. M. Forster. As a heritage film *Chariots*—despite, as I show, its ambiguous portrayal of national identity—has usually been "construed as the embodiment of Thatcherite patriotic rhetoric."[7] More generally, heritage films have been critiqued as inherently conservative, despite often presenting conflicting ideals in form and narrative. As Andrew Higson argued in his seminal 1993 article "Re-presenting the National Past: Nostalgia and Pastiche in the Heritage Film": "the past is displayed as visually spectacular pastiche, inviting a nostalgic gaze that resists the ironies and social critiques so often suggested narratively."[8] A connected criticism of heritage films in general, but of *Chariots of Fire* in particular, is that of misrepresenting the past or, to put it differently, quietly accepting a plethora of historical inaccuracies in the name of "artistic license." In this chapter I interrogate this criticism in depth by exploring the construction of emotional authenticity in the film.[9]

While aspects of earlier discussions surrounding the heritage film as a genre and critical category inform my argument in productive ways, the following analysis comes from a perspective that highlights the film's role in myth creation and the complex construction of national identity(ies), which I argue defies any straightforward notion of a unified national identity in the British context. In order to shift the debate about *Chariots of Fire* in a new direction, I explore the ways in which the film first constructs a new set of mythical British heroes from figures who had been largely lost to cultural memory and subsequently reclaims these national heroes in the name of contemporary national identity. These two strands of mythmaking combine to produce a complex film that at one level presents the idea of British national identity as fractured, multifaceted, and difficult to contain (not least through the disruptive elements of the time-image) but that ultimately seeks to affirm the possibility of a unified national consciousness.

Most of *Chariots of Fire* is set between 1919 and 1924. The major aim of the narrative is to demonstrate Harold Abrahams's and Eric Liddell's athletic progress and the obstacles they must overcome in order to achieve their (shared) goal of a gold medal at the Paris Olympics. The central part of the narrative is bracketed by the opening and closing scenes showing Abrahams's funeral in 1978. I discuss this awkward flashback time structure (1978–1924–1919–1924–1978) below; for now, it is most important to note that the film is mainly set in the fairly recent and lavishly re-created past. Harold Abrahams, son of a Lithuanian Jew, is a high-achieving student and star athlete at Caius College, Cambridge, while Eric Liddell is a Scottish student, born in China to missionary parents, who is conflicted by the possibilities of his earthly talents and his devotion to his faith. When Liddell takes up serious training in order to make the Olympic team, his sister Jennie (Cheryl Campbell) increasingly worries that his running ambitions will interfere with his goal to become a missionary in China. Meanwhile, Abrahams battles anti-Semitism in the form of pervasive but subtle racism. In his determination to work with a professional coach, Sam Mussabini (Ian Holm), he faces opposition from the Caius College master, who adheres to a strict view of sports as an amateur leisure pursuit and therefore considers the hiring of a professional trainer a violation of this amateur code.

Despite these hurdles, both runners are chosen for the Olympic team, along with Abrahams's Caius College friends, Lord Lindsay (Nigel Havers), Aubrey Montague (Nicholas Farrell), and Henry Stallard (Daniel Gerroll). On the way to Paris, Liddell learns that the heats for the 100-meter race are scheduled on a Sunday, and because of his faith, he refuses to take part in the heats, therefore eliminating his chances for a medal. Having arrived in Paris, he continues to refuse "to run on the Sabbath," despite the pressure put on him by the British Olympic Committee and the Prince of Wales. Lord Lindsay, having scored a medal already, gives up his place in the 400 meters so that Liddell can run that race instead of the 100-meter race. This way Liddell and Abrahams do not meet in the 100 meters as expected, and the film finishes with a happy ending, resulting in a gold medal for both runners.

Saturated with lavish sets and steeped in nostalgia, the film covers many diverse issues that are not confined to the interwar years, such as class struggle, latent anti-Semitism, the increasing professionalization of modern sports, muscular Christianity, and questions of national loyalty. The following analysis examines these larger themes as they become incorporated into the mythmaking processes in the film. In order to argue that the film engages in active myth- (and history-) making to construct a contemporary representation of national identity, I begin by demonstrating how the film creates a framework of authenticity that gives greater credence to the overall narrative and veracity to the vision of national identity that underlies it. I then analyze how the nostalgic style in the mise-en-scène contributes to the building of this myth of a unified national identity, and finally I examine how the film both supports and undermines this national identity through its formal and narrative structures.

Emotional Authenticity in *Chariots of Fire*

Chariots of Fire builds a framework of authenticity on many levels. First, the film puts real people and events at the center of its narrative. However, while these are real, the actual audience's level of familiarity with the sporting events, athletes, and outcome of their Olympic quest was quite limited at the time of the film's release, particularly when compared to events such as Germany's Miracle of Bern, examined in chapter 2. While Abrahams went on to become a well-known sports commentator and administrator, Liddell died in relative obscurity in China during the Second World War.[10] Constructing a framework of authenticity depends partly on audience familiarity: naturally the more familiar the events and persons depicted, the more difficult it is to convincingly establish verisimilitude. For example, while even nonsports fans would be familiar with more recent sports stars such as Cristiano Ronaldo or Usain Bolt due to their enduring presence in a variety of media, the same could not be said of Abrahams and Liddell and their performances at the Paris Olympics among 1980s audiences. This is, of course, in part due to the rapid development of television broadcasting—and the media in general—since the beginning of sports broadcasting in the early 1950s and the lack of such reportage in the 1920s.[11] In 1920s Britain, athletic meets were reported mostly through newspapers and newsreels in cinemas and were otherwise, quite literally, live events that required the interested spectator to *be* at the event.[12]

This lower level of audience familiarity with the actual events left room for the filmmakers of *Chariots of Fire* to alter history, sometimes significantly, in favor of a dramatic storyline. For example, in the film Eric Liddell hears for the first time that the heats are scheduled on a Sunday while already en route to Paris. Liddell then gratefully accepts Lord Lindsay's place in a different race, although he supposedly has not trained for the event. Not only is Lord Lindsay a fictional character, but by all reports Liddell knew well in advance that he would run the 400 meters and trained accordingly.[13] What distracts audience attention from this use of "dramatic license" is the well-developed sense of visual historic accuracy in the mise-en-scène: the set design (e.g., the separation of the running tracks by thin cords instead of lines on a synthetic ground), the costumes (e.g., the dinner suits at Abrahams's dinner with the headmasters of Caius College, the running outfits), and the props (e.g., the cars, the running shoes, the spades to dig the holes in the track for the runners starting positions at the race).

Typical for sports films set in the past, *Chariots of Fire* also "rings true" on the narrative level. The film captures its 1920s setting perfectly through characters' use of language, references to contemporary issues (such as the appearance of disabled war veterans), the modes of reportage depicted, and so on. For example, Harold Abrahams's rise to sporting prowess is visualized through a swirl of black-and-white newspaper cuttings.[14] This helps to build a technical and visual framework for emotional authenticity: "the care with detail and atmosphere . . . lends historical accuracy," as Ed Carter observes, despite the many historical inaccuracies in the *story* of the runners.[15] In sharp contrast to the historical faultfinding of scholars such as Carter stands screenwriter Colin Welland's account: "I did endless research for the film. I went to the National Film Archives and said 'What have you got on the 1924 Olympics? Abrahams and Liddell, who won the gold medals.' And I sat there looking at these two young men on silent film, and said 'Don't worry boys, I'll make a good job of it.' And that's when I committed myself to them. . . . I interviewed everybody who was still alive."[16]

For Welland, a sense of emotional "truth" to the characters wins out here over the "endless research." Similarly, my emphasis here is on exploring how the film creates an *atmosphere* perceived by audiences as historically truthful, embedded in the mise-en-scène, and prioritizes this over the accuracy of (hi)story. It is, I argue, the former that functions as the framework that supports the film's emotional authenticity and thus ultimately strengthens the story's impact on the audience.

This impact is further strengthened by the film's aforementioned unusual and complex timeline, which begins in 1978 with Harold Abrahams's funeral, then moves to 1924 in a brief flashback introduced by Lord Lindsay, but which is subsequently told from the point of view of—and thus narrated by—Aubrey Montague and begins with the now iconic shots of the athletes running along the beach to Vangelis's anachronistic, yet stirring, electronic score. The second flashback to 1919 shortly after shifts the perspective more obviously to that of Montague's character, whose point-of-view narrator then slowly and subtly changes to an omniscient narrator until it shifts back toward Montague's perspective just before the end, giving the story a personal touch, not unlike a memoir. The opening late 1970s funeral scene functions as a vehicle to connect the then (nearly) contemporary early 1980s audience to the events in the past, as David Puttnam explains: "We were very keen that the film shouldn't be seen as just a period piece. We wanted to place those men in—as close as we could—into a contemporary context. And that was echoed in both the first and the last lines in the movie. These men really did live—they lived in our lifetime."[17]

The effect of the first flashback is thus to make this exceptional sports story matter to a 1980s audience and add a sense of realism to the unfolding events. Combining the technical and atmospheric framework of authenticity with not only a personal link through Aubrey Montague's memoir-like voice-over but also the creation of a tangible connection between the historic athletes and the contemporary audience served to produce a powerful sense of emotional authenticity in the film.

Mythmaking and Visual Style

Rather than having been considered a sports film, *Chariots of Fire* has often, as noted above, been included in the group of films that have collectively been called "British heritage films," from *A Room with a View* (Ivory, 1985) to *Howards End* (Ivory, 1992), and it does indeed share that group's lavish visual style.[18] My goal here is not to tread down the now well-worn paths on either side of the heritage film debate—are they essentially conservative or progressive, superficial or socially critical cultural products? Instead, my concern is with extending the aspects of this debate concerning visual style and to ask how this style contributes to producing the myths of the runners and enhancing their impact as part of a contemporary nation-building project.

The visual style of heritage films has been described by Andrew Higson as "pictorialist" or akin to a "cinema of heritage attractions."[19] It is a lavish style that moves slowly and displays the mise-en-scène to its best advantage rather than necessarily advancing the narrative, and thus the shots tend to lean toward deep focus and wide-angle framing, rather than fast editing and close-ups.[20] While much of this is true of the visual style of *Chariots of Fire*, the overt use of close-ups and the heavy use of slow-motion sequences offer a departure from the heritage film norm. For example, the sequence of Abrahams's climactic 100-meter race at the Olympics is divided into four parts: the preparation before the race, which is partly in slow motion, the race itself in "real time," then a slow-motion repeat of the race intercut with the key characters congratulating Abrahams, and finally the reaction of his coach, Sam Mussabini, in his hotel room upon seeing the Union Jack raised in triumph. The race preparation and the race replay are particularly noteworthy, as they make the most use of slow motion and close-ups. During the preparation, the camera moves ever closer as the runners stretch, loosen up, dig their starting holes, and bend down to assume the starting position. The shots have clearly been selected for their affective power to display the runners' tension and therefore raise that of the audience. By repeatedly delaying the start of the race, the tension is heightened further. An extreme close-up, filmed in soft focus, of Abrahams's good luck charms swinging back and forth symbolizes his life hanging in the balance. The race itself lasts a few seconds longer than it realistically would have, which is due to several cutaways of the excited audience and a barely perceptible slow-motion finish.

The race replay further serves various functions much more typical of sports than heritage films. On the most basic level it gives 1980s audiences what they are used to in terms of sporting coverage: replays and varying angles. Yet again, the camera moves into close-ups to linger on Abrahams's face in intense concentration and on his feet pounding the soft ground. These shots are not dissimilar to those often critiqued shots of female bodies that, as Laura Mulvey asserts, have "the quality of a cut-out or icon, rather than verisimilitude."[21] Yet unlike the kinds of close-ups more commonly associated with the objectification of women, the shots in *Chariots of Fire* are devoid of any erotic appeal and are motivated more by the narrative—indeed, one could argue that they are unnecessary considering that they are "merely" a replay of the race that has already been shown. Their primary function, I suggest, is to increase, quite literally, the size of the athlete's bodies and turn them into larger-than-life heroes. This objectification is based less on erotic appeal than on an austere admiration that effectively distances the viewer from the character.

This process of elevation from mere runner to iconic hero and mythic figure is helped along by Vangelis's psychedelic score and the near absence of diegetic sound. The score supports these scenes' tense, surreal, and dreamlike quality, further eroding any sense of realism. This is most evident during the preparation for the race where the score dramatically turns into (slow) beats that resemble the sound of a heart beating, thus impossibly fusing nondiegetic sonic, narrative, and physical tension of both the character *and* the viewer. Meanwhile, the few muffled, yet highlighted diegetic sounds, such as the digging in the ground for the starting holes during the race preparation, or the crunching of the soft ground underneath the feet of Abrahams's friends as they run to congratulate him after the race, further emphasize the dreamlike nature of this sequence. The deliberate break with the previously adhered to—and quickly restored—mode of realism in these scenes effectively liberates the characters from the narrative, allowing them to transform into larger than life mythical heroes.

Mythmaking and Narrative

Apart from being visually aggrandized, the runners are also narratively elevated to heroic stature, which is another common strategy employed in sports films. The film begins with a biblical quote from Ecclesiasticus during Abrahams's funeral service: "Let us praise famous men and our fathers that begat us. All these men were honored in their generations and were the glory in their day."[22] Lord Lindsay continues in a suitably pathos-filled voice: "We are here today to give thanks for the life of Harold Abrahams. To honor the legend. Now there are just two of us—young Aubrey Montague and myself—who can close our eyes and remember those few young men with hope in our hearts and wings on our heels." These introductory remarks seamlessly segue into Vangelis's equally emotion-laden score as the athletes run along Dover beach, immediately setting the mood for the rest of the film. This is a story not about mere mortals, we are given to understand, but about "famous men, who were honored in their time," and who are now "legends." It is significant that their importance "in their day" is emphasized early on in order to leave no doubt in the audience's mind, regardless of whether they had achieved this legendary status in reality. The wistfulness and sense of nostalgia point toward a deliberate redressing of this potential imbalance through the film—it leaves no room for any doubt. The film links the retold past to the contemporary audience by way of the oddly convoluted flashback structure of the film, thus lending extra credibility to the claim of the athletes' grand status of being "the glory in their day."

While Harold Abrahams is mostly defined by his ambition—and to a lesser degree his Jewishness—Eric Liddell is predominantly framed as a devout Christian with a God-given gift. After the funeral service scene, the flashback introduction to the youthful Abrahams showcases his "intensity," his ambition, and his drive to win; it highlights his Jewishness as well as the anti-Semitism that is directed against him, and hints of his desire to be welcomed into English society. Indeed, both Abrahams and Liddell are defined in relation to their national and religious allegiances early on in the film: the son of a Lithuanian Jewish immigrant, Abrahams "took up the King's commission" and therefore clearly states his allegiance to the British Crown, while Liddell, whose first appearance is at a Scottish track meet in the highlands, is depicted as a man equally divided between his pride as a Scot and his devotion to his faith.

The religion of both men is crucial to their identity and to how the audience understands their characters. However, whereas Liddell's faith is presented as making him virtuous, kind, and a man of principle with strong Christian values, Abrahams's Jewishness supposedly makes him defensive—to the "point of pugnacity" as one of the Caius College masters puts it—and somewhat arrogant in his success. Liddell's faith is portrayed positively: it is not ambition that is driving him, but devotion to God, and his faith only becomes an obstacle when his devotion is first doubted by his sister and then attacked by the Olympic Committee. In contrast, Abrahams's Jewishness is an inherent obstacle that, in the face of pervasive anti-Semitism, does not and cannot be overcome—it can only be masked, or so he believes, by his entrance into a different realm: the world of success. While for Liddell religion is a matter of "belief," Abrahams experiences religion primarily as race and, more specifically, as racial discrimination. The ambition driving him is at least partly due to this experience and provides an additional layer to his success when he is eventually accepted as "the toast of England," as a newspaper headline informs the audience on his return to England, and as an "Englishman," as he sings in the Caius College production of Gilbert and Sullivan's *H.M.S. Pinafore*. Success is represented as trumping race, religion, and inequality and embodying a sense of English nationhood. Liddell's desire, on the other hand, is not to become an Englishman—he declares himself a proud Scot within the first few minutes of his on-screen appearance—but rather to praise God through running.

Other challenges are also put in each man's way in order, in the manner of the heroic quests of antiquity, to verify their outstanding athleticism. For example, in his first days at Caius College, Abrahams becomes the first person to "win" the Great Court Run at Trinity College, which involves running the perimeter of the court during the interval that the clock takes to strike twelve times. Meanwhile in Scotland an entirely unprepared Liddell wins the 200-yard race at the track meet where he is scheduled to hand out trophies to little boys. Their subsequent successes are charted by their wins on the track, which are accompanied by newspaper clippings swirling across the screen. When Abrahams finally seeks out his Scottish competitor, he witnesses an extraordinary event: as Liddell runs the 400 meters he trips, falls down, picks himself up, catches up with his opponents, runs past them, and wins the race. One of Liddell's most telling characteristics is his unusual running style that is characterized by his head falling backward and his arms swinging wildly just before the finish. This running style makes him look as if he is possessed by a higher power and during the running events serves to heighten the competition between the two athletes. Both Abrahams's and Liddell's extraordinary deeds signify not only their considerable athletic prowess but also their determination and will to win.

When the two men are finally scheduled to run against each other at the Olympics, however, this normally climactic competition is defused by Liddell's refusal to run on the Sabbath. Instead, Abrahams and Liddell are ultimately united under the Union Jack—albeit in different races—to compete against a common "enemy": the sprint stars of the United Stars, in particular Jackson "The New York Thunderbolt" Scholz (Brad Davis) and Charlie Paddock (Dennis Christopher), "the fastest man in the world." It is at this point that the film's unifying mission becomes visible as the previously separate national identities of England and Scotland are subsumed by a single British one. The Americans with their professional training—which stands in stark contrast to the amateur spirit invoked by the masters at Caius College, who reproach Abrahams for hiring a coach—loom large as the untouchable record holders. The trope of the "unbeatable" opposition, successfully used ever since Julius Caesar's efforts to attain more and more troops to fight the "terrible" Gauls, is frequently given an outing in sports film contexts, where it tends to be visualized through training or match sequences featuring the opposing team, in which they appear physically dominant and outstanding in their sport. This is similarly the case with the depiction of the Americans in *Chariots of Fire*, whose untouchability only serves to add to Abrahams's and Liddell's achievement when they finally beat their star-spangled opponents.

As these examples suggest, Abrahams and Liddell each share some of the traits of classical heroes outlined by scholars of myth and ritual such as Otto Rank, Lord Raglan, and Joseph Campbell.[23] Some of these traits are reflected in Abrahams's and Liddell's life stories: Abrahams and Liddell are both born under unusual circumstances (Abrahams is the son of a Jewish Lithuanian immigrant; Liddell is "oriental born" to his missionary parents), and both are implicitly descended from the gods (thus the Caius College master says about Abrahams, "Perhaps they are God's chosen people"; while Liddell seems to have divine running talents). They are being called on a quest and must prove themselves by winning many races on the long journey to the ultimate trial of the Olympic Games. Abrahams even briefly descends into the underworld, albeit admittedly one of his own making, when he loses hope after his loss to Liddell, only to be redeemed in the final scenes. While the characters and their quest do not uniformly adhere either to the patterns laid out by Rank and Raglan, nor to Campbell's classic stages of the quest (departure, initiation, return), they do follow the historical patterns of hero-myths closely enough to further strengthen the magnitude of their achievement. This demonstration of each man's "heroic" importance in history is a prerequisite of creating relevant heroes for the contemporary British nation: only if they can be made to appear as national heroes *in their day* can they be called upon to rise again in the name of national unity for a contemporary, 1980s audience.

National Identity in *Chariots of Fire*

Chariots of Fire thus effectively combines an atmosphere of authenticity, embedded in the narrative as well as in the mise-en-scène, with aggrandizing plot lines and allusions to classical mythological heroes, in order to lift Abrahams and Liddell out of historical obscurity and transform them into valid national heroes of 1920s Great Britain. The next step is to appropriate these characters as unifying heroes for a more recent, 1980s British audience. These characters, then, are required to represent both past *and* contemporary national identity. As might be expected, these competing representational demands at times come into conflict with one another.

As I noted in the introduction, sports films are filled with, in Mette Hjort's terms, "themes of nation," and this is certainly true for *Chariots of Fire*.[24] Starting with the quote from William Blake's allegorical poem "And Did Those Feet in Ancient Times"—best known in its incarnation in the popular hymn "Jerusalem" and referenced in the film's title—the film's nationalist themes range from allusions to Britain's role in World War I to Gilbert and Sullivan's comic operas and, of course, the various nationalisms surrounding the athletic competitions.[25] As noted above, both runners early on are associated with their respective national identities, but these seemingly straightforward English and Scottish affiliations are immediately complicated. Neither runner has the luxury of what could be considered a natural or self-evident national identity; rather, Abrahams and Liddell must both consciously make an effort to align themselves with particular visions of the nation. Consider, for example, Eric Liddell's speech at the track meet that serves as his introduction: "When we were in China, my father, here, was always waxing lyrical about his wee home in the glen. But being oriental born myself, like my brothers and my sister here, I suffered from a natural incredulity. But looking about me now, the heather on the hills, I can see he was right—it's very special. Thank you for welcoming us home. And thank you for reminding me that I am and will be whilst I breathe, a Scot."

Eric Liddell speaks with a recognizable Scottish accent and uses words and phrases such as "wee home in the glen" that clearly denote Scotland—yet despite these attempts to naturalize his national identity, it is equally clear that this is not one that could be claimed in essentialist terms, but is something he relates to only in a self-conscious way. This speech is one of the many small gestures the film makes toward the possibility of national identity as a construct. Abrahams, too, recounts his father's wish to make his sons "true Englishmen"—another gesture that marks national identity as a process. Unlike for Liddell, though, he soon finds out that being neither Anglo-Saxon nor Christian all but negates this possibility.

Paradoxically, the film thus simultaneously highlights the constructedness of national identity, while also invoking the possibility of an essentialist version of Britishness, of which being Anglo-Saxon and Christian are key parts. It is by pitting against each other these two diverging conceptions of national identity, one essentialist, one as a process and construct, that the film breaks with any notion of a simple and unified nationhood. Indeed, hidden underneath the lavish and nostalgic visual style is a much more complex representation of Great Britain—and of England and Scotland in particular—than might be expected at first sight. The tension between these competing versions of national identity is already on display in the film's unusual opening double-flashback structure. As noted above, the film starts with the funeral scene in 1978, then flashes back to 1924 to the iconic shots of the athletes running along the beach. Following directly is a voice-over that takes the audience even further back to 1919, when Montague and Abrahams first meet. Jim Leach has called the opening scene an "elaborate, temporal regression" and the structure of the film "dislocated," while Andrew Sarris has bemoaned the film's "three false starts to the narrative and half a dozen anticlimaxes at the end."[26] But the scene is not only awkward and narratively confusing; it is also a sign of the inherent tension in regard to national identity within the narrative.

These false starts and ruptures, such as the many times the athletic action is literally frozen as it becomes a photograph in the newspaper, can be usefully framed within Gilles Deleuze's theory of the time-image and the movement-image. In his two main works on the philosophy of film—*Cinema 1: The Movement-Image* and *Cinema 2: The Time-Image*—Deleuze develops a taxonomy of film concepts, or ciné-system, which, put simply, differentiates between two types of films, the time-image and the movement-image. The time-image is characterized by a discontinuous narrative and nonlinear timeline (a labyrinthine model of time) and representations of "any-space-whatevers," where characters just "are" rather than engaging in direct causal action, thus disrupting the flow and continuity of a classical narrative.[27] They are disorienting in their use of narrative time, and to illustrate this phenomenon, Deleuze singles out many of the films of the European new-wave cinemas, such as Fellini's *8½* (1963). In contrast, the movement-image with its linear narrative timeline and continuity editing is action driven by its protagonists and constitutes much of what would be called classical (Hollywood) cinema.[28] Deleuze's philosophy of time has been successfully applied to questions of national identity by David Martin-Jones. Examining various international films that play with the passage of time such as *Run Lola Run* (Tykwer, 1998) or *Memento* (Nolan, 2000), Martin-Jones shows how these films "self-consciously manipulate narrative time in order to negotiate transformations of national identity."[29] With its action-driven protagonists and teleologically progressing storyline, *Chariots of Fire* should be an excellent example of a movement-image, formally demonstrating a unity of national identity. At the level of narrative, however, the film is repeatedly disrupted by the intervention of the time-image, which as I show, serves to undermine this superficial demonstration of unity.

While Deleuze casts his two cinematic types as direct opposites, according to Martin-Jones there are many films that do not fit neatly into either category and where both time-image and movement-image exist in the same film. For the most part, as Martin-Jones points out, these are "classical narratives like Frank Capra's *It's a Wonderful Life* (1946) [that] briefly toyed with a labyrinthine notion of time by presenting two possible worlds. . . . However, this temporary departure from a singular, linear view of time was used to reinforce the legitimacy of one true time, and indeed, to conflate this 'correct' view of time with the film's one true vision of postwar American national identity. Thus, whilst evoking the labyrinthine model of time found in many time-images, this movement-image quickly returned its narrative to a classical framework."[30]

Most sports films can safely be considered to be even less complicated movement-images than *It's a Wonderful Life*. I argue, however, that *Chariots of Fire* has certain "moments" of time-imageness. Martin-Jones outlines some of the characteristics of time-images using the example of Fellini's *8½*, which "used a disorienting editing pattern to represent the equal validity of various parallel universes. By representing these labyrinthine variables as indiscernible from any one 'correct' version of reality, *8½* expressed the seeming impossibility of finding one informing, linear national narrative at a time of historical transformation in postwar Italy."[31]

National identity is thus tied to narrative time in Fellini's film through the use of "parallel universes" of, in this example, postwar Italy. As such, the ruptures of time within the film upset the representation of a fixed national identity. This is also the case, I argue—although admittedly to a somewhat lesser degree—in *Chariots of Fire*, where the elaborate construction of cinematic time and its disruption at various points underline the contradictory nature of national identity as already put forward in the narrative. Martin-Jones concludes that "time-images like *8½* use their disrupted narrative to comment on the illusion that movement-images, such as *It's a Wonderful Life*, attempt to create, that is to say, the illusion that there *is* one 'correct' narrative of national identity."[32] I argue that *Chariots of Fire* creates, disrupts and repairs the various versions of national identity it represents in order to suggest at least the possibility of multiple versions, without necessarily arriving at a singular "'correct' narrative of national identity."

While Deleuze's two categories of the movement-image and the time-image are opposite ends of the spectrum, Martin-Jones is particularly interested, as the above examples suggest, in the films in-between, which he terms "hybrid films" or "*time-images 'caught in the act' of becoming movement-images*."[33] These films disrupt the narrative of the film at a formal level, for example, by the deterritorializing use of jump cuts and other techniques that suggest a jumbled or discontinuous construction of time, yet these aspects are often reined in again by the reterritorializing force of the movement-image aspect of the film.[34] Martin-Jones concisely demonstrates the process of the "*time-image . . . 'caught in the act' of becoming a movement-image*" in the film *Sliding Doors* (Howitt, 1998).[35] The main protagonist Helen (Gwyneth Paltrow) exists in two alternative universes: in the first, "brunette Helen" does low-wage jobs and has a cheating boyfriend; in the other "blonde Helen" successfully runs a PR firm and is in a happy relationship. The first Helen gets to see the alternative Helen and eventually has to choose which life she wants to lead. Different visions of London accompany the two lives, and the audience and Helen herself are easily persuaded by the attractive and successful Helen and a cosmopolitan London that is full of entrepreneurial opportunities. According to Martin-Jones, a momentary crisis of national identity in regard to the European Union and the effects of globalization on London is resolved by demonstrating Helen's/London's—and therefore by extension, Britain's—success at finding her/its place as a global citizen/city in the new world order. In Deleuzian terms, the momentary deterritorializing pull of the time-image and its labyrinthine model of time has been restrained by the reterritorrializing success of the movement-image.[36] In situating *Sliding Doors* within the context of Britain at the turn of the century, Martin-Jones shifts Deleuze's work away from the global (Deleuze had seen the emergence of the time-image as a pan-European, if not global, effect of the crisis of World War II) and makes it pertinent to reflecting on constructions of nation.

National identity and its refigurations can become expressed through the influence of the time-image within hybrid films, but frequently only to reinstate "one unifying image of national identity" at the expense of a multitude of possibilities: "Both films [*Sliding Doors* and *Run Lola Run*] play with the labyrinth, momentarily allowing it to appear and thereby acknowledging a moment of national transformation. Their multiple narratives demonstrate the time lag during which an 'old' version of national identity is replaced by a 'new' one. However, they both firmly reterritorialise the labyrinth, thereby asserting that this transformation is now over and that the national narrative has been resumed."[37]

Sliding Doors, with its parallel universe, and the late-1990s German film *Run Lola Run*, with its narrative repeated in three different iterations, are more obviously playing with ideas of the time-image than *Chariots of Fire*. Yet while *Chariots of Fire* might not be as obvious a hybrid film in Martin-Jones's sense, it nonetheless displays moments of disruption that suggest the presence of the deterritorializing pull of the time-image. As Martin-Jones notes: "A film does not have to be a time-image, or a hybrid image to critique the dominant ideology usually found in the movement-image. Many movement-images critique the dominant view of national identity in their narrative. However, it is rare for one to also *demonstrate this critique formally*. Indeed, when it does so, its deterritorializing movement ensures that it becomes a hybrid image. This is the added dimension that hybrid films are able to negotiate, a formal demonstration of the process of national identity de- or reterritorialization examined in their narratives."[38] Similarly *Chariots of Fire* "formally demonstrates" the ambiguity of British national identity in various ways.

While time is in the main coherently structured throughout *Chariots of Fire*, the narrative and the formal construction of time are sometimes at odds with each other. This becomes particularly clear in the opening scenes with the multiple flashbacks. In *Sliding Doors* a flashback during a coma melds the two Helens' memories together and thus "the existence of blonde Helen's displaced memories within the universe of brunette Helen suggests a Deleuzian view of identity in time."[39] In *Chariots of Fire* the exact opposite is suggested: the scene starts out with Lord Lindsay calling up an old memory (the runners on the beach) that is then seamlessly taken over by Aubrey Montague through the commencement of his voice-over. Instead of one person with two simultaneous lives and memories suggesting the labyrinth of time, there are two people with apparently exactly the same memory, suggesting a singular, "correct" memory and national identity. On the one hand this further underlines the construction of authenticity outlined above in that it attributes a universal validity to the remembered events. On the other hand this uniting of what should be different memories demonstrates the strength of the reterritorializing pull of the movement-image in *Chariots of Fire*. A shot of the mourners in church, with the aged Montague in the middle, which directly precedes the fade to the runners on the beach while Lord Lindsay is recalling the past, does not successfully pass the voice of the storyteller from Lindsay to Montague. This is in part because Montague is not yet recognizable as one of the main characters and also because at this point Lindsay's voice-over is still dominating the actual telling of the story. Thus at the same time as the film formally presents the unity of memory in two ways—through the structuring device of the flashback and through the "merging" and thus unifying of the memories of Lindsay and Montague—narrative uncertainty is introduced concerning who is telling the story. Despite having taken so much care to construct the unity of memory formally, the film stumbles over its own constructedness and is momentarily unhinged by the confusion over the narrative voice that breaks the illusion of the unity of memory for a split second.

As well as attempting to collapse various individual memories into a unified history of events, the flashback serves a second function. It is also a demonstration of the importance of a history of "first causes" for the movement-image in that it begins with the end (Abrahams's glorious and glorifying funeral) and then immediately links this to a "false origin"—the beginning of the narrative, which is, however, constructed rather than natural—by cutting to the iconic scene of the runners training on the beach.[40] In establishing such a false origin and then working back to the already screened ending, the film leaves no room for divergence along the way and thus negates a labyrinthine version of time from the beginning, or, as Martin-Jones puts it, "there is no scope for a bifurcation of the path which the narrative will take through time."[41] On the level of the narrative it is clear that the film will end with Abrahams's funeral. The funereal pronouncement that he is a celebrated hero further negates any "bifurcation of the path" at this level. Left unclear at the beginning of the film, however, is the significance of Abrahams's funeral in an Anglican church, which signifies Abrahams's consummate acceptance into English society symbolized by his conversion to Christianity.[42]

Performing British Identities in Chariots of Fire

The performance of national identity in *Chariots of Fire* is both obvious and subtle, and at various points, I argue, it is briefly shaken by the deterritorializing pull of the time-image. Significantly, it is not only historical British, Scottish, and English national identity that the protagonists "perform" but also a vision of *contemporary* Britishness, which eventually subsumes the Scottish and English identities. The implied strength and vitality of this national identity is quite literally written onto their young and athletic male bodies. A number of critics of the nation and nationalism have examined the "performativity" of ethnic and national identities, extrapolating in particular from Judith Butler's concept of gender identity as inherently performative.[43] Tim Edensor, for example, argues that "performance is a useful metaphor since it allows us to look at the ways in which identities are enacted and reproduced, informing and (re)constructing a sense of collectivity."[44] In his analysis of the performance of national identity in film, Martin-Jones also draws a compelling comparison with Butler's work on gender and sexual identities, which, she argues, do not have their basis in a biological "first cause" but are instead endlessly repeated to give the idea that they are "natural" categories. Of heterosexuality, Butler states that "it requires to be instituted again and again, which is to say that it runs the risk of being *de*-instituted at every interval."[45] Like the forks in Deleuze's labyrinth of time, the potential for deviation from the norm in every repetition of the performance of gender identities or roles opens up a multitude of other possibilities. Similarly, national identity is constructed and maintained by constant reiteration of signs of, for example, Englishness, and thus the potential for the subversion or derailing of national identity is integrated at every interval of the repetition.

The most obvious performance in the sense of a "self-conscious and deliberate"[46] act of national identity, as opposed to unreflexive performativity, can be seen in a montage of Abrahams's training and success both on and off the sporting field. This montage tellingly begins just after he has told Montague about the prejudices and setbacks he faces in his quest to become a "true Englishman" due to his Jewishness. Despite his strong criticism of the English establishment ("this England of his [Abrahams's father] is Christian and Anglo-Saxon, and so are her corridors of power and those who stalk them guard them with jealousy and venom," he tells Montague with some bitterness), the film at the same time "appears to relish the visual pomp and splendor with which it is associated."[47] As Abrahams and Montague walk through the Cambridge grounds the university is depicted, in true heritage film style, in all its architectural glory, the splendid view dissolving Abrahams's criticism in visual beauty. When Abrahams promises Montague that he will "run them off their feet" and walks determinedly along the university grounds, the Gilbert and Sullivan song "For He Is an Englishman" functions as the sonic introduction and ironic overlay to the montage.[48]

The montage then artfully traces Abrahams's progress from solitary training to individual success to success as part of the Cambridge athletics team, before he is revealed to be the star of the Gilbert and Sullivan production *H.M.S. Pinafore*. Here Abrahams clearly moves from being a lonely outsider training on his own to a fully respected member of not only the prestigious Cambridge athletics team—Abrahams's status as the final runner is evidence of his importance within the team—but also of the Cambridge University Gilbert & Sullivan Society. Abrahams dutifully and actively performs key qualities of stereotypical Englishness in this sequence: intellectual rigor, evidenced by his studies at one of the nation's most prestigious and historical educational institutions; rugged athleticism; and engagement with English popular cultural and musical traditions.[49] All of these form part of what the college master calls "the education of an Englishman," and athletic ability—at which Abrahams excels above all else—plays a particularly important role: "Here in Cambridge we have always been proud of our athletic prowess. We believe, we've always believed, that our games are indispensable in helping to complete the education of an Englishman. They create character. They foster courage, honesty and leadership. But most of all an unassailable spirit of loyalty, comradeship and mutual responsibility."

Yet the inclusion of Abrahams's role as the quintessential "Englishman" in the Gilbert and Sullivan production has a further, less stabilizing function. While narratively affirming his ability to "perform" Englishness to an acceptable degree, the very fact that this is a performance highlights the constructedness of this identity. Similarly, although the movement-image does its best to maintain its causal linearity through Abrahams's physical movement, it is momentarily disrupted every time the movement is frozen and merges visually into a still newspaper photograph. In such moments, what the viewer had assumed to be the "present" suddenly becomes the past, and thus the process of constructing one "correct" history (over a multiplicity of histories in the labyrinth of time) is revealed.

There are also other, less self-conscious ways in which national identity is performed. These in particular can be linked to the kinds of 1980s ideas about British identity put forward by prime minister Margaret Thatcher, who had gained office in 1979, including a strong focus on meritocracy, entrepreneurial verve, individual success, and discipline.[50] In this context Abrahams comes to stand for a particular, Tory-approved version of the future, a symbol not only of where England was heading in the 1920s but where it "should" be at in the early 1980s. His drive to succeed and do so as an outsider from the British establishment proves to be at once a progressive symbol for a larger shift away from aristocratic privilege in British society (represented in the film by Lord Lindsay) and an underlining of the brand of conservatism exemplified not least by Thatcher herself, the daughter of a shopkeeper. Abrahams at one point directly attacks what he calls the "archaic values" of the college masters, for example, when he is summoned and then criticized for having employed a professional coach, which they consider to be against the spirit of amateurism aspired to by the college. Yet this very celebration of amateurism is mired in traditions of social hierarchy; the expression of a wealthy elite with the means to engage in "games."

It is exactly this amateur spirit and the laissez-faire attitude toward the "games" that the aristocratic dandy, Lord Lindsay, embodies. He arrives at the college court dash—the first opportunity for Abrahams to prove himself, and which he therefore takes very seriously—with a cigarette in one hand and a bottle of champagne in the other, announcing that he came to "push you [Abrahams] along a bit." In another scene he practices hurdling by placing a champagne-filled coupe (a wide, flat glass) on each hurdle. As he races through the course in the grounds of his family's country estate, his decidedly decadent motivation is to spill not a single drop of the expensive drink. As much as the audience is encouraged to admire Abrahams for his discipline, his determination, and his success, Lord Lindsay and his old-fashioned amateurism, mixed with a healthy dash of aristocratic eccentricity, is far more likeable and charming. His character further encourages the typical heritage film nostalgia for a bygone era of "Old England," which is also expressed visually through the lavish mise-en-scène. Abrahams's fierce ambition and sober cultivation of his athletic talent is in stark contrast to Lindsay's nonchalance, born out of the knowledge of his privileged status, regardless of his success on the sporting field.

Such divergent representations of Englishness and their varying appeal have prompted Sheila Johnston to call *Chariots of Fire* "Janus-faced" and Jim Leach to conclude that "such contradictions were very much part of Thatcherism."[51] Indeed, as much as Thatcher encouraged enterprise, progressivism, and success born of merit, she also favored moral absolutism based on Victorian values and pushed the idea of heritage and its industry as part of English—and to a lesser extent, British—national identity.[52]

Abrahams might represent the future, but the film lingers lovingly on the past. Noticeably absent in any of the scenes with Lord Lindsay is any kind of Deleuzian interruption—in his portrayal the reterritorializing pull of the movement-image is at its strongest, and any suspicions of alternative pasts, that is, pasts that might be different from that represented by Lindsay, are invalidated.

Lindsay is also represented in contrast to Liddell—for instance, in their only meaningful interaction, it is Lindsay who enables Liddell to participate in the Olympic Games. As we know, when Liddell learns that the heats for the 100-meter race are scheduled for a Sunday, he takes himself out of the competition, despite his months of training. His principled stance is not appreciated by the British Olympic Committee, and he is called into a meeting, at which the Prince of Wales is also in attendance. Despite having his loyalty to the future king and his country questioned, Liddell stands firm and upholds the morally "right" choice in that he does not stray from his (Christian) values. The conflict is resolved by Lord Lindsay nonchalantly offering to give up his place in the 400-meter race—as he says, "I've already got my medal." Paradoxically, Liddell may only run with the permission of the aristocratic elite; the generous Lord Lindsay's offer is part noblesse oblige, part amateur spirit and again displays a certain nostalgia or "cultural fascination with the aristocratic *ancient régime*."[53] It is interesting to note, though, that Lindsay "only" wins a silver medal, which suggests that his amateur training and chivalry about racing ultimately only lead to partial success. Instead, it is the professional approach and spiritual determination of Abrahams and Liddell, respectively, that reap the rewards and declare the amateurism of Lindsay to be outdated—and at least implicitly, out of tune with a Thatcherite model of "success."

Liddell performs his version of national identity in quite a different way than both Abrahams and Lindsay. His Scottishness is not only swiftly declared, as noted above; it is also firmly set in rural Scotland. Despite being supposedly a student at Edinburgh University, we never see him in an urban setting. His training—he is also accompanied by a coach, albeit not necessarily a professional one—lacks the sophistication of that of Abrahams. Whereas Abrahams practices on a proper track with his coach, Sam

Mussabini, employing what appears to be state-of-the-art training methods, Liddell is shown running across the Scottish hills and along the beach. Where Abrahams scowls, Liddell smiles as, in his mind, he is fulfilling God's wishes when he runs. In short, Liddell is the natural runner, and Abrahams the one who has learned his profession. This alignment with nature and spirituality harks back strongly to Victorian-era discourses of "muscular Christianity"—the belief that cultivation of one's physical body, in partic-ular masculine bodies, was central to fulfilling one's spiritual obligations.[54]

Liddell's affinity with nature also denotes Scotland as quaint and back-ward, as exemplified by his seemingly outdated training methods; it stands in contrast to the urban modernity of Abrahams. While Lord Lindsay represents the best of aristocracy and Abrahams the benefits of meritocracy, Liddell's muscular Christian is most closely associated with the "simple" people within his provincial church framework. His principled, moralistic, and disciplined life of Christian values embodies the conservative aspects of Thatcherism and introduces another facet of British national identity. At the same time, both Liddell and Abrahams remain partial outsiders until their victory at the Olympics, so that, as Martha Solomon concludes, "each man is not the other's enemy. Indeed, they share a common foe: a social order which does not fully respect their values and commitments."[55]

These conflicting versions of British national identity and belonging are represented at a structural level in several further scenes featuring the deterritorializing pull of the time-image. Throughout Abrahams's and Liddell's races, the multiple replays and camera angles not only pander to contemporary audiences' viewing habits, as outlined in the introduction; they also serve to again disrupt the linear chronology of the movement-image. In one key example, Abrahams watches Liddell run a 400-meter race in which he falls down, recovers, and overtakes all his competitors to win the race in a superhuman effort. During Liddell's fall, the film cuts away to the astonished spectators—Abrahams among them—and then back to Liddell, but now in slow motion. His slow-motion tumble and subsequent getting back into the race are intercut three times, first with a shot of Mussabini, who is observing the track meet, and then with a shot of Liddell's coach, Sandy (Struan Rodger), among another throng of spectators, and another shot of Mussabini urging Liddell to get up. Only the shots of Liddell are in slow motion and thus suggest a different time for him than for the rest of the spectators. As his movements slow down almost to a standstill, one can briefly glimpse a fork in the labyrinth of time: on one path Liddell gets up and continues the race; on the other he stays down defeated. After another cutaway to Abrahams, the shots of Liddell return to "normal" speed, negating any other possible simultaneous history. In similar ways many of Abrahams's races suggest small glitches in the reterritorializing pull of the movement-image. While all of these factors do not make *Chariots of Fire* a particularly strong hybrid-image, they do keep undermining the performance of national identity by questioning the validity of any single "correct" narrative.

The three key performances of English and Scottish national identity—by Abrahams, Liddell, and Lindsay—are ultimately brought together under the banner of the United Kingdom as the British athletics team leaves for the Olympic Games. One cannot be without the other: Lord Lindsay steps in to give Liddell a chance to run, and Abrahams needs the loss against Liddell in an earlier race as motivation to be at his best at the Games. The precariousness of this incorporation of the outsiders, Liddell and Abrahams, under the British flag is clearly demonstrated when Liddell refuses to race on the Sabbath, a dramatic tension that threatens to jeopardize the unifying project of the film. The rivalry between Abrahams and Liddell further endangers this project but is similarly defused by removing Liddell as a direct competitor of Abrahams's. This resolution is supported at the highest levels when the Prince of Wales comments to Liddell that "it's good to have you on the same side at last." Solomon comments on the unusual resolution of what had, until this point of the film, been the primary conflict: "Instead of partial frustration the audience gets total satisfaction."[56] At the crux of this "total satisfaction," I submit, is the affirmation of a shared British identity that has successfully overcome differences of regional identity, class, and religion. It is at this point of the narrative that the international rivalry of the Olympic Games, and in particular the contest between the United Kingdom and the United States, usurps the now defunct main conflict between Liddell and Abrahams. The introduction of a shared Other functions to stabilize the precarious unity of the British team, with the national heroes the film has so carefully constructed finally battling on the same side.

This chapter has examined the multifaceted representation of national identity in *Chariots of Fire*, a representation that draws on past and contemporary 1980s ideas of nationhood and that eventually unifies competing regional identities into a single British national identity on the cusp of the Thatcher era. Through historical verisimilitude the film constructs a framework of technical and visual authenticity—at times through anachronistic techniques—that enables what I have termed emotional authenticity. The film builds on this framework to construct mythic heroes in Abrahams and Liddell, drawing on traditional patterns of mythmaking in order to make these newfound national heroes relevant for contemporary audiences. Elements of both this mythical aggrandizing and the discourse of authenticity ultimately serve the complex representation of national identity in *Chariots of Fire*; a representation that is repeatedly ruptured and in need of containment. National identity is anything but straightforward in *Chariots of Fire*, a film that is both forward-looking (albeit in a 1980s conservative sense), pointing to the establishment of a social meritocracy, but also mourning a lost "Golden Age" of English aristocracy. The national identities performed by the characters of Abrahams, Liddell, and Lindsay are interrupted and almost derailed at various points in the film, a process formally demonstrated by the struggle between the deterritorializing and reterritorializing pull of the time-image and the movement-image, respectively.

These ruptures attest to the contradictions inherent in Thatcherite ideology and the tensions arising from the economically aggressive yet socially and morally regressive elements that characterized the early 1980s British political scene, and that would rise to greater prominence as the decade progressed. It is no accident that this film appeared at the beginning of Thatcher's period of rule. Whereas some scholars have argued that *Chariots of Fire* is a thoroughly "Thatcherite" film, I argue that it is, more precisely, a film that reflects the coming of Thatcherism, a period of transition and social change in a Britain frequently at odds with itself. The creation of mythic national "heroes" in order to unite a fragmented national community can also, from this perspective, be seen as a heralding—and thus endorsement—of Thatcherism. On the one hand the film's unifying project showcases the difficult processes of the transformation of national identity, particularly when this involves the incorporation of regional, religious, ethnic, or socioeconomic Others. On the other hand it highlights the constant potential for such national identity—and ideology—to be destabilized. Typical of the sports film genre, *Chariots of Fire* ultimately gives preference to the affirmation of a British identity that is outwardly united, despite its internal differences. In doing so, it suppresses the disruptive elements of the time-image that complicate this myth of national unity and threaten to reveal it as a constructed, fragile entity. Yet it never completely eliminates these troubling undercurrents, and this subtle underlying tension and complexity may well help to explain its continuing resonance with both British and international audiences. The narrative power at work here, I argue, is reliant on the deliberate creation of mythical hero figures and a sense of emotional authenticity in the mise-en-scène. These patterns of mythmaking are also in evidence in the following chapter, which examines a West German foundation myth of modern nationhood that sprang from a sporting event that has itself attained an almost-mythical status and that has been dubbed the "Miracle of Bern."

CHAPTER 2

UNIFYING GERMANY

The Miracle of Bern and National Identity

> Germany in the final of the soccer world championship—
> this is an incredible sensation, a true football miracle.
>
> Herbert Zimmermann in *The Miracle of Bern* (2003)

In one of the best modern examples of the power of sports to build national identity, the words of Herbert Zimmermann during his live radio commentary on July 4, 1954, at the Fédération Internationale de Football Association (FIFA) World Cup final between underdog West Germany and favorite Hungary are now part of the legendary status of European soccer. During that championship, the West German team surpassed all expectations to beat Hungary at the Wankdorf stadium in Bern, Switzerland. This victory—dubbed the "Wunder von Bern" (Miracle of Bern)[1]—became a founding myth of the then newly created Federal Republic of Germany, subsequently recognized as a vital moment in renewing the West German people's sense of dignity following the horrors of World War II and inspiring confidence in the still-young republic. For this event, however, the term "Wunder"/"Miracle" should not be understood as an expression of overt religiousness, in the sense of winning the tournament by the grace of God, as seen in Eric Liddell's divinely inspired running performance in *Chariots of Fire* in chapter 1. Rather, it is an indication of the perceived unlikelihood of the sporting success achieved by the West German soccer team. Just how strongly the Wunder von Bern has permeated the popular imagination beyond the realm of sports—where, for example, the radio commentary still serves as a blueprint for successful soccer commentary even today—can be seen in its representation in media and popular culture since 1954. Referenced in films from the New German Cinema feature film *The Marriage of Maria Braun* (Fassbinder, 1979) to the 1990s indie hit *Run Lola Run* (Tykwer, 1998), and in literature, in Friedrich Christian Delius's *The Sunday I Became World Champion* (1994), this beloved David and Goliath story has had a lasting impact on West German national identity.[2] Much like *Chariots of Fire* is revived with every Olympic Summer Games, so too is the Wunder von Bern recalled through songs, books, and documentaries, culminating in the 2014 musical *The Miracle of Bern*, to provide inspiration for every soccer World Cup championship.

In 2003 this legendary sporting event became the subject of one of the most successful German films of the year, reinvigorating the mythical story of how West Germany beat the odds to bring a new confidence to the nation. Sönke Wortmann's *The Miracle of Bern* portrays a slowly reorienting postwar society whose problems reverberated with its audience, a newly reunited German population still negotiating the effects of the fall of the Berlin Wall. The film depicts both the surprise win of the West German team and the impact this event had on young Matthias Lubanski (Louis Klamroth) and his recently reunited family in the West German mining city of Essen. As the family struggles to come to terms with life in postwar West Germany, and an estranged father recently returned from a Russian prisoner-of-war camp, the West German soccer team fights to take home the trophy and establish a new footing on the international stage for the young Federal Republic.

For the most part *The Miracle of Bern* has been has been examined in relation to notions of *Heimat* or what Lutz Koepnick called "Germany's new heritage cinema," a cinema defined, much like its British counterpart, by its presentation of "the texture of the past as a source of visual attractions and aural pleasures" and the transformation of "the past into an object of consumption."[3] Paul Cooke and Chris Homewood see these films as growing out of what Eric Rentschler has called the (German) "cinema of consensus," which showed "a marked disinclination toward any serious political reflection or sustained historical retrospection."[4] German heritage film, they argue, continues this trend of apolitical genre films, often relying on melodramatic conventions, making for pleasant and uncomplicated consumption.[5] Mattias Frey, meanwhile, arguing against a heritage film framework, frames the film as a revisionist male melodrama that is in direct conflict with earlier representations of the event of the Wunder von Bern, such as Rainer Werner Fassbinder's *The Marriage of Maria Braun*.[6] This chapter intervenes in this scholarship by examining themes of mythmaking and nation, showing how the retrospective cinematic retelling of a mythic narrative that would resonate emotionally with a post-Wall German viewing public entailed brushing over problematic and unflattering aspects of the immediate post-Nazi German past, as well as of continuing inequities between East and West in contemporary German society.

In contrast to *Chariots of Fire*, which, as argued in the previous chapter, created a new myth out of two forgotten sporting heroes, *The Miracle of Bern* instead *reconfigures* an existing myth that had long been circulating at the level of collective cultural memory. Specifically I argue that the film works to create a single, in Alison Landsberg's terms, "prosthetic memory" of the historical event for a new generation of both West and East Germans, for whom the notion of German division is less deeply entrenched, and it actively reaches out to a less obvious public of older East Germans, not just their West German counterparts, aware that the original event would not have had the same cultural impact for this demographic.[7] This new prosthetic memory enables the film to conjure a feeling of pan-German community and national unity through the historical event of the Wunder von Bern. I explore how this new, constructed memory—which at the same time elides other memories of Cold War division and pervasive postwar Nazi sentiment—is created with the help of the strong sense of emotional authenticity that the film produces, and by the concerted effort put into the creation of the main characters as identificatory figures. Whereas in *Chariots of Fire* emotional authenticity is used to create a new hero-myth out of historical figures, here it works to enable hyper-identification with fictional characters, who are retrospectively injected into the historical events to create a highly selective version of a unified German past.

The fictional family at the center of the film plays a crucial role in the process of reinvigorating a popular West German founding myth for a post-unification, pan-German audience. At one level the various family members, of a range of ages, genders, and political affiliations, provide multiple points of identification for a cross-section of German society. At another level the insertion of these characters into the mythical narrative of the events in Bern shifts the emphasis of the achievement away from the soccer players and toward the "ordinary" West German population. By fictionally incorporating the lives of the Lubanski family directly into the tale of the great soccer win, this shift involves a series of deliberate misrepresentations of actual historical events. The effect of these fictional gestures is to create the impression that the majority of the population actively participated in—indeed, to various extents "owned"—the "miracle" that became enshrined as the rebirth of Germany in the popular imagination following World War II. The film allows the "miracle" to be reclaimed by the people, that is, by contemporary audiences, who might see aspects of their own family history in that of the Lubanski family. In the process it works to bring unity to a still-fragmented nation suffering from vast economic and social inequalities, as the "new" states of the former German Democratic Republic faced the flight of a younger generation to supposedly greener, Western pastures, high unem-ployment, social discord, and the resentment of a West German populace at the ongoing costs of unification. These social inequities, which Wortmann's film strives to overcome in the name of portraying a unified nation both "then" and "now," not only pervaded German politics and debate at the time of the film's release almost one and half decades after the fall of the Wall but continue to do so today, almost thirty years after those momentous events.

The Miracle of Bern has three intertwining storylines. The first and central narrative follows young Matthias Lubanski and his family and the impact of the 1954 World Cup on their lives. Matthias's father, Richard (Peter Lohmeier), has just returned after eleven years in a Russian prisoner-of-war camp, and the familial relationships reach breaking point as he tries to adjust to their unfamiliar, "normal" life. The second storyline provides comic relief in the form of affluent newlyweds Annette (Katharina Wackernagel) and Paul Ackermann (Lucas Gregorowicz). Paul has been sent to attend the World Cup as a reporter, and Annette is keen to accompany him despite her disinterest in soccer. The last storyline, and the only one that can claim to be based on true events, however tenuously, serves as the reference point for the other two, following the German national team's preparation for, and struggle to win, the World Cup, as seen through the eyes of Coach Herberger (Peter Franke) and striker Helmut Rahn (Sascha Göpel), who is also Matthias's soccer idol. Matthias serves as Rahn's ball boy and mascot for his local matches in the industrial West German city of Essen, and Rahn has effectively become a father figure for Matthias during his father's long absence. In this way the film's revisionist version of German history begins at the level of the family, with the emotional trauma of missing fathers and broken families focusing on German suffering during the war rather than on being the perpetrators of war.

This chapter is divided into two parts. Based on the history of the event itself, the first section illustrates how emotional authenticity is produced in the film through impeccable attention to historical detail, and how this supports the creation of a single prosthetic memory as a means of reimagining the national past. The second section builds on this analysis to reveal how the development of emotional authenticity within the narrative is used to foster a hyper-identification with the main characters, who offer various entry points to the events in Bern. While some of the characters (Annette, Matthias) are literally injected into the event by being in direct contact with the soccer players and the crucial soccer game—and therefore, it is implied, actively enabling the Wunder itself—others, particularly Matthias's brother Bruno (Mirko Lang) and his father, Richard, offer their experiences of the time of the Wunder to a new audience, including former East Germans, who have a far less emotional relationship with this myth than former West Germans. In doing so the film reconfigures a national myth of the past to enable contemporary audiences the possibility of imagining a unified nation in the present.

Emotional Authenticity and Prosthetic Memory: Capturing History, Soccer, and Myth

In *Prosthetic Memory: The Transformation of American Remembrance in the Age of Mass Culture*, Alison Landsberg argues for the recognition of a "new form of public cultural memory" that is available through mass media—for example, the emotional experience of film viewing in cinemas.[8] Through such mediated experiences, she contends, it is possible for the spectators to "gain" memories of historical events that they themselves have never experienced in their own lives. These "prosthetic memories" are powerful as they have "the ability to shape [a] person's subjectivity and politics."[9] Just as nostalgic representations have the potential to encourage audiences to engage with the past in ways that inspire reflection, the concept of prosthetic memory builds on the affective power of the filmic medium, especially in the confines of the cinema.[10] The particular emotive capabilities of sports films, with their clear-cut highs and lows, right and wrong, winners and losers, and, above all, the heightened tension created by the on-screen sports contest, aid the creation of such prosthetic memories, which work to reinforce the myth of a virile, successful nation.

While Landsberg's work is situated within the context of American remembrance, her theory of prosthetic memories can be usefully applied to the postwar German context. Her stated goal is "to explore the ability of prosthetic memories to produce empathy and social responsibility as well as political alliances that transcend race, class, and gender,"[11] but the effect in *The Miracle of Bern* is somewhat less progressive: having acquired the prosthetic memory of the event of the Wunder von Bern, the contemporary audience is encouraged to embrace it uncritically in the name of renewed national unity. Facilitating this process of acquiring a prosthetic memory—of a "person sutur[ing] himself or herself into a larger history"—is, I argue, the underlying emotional authenticity produced by the film.[12] Without it, the prosthetic memory cannot be incorporated into the viewer's storehouse of experiences and thus effects the change in that person's worldview that Landsberg argues is possible.

In order to understand how emotional authenticity enables the prosthetic memory created by the film, it is necessary to consider the broader historical situation of Germany in the 1950s, the historical event itself, and the impact it is said to have had on West Germany. Nearly ten years after the end of the Second World War, the soccer World Cup marked only the second major international sporting event in which Germany had been allowed to participate. Germany's comprehensive war defeat had resulted in the occupation of West Germany by the United States and its Allies. Germans no longer felt in control of their own sovereignty, and national spirit and identity were at an all-time low.[13] As Florian Breitmeier and Arthur Heinrich point out, the West Germany of the early 1950s was subdued as people tried to put their lives back together. At the same time, the economy was recovering quickly, and the 1950s also became known for West Germany's so-called economic miracle.[14]

In addition, the two Germanys, East and West, were slowly developing new, separate identities, and the division increasingly appeared to be more than a temporary measure. The formal establishment of the Federal Republic of Germany and the German Democratic Republic in 1949 solidified this division and made a reunification in the near future unlikely. To a large extent the West German population steered clear of national politics, because, as Wolfram Pyta points out, "German nationalism in all its forms and varieties [had been] disqualified as a community-building force for the foreseeable future."[15] Instead West Germans were seeking refuge in their regional surroundings and trying to make a living while slowly rebuilding the country.

In short, postwar West Germany was a country not only in need of reconstruction, with many of its cities destroyed, but also with a new political system, culture, and identity. After the war, many families struggled to come together and find their place, especially with men returning from prisoner-of-war camps, who often had difficulty adjusting to a "normal" civilian life. These soldiers were often in shock about what they had experienced and what they had done. They experienced guilt and shame concerning the suffering, grief, and violence they had inflicted on others and pain over what they had endured. This sense of shame and devastation was shared with the civic population and led to a nationwide attempt to achieve normalcy that was characteristic of "a population that wished to move on and put the recent past behind it."[16] The popularity of the Heimat film genre during this period perhaps offers an insight into these times—a genre that is populated with "morally upstanding men and girlish women clad in traditional dress" and that includes the "repeated integration of (pseudo-) traditional Volksmusik . . . lengthy inserts of Alpine flora and fauna, often on the flimsiest motivation [and] the appeal to forms of humor and general values allegedly held by the peasants who people these films."[17] These films were seemingly apolitical, often focusing on romantic plots in picturesque landscapes, and presented a Germany as far away from war as possible.

The Miracle of Bern in many ways continues in this vein, concentrating on the suffering of the German people in the aftermath of war, at the expense of examining the suffering *caused* by the Germans and their war efforts, a more familiar subject for both national and international audiences in the postwar period. Stuart Taberner argues that the film is part of a "trend that began in the mid-1990s, to focus on the wartime fates of 'ordinary people,' on the apparent 'impossibility' of their circumstances, choices and varying (mis)fortunes. This development often subsumes the very different causes of German and Jewish suffering within a sentimentalized, universalized victimhood."[18] *The Miracle of Bern* is a perfect example of this nostalgic, uncritical treatment of postwar Germany.

For Benedict Anderson, the nation is an "imagined community" conceived of as a "deep, horizontal comradeship."[19] Accordingly national identity has been theorized as the means both to identify with and to strengthen the nation state through its assembly of symbols and rituals. Germany in the 1950s had not yet found the appropriate rituals and symbols—let alone narratives—that could emphasize the traditions and continuity of the nation, especially across as brutal a rupture as the advent of National Socialism and World War II. As historian Robert G. Moeller argues, "the problem for Germans after 1945 was not how to create a conception of the nation, but rather how to establish a sense of collectivity that did not draw on a nationalist rhetoric contaminated by its association with Nazism."[20] With the horrors of the war still clearly in mind, Germans had turned away from enacting rituals associated with celebrating the nation that had existed for thousands of years. These values had been fully discredited by the atrocities of the Second World War, and although a democratic nation-state had been formed in West Germany after 1945, it was widely perceived to be a fabricated apparatus that had no "natural" origin but that had been thrust upon the people.

The film shows these tensions to be tangible when, for example, Richard tries to impose his Nazi-infused, "old" value system on his sons. In one scene he slaps Matthias across the face and tells him not to cry, as "a German boy never cries." In another scene one of the war veterans complains that "we've lost the war and we'll lose this game" while watching the final in the pub. This loss of identity reflects the confusion and contradictions of the early postwar period, when the German language was still infused with nationalistic overtones and statistics showed widespread distrust in the new democratic system.[21] German society tried to steer as far away as possible from anything overtly political, and following each win of the national soccer team the newspapers were full of warnings about another uprising of nationalistic sentiment. Although the first fruits of the economic miracle had begun to be felt at an individual level—of which the film makes great comic use through the storyline of the affluent Ackermanns—the economic upturn alone was not capable of bringing the population together as a nation. In other words what Anderson describes as the imagined community necessary for a sense of nationhood was still much more imagined by the politicians than an actual community of the people. But the Wunder von Bern was about to change all this and give the West German population something it desperately needed—a collective emotional experience that could bind West Germany together as a community.

The film presents this period in West German history with great attention to detail (see fig. 1). The mise-en-scène is "hyper-saturated," to use Mette Hjort's term, with objects and symbols of 1950s consumer culture and everyday life.[22] This West Germany, however, possesses two sides: the drab surroundings of the Lubanskis, who struggle to make a living in the rough coal-mining area of the Ruhrpott in the region of North Rhine Westphalia and who represent the perceived postwar German victimhood; and the candy-colored, art-deco-filled world of the affluent Ackermanns in Munich in Southern Bavaria, who, in contrast, represent the bright German future thanks to the emerging economic miracle. With the unusually high budget for a German production of €7.5 million, the producers spared no expense with regard to costumes, makeup, set design, locations, and casting. Indicative of this commitment to historical accuracy is the filmmakers' order of 180 wigs of 1950s hairstyles from specialist wigmakers in Hollywood for the extras alone, an unprecedented extravagance in German

1. *The Miracle of Bern*: The gray streets of Matthias's home in the coal-mining area Ruhrpott; the fanciful art-deco apartment of the Ackermanns; 1950s cars and buses at the final; people gathering in front of the shop windows of an electronics shop to watch the final. *Das Wunder von Bern*. Bavaria Film International: Sönke Wortmann (2003).

film. Accordingly, in interviews Wortmann and his team stress the amount of research that went into their search for authenticity, citing, for example, the four weeks spent researching 1950s styles and costumes, or the months of location scouting for undisturbed 1950s streets with workers' cottages in the Ruhrpott area.[23]

The film captures not only an authentic-looking 1950s West Germany but also the mood and atmosphere created by the World Cup win. The tournament itself provided a perfect script for the creation of a myth in the form of the Wunder von Bern. The opponent, Hungary, had become an international soccer Goliath, the "Golden Team" that had been unbeaten for thirty-one games; not only were they the first team to beat England on home soil at Wembley Stadium, but they also had beaten the West German side at the group stage with a decisive score of 8–3. The media helped heighten this status by playing up Hungary's invincibility, enabling the West German victory to look even more heroic. As noted in the previous chapter, such a strategy of aggrandizing the opposition is a defining trait in the formation of classical myths and is also commonly employed in sports films.

The West German team, which had been discredited as a group of nobodies by the international soccer community, actually consisted of many highly skilled and well-known players, such as Jupp Posipal, who had been nominated for the FIFA World Team in 1953. Through clever tactics and deployment of his players' capabilities, coach Sepp Herberger brought his team to the final with successive victories over sizeable opponents Turkey, Yugoslavia, and Austria. In the final itself, West Germany was down two goals to nil after only nine minutes, making victory seem impossible and humiliation more likely. After another nine minutes, however, the score was equaled, and Germany was fighting off one Hungarian attack after another. Germany found itself on the attack in the eighty-fourth minute with German striker Helmut Rahn scoring the winning goal. An equalizing goal by the Hungarians was not given due to the offside rule, and finally, after ninety minutes of sheer drama, the referee ended the game, and reporter Herbert Zimmermann erupted with unbridled joy and excitement. This remarkable story of how West Germany beat Hungary in the 1954 final became a mythical rallying point that signified a new start for a country still struggling with a diminished sense of national identity.

Both Malte Hagener and Mattias Frey criticize the film for its lack of critical engagement with history as a mediated text, or, as Frey calls it, a "media memory."[24] Neither, however, fully appreciates the consequences of the soccer final as a mediated event at the time—the sale of forty thousand television sets prior to the World Cup final also made the experience of watching the game a distinctly collective one with some sales going to private homes, but the majority to pubs and clubs. Radios, while much more common, also provided spaces for collective experiences, with families, friends, colleagues, and so forth gathering to listen to the radio commentary. The film re-creates this atmosphere of collectivity in a scene that shows strangers huddled together in pubs in front of radios and TVs and around shop windows with TV sets. This effective montage clearly conveys a spontaneous moment of collective joy—"we" won, not just the soccer team—in a way that seems relatively untainted by nationalistic fervor. This experience of collectivity led to two developments. Nationally it gave the population an emotional success story seemingly far removed from politics; and internationally it marked, as historian Arthur Heinrich puts it, "something like a re-entry into the world, this time in a civilized fashion."[25] This sentiment found expression in the popular phrase "We are somebody again," which in the decades following the World Cup win found a solid place in the West German collective memory.[26]

The World Cup win was symbolically significant for the West German population, providing a boost to national self-esteem and pointing to the establishment of a new value system unblemished by National Socialism. In the years to come, however, this meant that some of the less savory moments of the event would be ignored or repressed, or even willingly forgotten. For there was a dirty underbelly to the events that smacked of a resurgence of Nazism and undermined the clean "miracle" story—one that had not gone unnoticed by either the national or international media. For example, at the awards ceremony the thousands of German fans who had witnessed the final at the Wankdorf Stadium sang the banned first verse of the West German national anthem, "Deutschland, Deutschland über alles" (Germany above everything), instead of the sanctioned, but lesser-known, third verse. This was broadcast as part of the radio reportage of the match to all of Germany and was commented on with outrage and fear of a resurgence of Nazism by the national and international press.[27]

The film deliberately reinforces the German public's amnesia about the darker aspects of this success story. As it looks nostalgically to the past, in what may be considered an example of a German "cinema of heritage attraction,"[28] *The Miracle of Bern* generously obfuscates the more problematic aspects of the historical event, such as replacing the crowd's singing of the national anthem with a roaring triumphant score and omitting the Hungarian offside goal in order to eliminate any doubts as to the legitimacy of the German win. Paul Cooke and Christopher Young argue that this is in line with other mythical hero narratives, as "Wortmann's de-selection of certain more problematic moments of the 1954 narrative is indeed an archetypal epic move . . . , and one that shows the continuing boundaries of German 'normality' that this epic can still not cross."[29] Rather than examining these largely forgotten "problematic moments," the film creates a revisionist history of the events of 1954.

Florian Breitmeier argues that myths develop at times of historical and societal rupture, when the need for the evaluation and legitimization of value systems in relation to the past is especially urgent.[30] For West Germany the time after the war was such a time of rupture and affected the population at all levels so that, as Heinrich points out, "by the time of the final round on Sunday, July 4, an entire people was on the ball."[31] The World Cup audience had extended to encompass not just soccer fans but all sections of the population, from housewives to children, and from managers to factory workers. *The Miracle of Bern* represents these various groups through the intertwined stories of the affluent Ackermanns, the working-class Lubanskis, and the mixed personalities of the soccer team.

While the older generation gained most in terms of perceived international rehabilitation, the World Cup win against such a formidable opponent engraved into the minds of a younger generation the message that anything was possible, and all odds could be overcome. This message could not have been conveyed nearly as strongly by party slogans or government programs, and together with the nation's economic resurgence the win presaged a powerful vision of a prosperous future. The young were emotionally touched more than the older generation, who were jaded by the National Socialist use of sports in their propaganda, with Leni Riefenstahl's *Olympia* films a shining example. It was this younger generation who would subsequently keep the story alive, actively revisiting it throughout their lives as a reference point for the foundation of West Germany, as evidenced, for example, in Delius's story about how "he" became a world champion through the soccer team's win.[32]

This process was helped along by successive governments that were ready to use this particular sporting achievement as a symbol of West Germany's achievements. In particular, though, it is the emotional impact of the event on young and old alike that lifts it above the usual soccer statistic and explains its continued relevance. As Pyta argues, the historical reception of the soccer match "shows in a particularly succinct manner the transition of a symbol to the status of a myth," distinguishing itself "by a special narrative structure which is in a position to release emotions and emotionally strengthen a collective identity."[33] It is this emotional value that Wortmann uses in his filmic reconfiguration of the myth, because only by achieving a sense of emotional authenticity is it possible for him to introduce small but important changes to the Wunder von Bern. In doing so the film seizes on the mutability of myths.

The Wunder von Bern has had many incarnations, most obviously as a constant reference for every subsequent international soccer match of the West German national team. Despite three more World Cup wins, in 1974, 1990, and 2014, it has never been dethroned as the quintessential West German soccer success story, because it rose above the limits of soccer fandom to signify a universal sense of national community. While Patzner attributes the reason for the persistence of the Wunder von Bern narrative to its mythological qualities, Pyta ascribes its success, on the one hand, to its appeal to comradeship and, on the other hand, to the Federal Republic's lack of other appropriate historical figures or victories that might function as a rallying point for the new state. As noted above, the new Republic sorely lacked symbols that could transmit abstract ideas of nationhood and national identity free of the burden of the recent past. Consequently, the soccer players and the World Cup became "the imaginative focal point of the cultural condition of the West Germans."[34]

Commentator Herbert Zimmermann played a decisive role in giving the German population a new set of heroes that they were all too ready to embrace, when he excitedly shouted the now famous words: "Over! Over! Over! The game is over! Germany is World Champion! Beats Hungary 3–2 in the final in Bern!" These soccer-players-turned-heroes were no fearless Teutonic Siegfrieds; they were ordinary young men with ordinary jobs and young families, who, more importantly, were considered politically untainted. This "ordinariness" meant that everyone in Germany could identify with them, as Breitmeier observes: "The players symbolized the anti-hero who could only become famous and mythical because he, in contrast to previous heroes, did not distinguish himself from ordinary people in attitude or habitus. Only because of this were many people allowed to hope that one day they might be able to equal the new heroes. In 1954 people became 'stars' who indicated to those who admired them that the achievement at Bern was in principle achievable by everyone."[35]

They represented a new set of admirable and untainted virtues such as perseverance, humility, and propriety, which would form the basis of a newfound German identity. These "11 friends," as they were called, of the national team were easily instrumentalized for the new German value systems in need of the legitimization to which Breitmeier referred, and such legitimization was actively constructed by the Adenauer government through its celebration of the win. This identity, so desperately needed at the end of a reorientation phase following the war, would allow Germany to join the international community once again and would restore some dignity to its collective ego. It is this emotional and cultural condition and its heroes that the film convincingly revives.

Having created the look and mood of 1950s West Germany, the filmmakers also needed to reproduce persuasively the famous soccer sequences in order to achieve what I am calling emotional authenticity. The complexity of this challenge is not to be underestimated, given that the 1954 World Cup holds the status of one of the first major media events in German history. When the soccer final was broadcast on television and radio, an estimated sixty million Germans watched the match live on television and listened to reporter Herbert Zimmermann's iconic commentary. Indeed, three television manufacturers reported completely selling out of their warehouse stock.[36] This meant that not only was the soccer final a collective event, as discussed above, but it was one that had a powerful visual memory attached to it. Almost the entire nation had seen the set pieces of the match, including the winning goal, and with every subsequent World Cup, the few surviving fragments of the television broadcast served as reminders of past glory, creating a living memory that the film needed to capture successfully.

This is evident in the research and depiction of the actual World Cup games (see fig. 2). The painstakingly re-created and well-known set pieces of the matches, and Zimmermann's perfectly reenacted original commentary, serve to cement the film's sense of authenticity, as do the documentary-like

2. *The Miracle of Bern*: The winning goal by Helmut Rahn in 1954; the film's soccer coach explaining the soccer choreography in 2002 to match the original game. *Das Wunder von Bern*. Bavaria Film International: Sönke Wortmann (2003).

titles introducing the matches and a litany of sports historical details, from re-creating television bulletins of interviews with the soccer players to Adi Dassler's (the founder of sports brand Adidas) invention of exchangeable screw-on cleats. Unlike in *Chariots of Fire*, the filmmakers faced the challenge of portraying soccer players who were widely known. In their search for actors to portray these heroes the filmmakers auditioned over one thousand soccer players in the hope that they could be taught to act. Conscious of the importance of credible sports action, they argued that a modern audience knowledgeable in soccer would reject actors "faking" the plays.

The soccer sequences were then filmed with multiple cameras by sports television camera operators for maximum emotional impact, thus going far beyond simplistic play-by-play choreography. Malte Hagener points out that whereas "in most football films the on-pitch action is heavily edited, *The Miracle of Bern* takes into account that most spectators (at least in Germany) qualify as 'experts,' through the intense media coverage of football, in particular on television."[37] This complex combination of attention to historical detail and mood, recognizable historical figures, and anachronistic but familiar film techniques chosen for their affective quality created a powerful sense of emotional authenticity in *The Miracle of Bern*. This emotional authenticity, in turn, forms the basis for the creation of a prosthetic memory aimed at unifying a fragmented post–Cold War audience. While some audience members might not have been alive at the time of the Wunder von Bern, for others it simply did not have the same impact because they were born or raised in the "other" Germany. Importantly, however, prosthetic memories are "not natural [and] not the product of lived experience . . . but are derived from engagement with a mediated representation."[38] If, as Landsberg contends, there is a possibility "of prosthetically appropriating memories of a cultural or collective past," then *The Miracle of Bern* offers contemporary German spectators the chance to participate in the celebration of the 1954 World Cup as part of a new collective past.[39]

Emotional Authenticity and Hyper-Identification

The film's multiple characters and storylines emphasize the importance of ordinary German people in this event and generate a multiplicity of identificatory options, including the Lubanski family, the Ackermanns, and the German national team. The film's fostering of strong identifications with these protagonists greatly enhances the audience's ability to acquire a prosthetic memory of the Wunder von Bern. Rather than celebrating aloof and inaccessible soccer stars in the vein of, for example, today's Cristiano Ronaldo, the film demythologizes the soccer players by depicting them as "normal" people and subordinates their storyline to the other two. In doing so it transfers much of the actual achievement of the Wunder von Bern to ordinary people such as the Lubanskis and Ackermanns, a more accessible point of entry and identification for contemporary audiences to experience the past and absorb a new prosthetic memory of the event.

The film's insertion of its fictional characters, in particular Matthias Lubanski and Annette Ackermann, into the actual final of the World Cup helps make this prosthetic memory emotionally valuable, allowing audiences, as Pam Cook describes, to "connect emotionally with representations of the past"[40] in ways that have the potential to encourage active reflection and thus impact on the audience's experiences in the present. By creating an emotional connection with this particular past, and especially by assigning agency to ordinary people, the film offers its audience ways to work through the more recent rupture in pan-German history symbolized by the Berlin Wall.

The Lubanski family offers the primary point of identification and is established early on in the film as the archetypal 1950s working-class family. Christa (Johanna Gastdorf), the mother, has inventively carved out a living for her family by taking on the running of a corner pub, in which her daughter Ingrid (Birthe Wolter) helps out as a waitress. Christa is less a fiercely independent woman than one forced to become a breadwinner out of necessity. She represents a generation of women who had to deal with the absence of husbands, sons, and brothers—a generation of male wage earners. Instead, these women entered the workforce and helped rebuild the country, as "women of the rubble" (*Trümmerfrauen*), who literally cleaned the cities of war debris, or as members of the workforce.[41] Like millions of other German women, Christa is uncertain as to whether her husband is still alive, let alone knowing if he will ever return home. The postwar ethos of hard work is displayed as everyone in the family pitches in to earn money: elder son Bruno (Mirko Lang) by playing in a band, and even young Matthias does his bit with an entrepreneurial scheme to resell cigarettes he makes out of used cigarette butts. The Lubanskis evoke familiar images and ways of life in postwar Germany, such as the need to be inventive, and this resonates easily with a German audience brought up in the shadow of World War II.

In stark contrast to the struggling Lubanskis, the wealthy Ackermanns are clearly early beneficiaries of the economic miracle. They illustrate the new consumer culture, with wife Annette, for example, exclaiming in front of a full wardrobe: "I have nothing to wear!" Their apartment is furnished with the latest design objects, and Annette's closet is filled with colorful petticoats, hats, gloves, and high-heeled shoes. While the scenes in the Ruhr valley, which is famous for its coal mining and industrialized landscape, are visually dominated by factory smokestacks, dreary colors, and dirt and grime, the scenes involving the Ackermanns are candy colored and over-flowing with the latest consumer goods. Their inclusion as representatives of the upper-middle-class is of central importance, not only because it adds comic and visual relief from the drabness of the Lubanskis' lives but also because it opens up another point of identification with 1950s West Germany, which is here coded as positive. In doing so it demonstrates how this particular soccer game came to permeate virtually all sections of the West German population, even across socioeconomic borders.

These diverse protagonists offer a microcosm of social issues within German society of the time. As noted above, Christa is emblematic of the particular struggles women faced, while her daughter, Ingrid, draws on the stereotype of the *Ami-Liebchen* (Yank's sweetheart) or "fraternizer," as she is considered later in the film by her father, Richard, when she dances with an American soldier at a concert of Bruno's band—which, of course, plays American music.[42] Bruno himself embodies the fear of the Americanization of German youths in the 1950s with his rock 'n' roll band and slicked-back hair, reminiscent of a young Elvis Presley. Matthias and Richard bracket the war experience at opposite ends: Matthias represents the innocence of the generation born at the end of the war, whereas Richard personifies the "fellow travelers" of National Socialism and the men broken by the experience of war. Richard's embodiment of past and present in friction is particularly important in relation to the reunified Germany of the 2000s, the context in which the film was released. As with the original myth of 1954, Wortmann's reinvented myth came after another time of rupture— Germany's reunification in 1989–90.

The film's depiction of a slowly reorienting postwar society reverberated with a population still negotiating the social and political implications of the fall of the Berlin Wall. With the end of the Cold War, East Germany effectively became part of West Germany and, at least at the beginning, had to asymmetrically absorb most of the changes in this merger. What West Germany considered a process of democratization in the former East was effectively an invalidation of the East German state, social, and cultural institutions. West Germans also needed to come to terms with this process, which involved large flows of money to support the new German states, including a solidarity tax paid by every taxpayer in West Germany. Tensions around the flows of money and the cultural and democratic developments in the former East and West remain high to this day, and the negotiation of this "inner unity" is still underway, with the ultimate goal of removing the "wall in the heads" of Germans on both sides. Recent years have seen a development of nostalgia for the "old East" (*Eastalgia* or *Ostalgie*, a play on the German word for nostalgia: *Nostalgie*), and some critics have seen a corresponding development in the West (*Westalgia* or *Westalgie*).[43] These nostalgic tendencies might be useful in furthering the project of inner unity, for nostalgia, as Cook contends, "can be perceived as a way of coming to terms with the past, as enabling it to be exorcised in order that society, and individuals, can move on."[44] The nostalgic past presented in *The Miracle of Bern* serves the double function of "moving on" from two ruptures of the past and negotiating identities in flux: postwar Germany in the aftermath of war and reunification Germany as it struggles to consolidate its two parts. Through Richard, the film invites its audience, and particularly Germans who have grown up in the German Democratic Republic, to identify with a man facing the effects of dramatic social and political changes in his own country. As Richard slowly but surely adapts to the changes and opens up to his family, the possibility for positive change is not only suggested but confirmed, and it offers reassurance to an audience still struggling toward unity.

The construction of the 1954 soccer heroes as ordinary Germans that is celebrated in the film is to some degree at odds with the reality of soccer in Germany in the 2000s. Only a couple of years after the premiere of the film, in the lead-up to hosting the 2006 soccer World Cup, the German Soccer Association would celebrate a German national team for its diversity, highlighting players with immigrant roots from Turkey, Africa, and Poland, as well as postwar German American families. Rather than attempting to incorporate such contemporary ethnic diversity into its vision of unity—which would inevitably have involved some further anachronistic fictionalizations—the film instead mobilizes the 1954 players as "ordinary" German heroes in order to promote, above all, inner unity between East and West.

The film makes the process of democratization visible (and palatable) through the disoriented war veteran Richard. His unexpected return at the beginning of the film throws the carefully balanced family life of the remaining Lubanskis into turmoil. The family struggles to incorporate him into their world of shared responsibility and support, which is very unlike the traditional, authoritarian family model that Richard remembers from his own childhood. He uses verbal and physical force, punishing Matthias with a belting for trying to run away, and in a misguided attempt to placate his family, he butchers and cooks Matthias's pet rabbits for a family feast. Richard and elder son Bruno's relationship also becomes increasingly volatile. Their conflict is particularly poignant, because it is set up not only as a father-son clash but also as a conflict of political systems. Bruno is an avid Communist Party supporter, while his father still adheres to the values of National Socialism. This conflict foreshadows the generational clash that would dominate the late 1960s, with many sons and daughters questioning their parents' involvement under the Nazi regime. Adding further to the discontent in his family, Richard plans to close the pub that has supported them prior to his return as soon as he has found work, and he soon finds himself at a loss, uprooted, and disoriented. He no longer knows how to get by in this newly democratic postwar Germany.

Richard is stuck between two worlds. On the one hand he is still infused with the Nazi past, while on the other hand he tries to forget the horrific time in the prisoner-of-war camp that stripped him of humanity and that he barely managed to survive. Richard's difficulties represent those of a generation of men who returned long after the war was finished, at a time when Germany's population had already turned decisively away from its recent past. These experiences are clearly at odds with those of his family, who have successfully moved on and managed to build a life out of the rubble of the war. However, Richard's prisoner-of-war experience eventually provides a basis for the first tentative steps toward bonding with his family again, as he finally decides to share his experiences and accept their support, thus signaling the possibility for change. Richard's storyline resonates with the audience because of its carefully crafted emotional authenticity. As Hjort shows with her theory of "aboutness" and "thematization," the details of everyday life can work to build an enduring sense of nation.[45] In addition to the monumental reconstruction of historical accuracy described above, the film fosters moments of familiarity—of dress, habitus, and everyday situations that connect the viewer emotionally to the times.

Tobias Hochscherf and Christopher Laucht read Richard's slow change to adapt to the "new" country in which he finds himself as a symbol of the "process of the democratization of the FRG."[46] Both Richard and Coach Sepp Herberger, as members of an older generation, need to change in order to find success—Richard in his family and Coach Herberger on the soccer pitch: "their evolution from authoritarian leaders to members of a team symbolizes the change in German society from a totalitarian regime to a democratic society."[47] This evolution, however, is not limited to the changes in postwar West Germany. By becoming the link between the past and the present, Richard symbolizes the disorientation of a generation of East German audience members that have grown up in the GDR and now find themselves socially, culturally, and politically uprooted in post-unification Germany. Richard's modeling of the democratization process not only encourages identification with his struggle but also showcases its solution.

Richard's eventual change of heart and rejection of his Nazi-infused understanding of the world, which leads him to open up to his family, comes too late to salvage the relationship with his eldest son, Bruno, the rebel of the family. Bruno is part of a new generation, disdained by their fathers for questioning their role in the war, and has run off to East Germany, filled with enthusiasm for the socialist movement. Bruno's defection to the East after the rapid dissolution of the relationship with his father represents an attempt to (prosthetically) integrate East Germans into the Wunder von Bern.

Rather than the film, as Matthias Uecker argues, "appear[ing] as an affirmation of a specifically West German success story which has no place for the East," I argue that the film's positive and uncritical portrayal of Bruno and his enthusiasm for the GDR carefully avoids alienating former East Germans and sets Bruno up as a vehicle to invite East German participation and thus reclaim the myth of 1954 for all of Germany, not just the West.[48] There is little evidence as to the importance of the match to the East German population at the time. The official party newspaper of the Socialist Unity Party of Germany (SED), Neues Deutschland, however, might offer a clue as to the official party line. While congratulating the West German team on their win, the article on the last page of the paper offers an appreciation, at best lukewarm, of the West German team's effort and praises the (Eastern bloc) Hungarian team for still being the world's best soccer team despite the loss in the final. It also heavily criticizes the nationalistic overtones of the celebrations—discussed above—and the immediate instrumentalization of the win by the West German chancellor Konrad Adenauer. Thus while East German sympathies on a private level may well have laid with the West German team, officially this was almost certainly not the case. In another act of historical revisionism, the film ignores the unsavory official reaction in order to speculate on ordinary East Germans' allegiances.[49]

This cinematic act of integration is achieved through the inclusion of a single shot in a montage that shows how, indeed, *all* of Germany is tuning in to the live coverage of the match. After revisiting easily recognizable but now deserted hubs of activity from earlier on in the film, such as the offices of the newspaper for which Paul Ackermann works, or the street in which the Lubanskis live, this montage adds new locations that emphasize how

3. *The Miracle of Bern*: Bruno (Mirko Lang) watching the final with his new friends in an FDJ club. *Das Wunder von Bern*. Bavaria Film International: Sönke Wortmann (2003).

the events penetrated into all corners of West German society. These range from a monastery, in which monks are listening intently to the radio, to a shop selling TV sets, in front of which throngs of people try to catch a glimpse of the soccer action on the display TVs in the window.

Swept up in this montage is a shot of Bruno, now dressed in the bright blue shirt of the Free German Youth organization (Freie Deutsche Jugend, or FDJ), the East German youth organization whose main purpose was to introduce the ideas of Lenin and Marx to the youth of the GDR (see fig. 3). While not officially affiliated with the GDR's leading socialist party, the SED, it effectively served as that party's youth organization. Bruno is shown sitting among other FDJ youths watching the telecast of the World Cup final in a room dominated by a painting of Lenin. This carefully placed shot, and the intensity with which the young people are following the telecast, clearly signifies their affinity with one singular Germany, as opposed to the reality of the two states. Bruno's enthusiasm for the GDR simultaneously feeds into the contemporary wave of *Ostalgie*, helping revalidate this second "other" Germany as a worthy place. Although Bruno's idealistic expectations have in hindsight been invalidated, the film resists the stereotypical depiction of the GDR as a totalitarian and oppressive regime and instead suggests that when it came to soccer, there was only *one* Germany. This inclusion of East Germans is of central importance, turning an essentially West German myth into a pan-German one suitable for a new millennium.

While Bruno's and Richard's World Cup experiences offer audiences a way to bridge the past and the present, the injection of Annette and Paul Ackermann into the events works to involve and engage the audience emotionally in the past. Through the omissions of the unpleasant parts of the event and the addition of these new fictional elements, director Wortmann reinvents the myth of 1954, by including scenes that are entirely, and obviously, fictional, and asks the audience to "become involved in re-presenting the past."[50] In particular, two highly charged scenes not only work to generate an affective response from the audience but also ask them to change their relationship to history. By rewriting the Wunder von Bern as a story of ordinary citizens making history, it thus creates a prosthetic memory for both West *and* East Germany.

This is achieved by finally bringing together the storylines of the Lubanskis and the Ackermanns with that of the soccer team at the match in Bern. The first of these scenes depicts an emotional eruption by Annette Ackermann. Her character symbolizes the millions of individuals who were generally uninterested in soccer but became swept up in the excitement of this particular tournament, thus paving the way for a truly collective experience. Convinced that Germany will win, she has made a bet with her journalist husband Paul: if Germany wins, she will name their children; if Hungary wins, he may choose the names. With Germany down 2-0, Paul announces that their first girl will be named Roswitha, an impossibly old-fashioned name, and accordingly Annette reacts with great disdain. In her desperation she begins chanting, "Go Germany! Go Germany!" and to her astonishment the crowd joins in. As her lonely chant turns into a roar by the German crowd, the despondent captain Fritz Walter suddenly takes notice. A slow-motion tracking shot of Walter starts at eye level, then moves in a half circle down to a low angle, making him appear bigger and bolder. At the same time, his expression changes from despair to determination, and his body straightens up as he surveys the cheering crowd. With this newfound determination he begins to lead the charge to equalize the two Hungarian goals.

This is the moment at which the everyman Fritz Walter, amateur soccer player, ex-prisoner of war, and laundromat owner, becomes a hero. He does so not only as the perfect, clean-cut representative of ordinary West Germans, but because he is encouraged by another ordinary (although clearly wealthy) German—Annette. This scene underlines her symbolic importance, as the once disinterested upper-middle-class woman becomes the catalyst for the German team's resurgence in the reimagined myth. Without *her* outburst, there would have been no change of atmosphere, necessary to motivate the German side to challenge the Hungarian team.

The second fictional addition relies upon the emergence of a father-son element. It involves Matthias and his father figure, Helmut Rahn, the striker on the soccer team. At the beginning of the film Rahn tells Matthias that he can only turn around the tight matches when Matthias is present, effectively making him the player's mascot. In an attempt to salvage the relationship with his son, Richard has taken Matthias, who is both the catalyst for and now beneficiary of his father's gradual change, to Bern for the final. This trip signals the impending end of the familial tensions brought on by Richard's return from the prisoner-of-war camp. In the dramatic high point of the film Matthias sneaks into the stadium to the voice-over of Zimmermann's increasingly excited commentary, a scene that is intercut with frenetic shots of the action on the pitch. Just as Matthias arrives at the side of the pitch, the soccer ball rolls toward him. This part of the scene—in which Matthias picks up the ball and throws it to the disbelieving Rahn for a free kick—is shot in slow motion and accompanied by an elegiac score, lifting this sequence out of "'reality'" and into the realm of the mystical, with Matthias literally lending the magic touch. Snapping suddenly back into "reality" and Zimmermann's commentary, Rahn storms toward the Hungarian goal and shoots the winning goal. This suggests, of course, that without the fictional Matthias, there would not have been a Wunder von Bern.

The two fictional scenes involving Annette and Matthias highlight the shift in the film from the mythic narrative of the soccer players to the ordinary population. Since the 1954 final constitutes a seminal moment in the postwar West German imagination and has often been seen to have contributed to the nation's "rebirth" in the 1950s, this amounts to a significant shift in the public perception of the myth. The rewritten myth relies on the ordinary people of Germany, rather than a team of soccer players; it is they who are shown to be responsible for it. As such, this miracle of national resurrection can be mobilized to serve the needs of a contemporary, still-fragmented nation in the new millennium. Rarely has a sports film carried such an array of identificatory signifiers designed to heal the wounds of a divided nation.

Against the backdrop of an unsettled post-unification audience in a nation lacking both social cohesion and suitable national heroes, the timing of the release of Wortmann's film, which introduces a set of nostalgic heroes for a pan-German audience, could not have been better. While East Germans had been stripped of their state and national identity in 1989, West Germans struggled to incorporate these familiar strangers much in the way that the Lubanski family struggles to welcome Richard back into their world. Grounded in emotional authenticity, the film creates a prosthetic memory of the event that can easily be absorbed even by those audience members unfamiliar with this West German foundation myth. While *The Miracle of Bern* works with a different strand of myth—and in a different spatial and temporal context—it follows a similar trajectory to *Chariots of Fire* in that it seeks to unify a disturbed national identity. By including multiple emotionally appealing identificatory figures in its protagonists, while simultaneously refusing to directly thematize any East-West division, *The Miracle of Bern* manages to naturalize the experience of this sporting event as a truly collective moment that, then as now, has the power to bring the nation together as a single, pan-German imagined community. The following chapter examines these tendencies of sports films to mythologize historical events even further by tracing the evolution of one of the central myths of American culture—the American dream—through the *Rocky* (Stallone/Avildsen, 1976–2006) franchise over a period of thirty years.

CHAPTER 3

_____

ANXIOUS IN AMERICA

Rocky Balboa and the American Dream

> This is the land of opportunity, right?
> Apollo Creed in *Rocky* (1976)

So strong is the cultural currency of the *Rocky* films (Stallone/Avildsen, 1976–2006, and their descendants *Creed* [Coogler, 2015] and *Creed II* [Caple Jr., 2018]) and their association with the American dream that, thirty years after the first film premiered, countless people pilgrimage to the steps of the Philadelphia Museum of Art to run up those steps "like Rocky did," as Michael Vitez vividly describes:

> One day not long ago, a taxicab pulled up to the curb in front of the Philadelphia Museum of Art. A man hopped out and started running up the steps. A woman jumped out after him and began filming him. He sprinted to the top, turned to face the city below, and danced and pranced and thrust his fists into the air in celebration, just as if he were Sylvester Stallone in *Rocky*. . . . This kind of thing happens all the time, every day of the year. From all over the Philadelphia region, the nation, and the world, people are drawn to these steps to run them like Rocky did.[1]

This phenomenon illustrates how deeply engrained the story of the down-and-out boxer Rocky Balboa, as played by Sylvester Stallone, is in the American national psyche. The original *Rocky* (1976) film has been associated with the American dream not only because of the story of small-time boxer Rocky Balboa's rise to glory but also because of its production history. Sylvester Stallone had much in common with his film alter ego: he was an unemployed actor who had one last chance to prove he was not, as Rocky puts it, "just another bum from the neighborhood." Significantly Stallone made his own chance of a lifetime by writing a script and insisting on playing the lead role. Echoing the fictional success of Rocky in his World Championship bout against heavyweight champion Apollo Creed (Carl Weathers), Stallone became an overnight star and his film an outstanding financial and critical success, winning the Oscar for Best Film in 1977. Stallone's own meteoric rise to fame and fortune is thus as much part of the *Rocky* myth as the film itself.

Yet despite the happy endings and success stories of the *Rocky* franchise, there is a strong undercurrent of uneasiness and anxiety present in the films. This is not about the obvious physical and mental demands of boxing, but rather a larger struggle regarding the availability of the mythical American dream: does it still exist? And if so, who has access to it? Most importantly, is this concept—so central to American self-perception—under threat of losing its relevance and viability? I argue that the true battles fought in the *Rocky* films are those brought against the known and unknown, solid and shifting, group and individual aggressors against the very idea of the American dream. The battles embodied in the conflicts between Rocky and his opponents are also always ideological in nature, with a symbolic significance that expands to the level of national mythmaking.

The Idea That Built a Nation: The American Dream

In the words of former president Bill Clinton, "America is far more than a place. It is an idea."[2] In this it is different from many countries, most notably those of the Old World of Europe, that at the time of the Puritan exodus in the seventeenth century to the New World were characterized by hereditary monarchies, oppressive class systems, and racial or ethnic borders. Historian Jim Cullen summarizes these differences as follows: "Over the course of human history, peoples have used any number of means to identify themselves: blood, religion, language, geography, a shared history, or some combination of these. Yet the United States was essentially a creation of the collective imagination—inspired by the existence of a purportedly New World, realized in a Revolution that began with an explicitly articulated Declaration, and consolidated in the writing of a durable Constitution."[3]

As a result of this idea of American exceptionalism—the United States of America as unique among the world's nations—America can be perceived as "the world's most free society, characterized by social mobility, meritocracy and egalitarianism unimpeded by barriers of class."[4] Francis D. Cogliano argues that the values of this positive reading of American exceptionalism are not only closely related to American identity but are at the heart of it.[5] The American dream is another construct that is closely bound up with the idea of American exceptionalism and, as I argue, is equally at the heart of American self-perception. Notwithstanding the existence of a founding myth in all cultures and modern nation-states,[6] accounting for how the nation came into being in an affective narrative, this particular one has proved to be both vague and definite and, perhaps most surprisingly, always current. The difficulty of defining the American dream has been noted by many scholars, and there are as many definitions as there are authors, or, indeed, dreamers.[7] However, the idea was perhaps most famously voiced by Thomas Jefferson in the Declaration of Independence: "We hold these truths to be self-evident, that all men are created equal, that they are endowed by their Creator with certain unalienable Rights, that among these are Life, Liberty and the *pursuit of Happiness*."[8]

Most critics see the idea of the American dream as intricately bound up with American history, starting with the Puritan pilgrims and their desire to build a new life in the New World. The Puritan work ethic, as communication theorist Walter Fisher points out, is one pillar of the American dream.[9] Horatio Alger's stories of impoverished boys who "pull up their bootstraps" and become successful—that is, improve their financial and social standing—popularized this version of the American dream.

What "success" means, however, remains contentious. Some scholars argue for a very generalized understanding of the American dream, such as Calvin Jillson, who defines the American dream as one that is "broader and more basic and [one] that has been remarkably stable since well before the

American Revolution. That dream was of an America that offers citizens and immigrants a better chance to thrive and prosper than any other nation on earth."[10] Other scholars aim for more precision in their explanations of what this actually means. Jim Cullen, for example, approaches the American dream in a more literal way (e.g., the dream of home ownership in the 1950s), while Wilbur W. Caldwell approaches the dream from a more theoretical viewpoint (e.g., the dream of progress).[11] Needless to say, a concrete definition of the American dream remains elusive. Its ambiguity and timelessness appear to be part of its appeal, making it more accessible than similarly historically important concepts such as "democracy" or "the Constitution," as Cullen argues: "The omnipresence of 'the American Dream' stems from a widespread—though not universal—belief that the concept describes something very contemporary. At the same time, however, much of its vitality rests on a premise . . . that it is part of a long tradition."[12]

This duality of being both contemporary yet steeped in history showcases the myth's most striking characteristic—for it to fulfill its function as the "glue" that holds the nation together it has to be adaptable to a great many sociopolitical, cultural, and historical contexts. As Robert Jensen contends: "Whether celebrated or condemned, the American Dream endures, though always ambiguously. We are forever describing and defining, analyzing and assessing the concept, and with each attempt to clarify, the idea of an American Dream grows more incoherent yet more entrenched."[13] The continued relevance of the American dream as a means to success—however defined—is perplexing in the face of the well-documented structural and economic inequalities that simply do not allow access to the dream to many sections of the population in the United States.[14] Writing in 1996, Jennifer L. Hochschild describes the paradox that "poor blacks now believe more in the American dream than rich blacks do, which is a reversal from the 1960s," despite being very aware that they face greater challenges to achieve success than their white counterparts.[15] Meanwhile, middle-class black Americans became increasingly disillusioned with what Alexis de Tocqueville had called "the charm of anticipated success."[16]

Communication theorist Walter Fisher elaborates on this idea of "anticipated success," splitting the American dream into two myths: a materialistic myth of success and a moralistic myth of brotherhood: "The egalitarian moralistic myth of brotherhood . . . [involves] the values of tolerance, charity, compassion and true regard for the dignity and worth of each and every individual. [The materialistic myth of success deals with] the puritan work ethic and relates to the values of effort, persistence, 'playing the game,' initiative, self-reliance, achievement, and success."[17]

Other scholars likewise see the American dream as twofold, with a materialistic and an idealistic side that are constantly at odds with each other.[18] Both of these sets of values correspond well to the changing dominant models of American masculinity: born of the religious convictions of the Puritan settlers, remasculated at the frontier in the form of the rugged pioneer (or, as Michael S. Kimmel puts it, the "masculine primitive")[19] and culminating in the resourceful self-made man.

Aaron Baker describes the ideal masculinity of the athlete as a "heroic individual" who "overcomes obstacles and achieves success through determination, self-reliance, and hard work."[20] This "heroic individual" in the pursuit of the American dream is closely linked to the history of American manhood, in particular the idea of the self-made man, who according to Kimmel's study *Manhood in America* represents the dominant model of American masculinity. Kimmel describes the self-made man as "ambitious and anxious, creatively resourceful and chronically restive, the builder of culture and among the casualties of his own handiwork, a man who is, as the great French thinker, Alexis de Tocqueville, wrote in 1832, 'restless in the midst of abundance.'"[21] The birth of the self-made man is linked to the time of economic boom shortly after the American Revolution in the latter half of the eighteenth century—a time in which the constraints of the English motherland were thrown off, and the "old standard rooted in the life of the community and the qualities of a man's character gave way to a new standard based on individual achievement."[22]

Coupling this emphasis on individual achievement with economic success in a time of renewed American self-definition and capitalist expansion following the American Revolution makes clear how interdependent the formations of masculinity, the American dream, and American national identity are. As "America expressed political autonomy," the changing images of masculinity from the independent, resourceful, and rugged pioneer of the American frontier to the self-made man of the American Revolution turned out to be crucial ideals in the national journey toward "economic autonomy."[23] But, as Kimmel points out, the "flip side of this economic autonomy is anxiety, restlessness, loneliness. Manhood is no longer fixed in land or small-scale property ownership or dutiful service. Success must be earned, manhood must be proved—and proved constantly."[24] Thus the American self-made man chases the American dream to prove his manhood with (economic) success.

It is above all the latter variant that serves as a role model for the character of Rocky. The *Rocky* films create a nostalgic vision of manhood that, as the franchise continues, frequently conflicts with more contemporary forms of masculinity. Furthermore, because Rocky's masculinity is so closely intertwined with the American dream, the inherent ambiguity of this concept produces a considerable problem: for the American dream to work, it needs a certain chance of failure—it cannot be "a self-evident falsehood or a scientifically demonstrable principle."[25] This results in an atmosphere of heightened anxiety, with Rocky continuously forced not only to prove his masculinity and validate it as the premier model of American manhood but also to defend the American dream so closely bound up with it. In the *Rocky* films we can see at work the myth of individual and national aspirations *as one* expressed through the American dream.

The 1970s: *Rocky* and the Civil Rights Movement

The original *Rocky* is the story of out-of-luck small-time boxer and mob strong arm Rocky Balboa and his unexpected shot at the World Heavyweight Championship title when the challenger of the current champion, Apollo Creed, withdraws from the fight. Despite initial skepticism, Rocky rises to the occasion and "goes the distance" over the entire fifteen rounds, taking the champ to the brink of defeat with the help of his faithful trainer, Mickey (Burgess Meredith), and newfound girlfriend, Adrian (Talia Shire). While he does not win the fight, he celebrates a moral victory over his own doubts and restores his self-respect and dignity as a man.

The film has been described, among other things, as a neoconservative backlash against the civil rights movement,[26] as the white man getting back at the upwardly mobile black man,[27] and as an anti-modernist statement[28] that found an audience ready to move on from the unpleasant first half of the decade that had brought Watergate, the oil crisis, and a public left disoriented after the challenges of the counterculture and civil rights movements.[29] With the 1976 bicentennial approaching, the nation was turning around to look at the bright side, as Daniel J. Leab observes: "No-where on earth . . . do the hopes for the future appear more exciting than they do in the U.S., rich in spirit . . . power . . . and people."[30] In this vein, film scholars Leonard Quart and Albert Auster identify a fissure that separated the cinematic history of the 1970s into two distinct halves: "In contrast to films of the first half of the decade, which either attacked American capitalism and culture for its corruption, murderousness, and creation of ersatz values, or saw criminality aided by liberalism overwhelming traditional institutions, many of the second-half films affirmed traditional American values such as a belief in mobility, family, technology, and religion."[31]

Obviously *Rocky*, together with other commercially successful films such as *The Exorcist* (Friedkin, 1973) and *Star Wars* (Lucas, 1977), fits into the second category, as its conservatism has been pointed out by many scholars.[32] Part of this stems from what would now, and even by 1970s standards, be considered a rather old-fashioned model of masculinity. Keeping in mind that any society is characterized by a multiplicity of masculinities, the dominant postwar models of American manhood had come quite severely under attack from the counterculture and civil rights movements.[33] The resulting social changes challenged the traditional model of the male patriarch, protector, and provider to which Rocky seems to ascribe. With a throwback to this superseded masculinity the makers of *Rocky* hit the nerve of the male Zeitgeist, reassuring and reorienting the spectators with affirmation of traditional gender roles. Responding to these changes and challenges, as Victoria Elmwood observes, *Rocky* offered "masculine status and national citizenship to a previously rejected group [i.e., black men] in exchange for their allegiance in a quest for the remasculinization of white men (and, by extension, the nation) as well as offering a bond of solidarity in rolling back the advances made by feminism."[34]

In *Rocky* this remasculinization project rests partly on a particular version of the American dream, reaching back in history to revive a masculinity built on the Puritan work ethic and concept of self-denial. To some degree both Rocky Balboa and his opponent, Apollo Creed, are self-made men, with Apollo initially the more obviously successful one: he is the current undefeated heavyweight champion and has also turned his sporting success into financial gain, whereas Rocky merely drifts along in his life, threatening to sink further to the bottom of the social ladder until he gets his big chance.

The two characters take quite different trajectories from this point forward, however, as Rocky tries finally, and earnestly, to make something of himself and follow his (American) dream, while Apollo discards his previous commitment to his own dream and underestimates Rocky's determination and belief in the very possibility of the American dream. Both characters symbolize the potential and viability of the American dream: Rocky because the audience can literally see his struggle to achieve it, and Apollo as a previous benefactor of its possibilities—the champion who rose from the slums of Los Angeles. They are, so to speak, on asynchronous timelines of the American dream, with Apollo both a shining example of its possibilities, sporting success, wealth, and fame, as well as a cautionary illustration of its potential pitfalls. As the appointed villain, Apollo is characterized as a greedy, arrogant, showboating capitalist, who—thanks to his wealth—has become too civilized, indeed almost effeminate, and in his vanity he has lost touch with the more rustic, working-class masculinity necessary for the fulfillment of the American dream in the traditionalist Rocky universe.

Rocky is always closely associated with a masculinity built on self-reliance and toughness, which is showcased in particular by the training sequences. Rocky's world is identifiably lower working class: the houses are run-down, the boxing gym is grungy, his clothes are well worn and scruffy, and his training is rough and basic. His training gear is likewise simple and devoid of any fancy machinery, therefore assigning any success that Rocky might subsequently have to sheer will and determination, unrestricted and untainted by his lack of financial means or access to more sophisticated methods. Adaptability, hard work, and endurance—as demonstrated by Rocky in these training sequences—are clear signs of Kimmel's self-made man and also, of course, are necessary attributes for achieving the American dream.

Moving Rocky ever closer to a primitive and savage ideal of manhood that harks back to the time of the frontier and the Wild West is his unique training method of using cattle carcasses as punching bags. Significantly the first time he punches a carcass follows an argument with his friend Paulie (Burt Young)—who works at a meatpacking plant and supplies Rocky with steaks—about Paulie's shy sister, Adrian. Provoked by Paulie's attitude toward and crude language about Adrian, Rocky angrily starts punching a carcass hanging from a hook when words fail him in his defense of Adrian's honor. The cracking ribs of the cow carcass and Rocky's bloodied hands serve to emphasize Rocky's primitive manliness, showcasing both his brute strength and his role as protector of the "fairer" sex.

Elegantly dressed in suit and tie, Apollo is mostly seen in wealthy sur-roundings—in particular, his manager's office—discussing the business side of the fight. He is clearly not taking the actual fight very seriously, despite the boxing championship having constituted his road to success. His arrogance has extended so far that he takes this success—that is, his own American dream—for granted, and in doing so, he begins to disrespect it. Having achieved his dream, he has moved further and further away from the masculinity of the self-made man, for whom success is personal achievement—that is, the boxing championship—and money and fame are just by-products of this success. When money and success become the primary focus, the American dream fades and turns into greed. As J. Emmett Winn argues in his analysis of the American dream in films such as *The Firm* (Pollack, 1993), *Wall Street* (Stone, 1987), and *Working Girl* (Nichols, 1988), "upward mobility is attainable by the morally sound character."[35] That Apollo Creed is no longer a morally sound character, and thus that his expulsion from the dream is due to the individual failings of his character rather than any institutional or structural obstacles, is revealed at the beginning of the title fight. Dressed as George Washington, Apollo enters the arena in a scene of great spectacle on a giant float flanked by human Statues of Liberty. His flamboyant display of patriotic symbols is intended to start off the American bicentenary year with a bang. Yet the spectacle is excessive—the scantily clad "statues," for example, undermine the earnestness of these signifiers of nationhood and the believability of the vision for which they stand. Despite his talk of patriotism and believing in the American dream, by turning the fight into a spectacle that places the sporting event in second place, Creed effectively demonstrates that he does not sincerely believe that he has given Rocky the chance of his lifetime. In other words, despite having lived his own American dream, his actions defy his professed belief in that dream.

By making Apollo Creed the villain, and intertwining his success with his masculinity and identity as a black man, the film implies that the upward mobility of post–civil rights movement black men comes at the expense of working-class white men like Rocky. This depiction of Apollo Creed, as Seán Crosson argues, "builds on a particularly racist construction of African Americans as representing the worst excesses which the White man should avoid" and is most evident in the final fight scene.[36] This also criticizes a perceived shift in masculine values, presenting Rocky as the morally superior model of American manhood. While Rocky's masculinity recalls the hardened, barely civilized pioneer, Apollo embodies a vain, greedy, and decidedly urban masculinity that has more in common with the flamboyance of 1970s disco dance floors than the wilderness of the frontier. As the ringside commentator puts it, this is a battle of "the cavalier against the caveman." Within the logic of the film, this is also the only version of manhood that has access to the American dream, as is demonstrated when Creed is brought to the brink of defeat by Rocky. Creed's version of masculinity is not beyond redemption, however, as is shown in the later scenes of the fight. When his trainer wants to stop the bout because of an injury, Creed refuses: he "mans up" and continues the fight, thus honoring the concepts of perseverance and determination so central to the nation's founding fathers. Ultimately, both fighters' bruises and exhaustion not only serve as visual reminders of the dramatic struggles with which one has to engage to achieve one's goals but also recall the determination of one of the nation's most beloved symbolic figures: the self-reliant pioneer of the frontier.[37] The film thus rehabilitates Apollo as his masculinity is remade in the ring, and therefore defuses the threat to the concept of the American dream posed by his other self—the narcissistic, materialistic dandy.

In the end Apollo Creed wins the fight and retains his championship title. However, Rocky's loss is framed as his greatest success: in a fight that nobody had ever expected him to win, he achieved more than any challenger before him, knocking down the seemingly invincible Creed at one point and staying in the fight for the full fifteen rounds. Indeed, having realized the enormity of his task the night before the fight, Rocky modifies his goal from "winning" to the more modest "going the distance." This modesty underlines the idealism of his version of the American dream—the notion that "winning" is about how one fights the fight. It is more important to give one's absolute best, rather than achieve the kind of outright success that leads to materialistic greed—the perverted interpretation of the dream embodied by Apollo. Further legitimizing Rocky's version is the crowd's shifting support during the course of the fight: while they begin by celebrating the reigning champion with chants of "Creed, Creed," they are soon moved by the tenacity of the underdog challenger and change their calls to "Rocky, Rocky." Facing up bravely to an impossible task has thus earned Rocky the respect of the audience and situates him as the moral hero of the film, reinstating the credibility of the traditional myth of American manhood and the American dream. In this way *Rocky* embodies the narrative trajectory and values of the sports film that seeks to associate an uplifting struggle with the heroic face of national identity.

Moving into the 1980s: *Rocky II* and *Rocky III*

Having set the scene in the first *Rocky*, *Rocky II* and *Rocky III* further delineate the boundaries around the American dream and the kind of masculinity that is necessary to achieve it. Four years after the first *Rocky*, *Rocky II* begins with the fight scenes from the previous film, followed by some brief scenes between Rocky and Apollo in a hospital. By this stage Apollo is so enraged about having only barely won the fight that he challenges Rocky to a rematch, despite his initial reaction after the final bell: "Ain't gonna be no rematch." Regardless of these initial scruples and the disapproval of both Adrian and Mickey, due to Rocky's severe injuries, Apollo pressures Rocky to agree to a rematch. Mickey is quickly convinced of the necessity of a second fight, but Adrian's continuous opposition hinders Rocky's training. It is clear that Rocky cannot "do it" without the support of Adrian, now his wife. After

Adrian prematurely gives birth to their first child and falls into a coma, Rocky wants to cancel the fight, but Adrian wakes up, has a miraculous change of heart, and tells him to win the fight for her. Thus training begins in earnest, and after another grueling fight, Rocky is finally pronounced the new World Heavyweight Champion. The film ends with an in-the-ring interview, in which Rocky yells out to Adrian at home: "Yo, Adrian, I did it!"

The film essentially answers two questions left open in the first film. First, there is the question of the legitimacy of Rocky's endurance, and thus his manhood and suitability to represent the American dream. If, as is now suggested in some quarters, Apollo "carried" him for fifteen rounds to make the fight more interesting to the audience, then Rocky has not yet proved that he is not "just another bum from the neighborhood." So strongly have the seeds of doubt taken hold that Rocky goes to Apollo's room in the hospital to ask him: "Did you give me your best?" to which Apollo just sighs a "yes" without making eye contact. This persistent question, as to whether Apollo "carried" Rocky, becomes a significant marker of the legitimacy of Rocky's abilities, not only for this film but for all of the films in the series, as it continues to provoke anxiety over Rocky's "hard body" masculinity—"heroic, aggressive, determined."[38] The second unanswered question from the original film concerns what happens when the dream is realized. The answer is, at first, not a particularly reassuring one: Rocky's upward mobility is hindered by his lack of education, and his financial security is threatened as the money from the first fight quickly dwindles after a spending spree that includes the staples of the American dream—a car and a house. By the end of the film the validity of the dream is firmly reestablished and even celebrated as Rocky becomes World Heavyweight Champion, disposing of any doubts over his physical prowess and manhood and suggesting a future with all the money and fame this win promises.

Rocky II thus first shows the dream fulfilled, then revoked, and finally fully reinstated. Rocky's attempts to live what James Truslow Adams once called a "fuller and richer life"[39] after his loss to Apollo in the first fight are not fully realized because he has not yet truly reached his goal of the heavyweight championship. His morally superior dream of "going the distance" does not appear to sit right with an audience on the brink of the increasingly materialistic 1980s, which would culminate in the "greed is good" attitude of the yuppies of Wall Street, made famous by the film of the same name. To be a true success, the film suggests, the morally superior goal is not enough—Rocky needs to win "properly" to claim his American dream. Proven masculinity, materialistic success, and the American dream thus come to be irrevocably intertwined, as the usually taciturn Rocky explains more eloquently than ever before in an argument with Adrian:

ROCKY: It's just that . . . I don't want just to get by the hard way, you know? I want you to have good things, I want the kid to have good things.

ADRIAN: We'll have 'em.

ROCKY: I just think we need 'em now, don't you?

ADRIAN: Well, Rocky, please, you don't have to prove anything.

ROCKY: Adrian, it's all I know.

ADRIAN: I don't want you to do it.

ROCKY: It's all I know. Adrian, you know, I never asked you to stop being a woman, you know, please, I am asking, please, don't ask me to stop being a man.

During this whole conversation, Rocky is standing and literally looking down at Adrian, conveyed by point-of-view shots over Rocky's shoulder. Thus not only is Adrian literally looked down upon, but she also is framed by both her husband's body in the foreground and the bed that she is sitting on in the background, making it a closed and almost oppressively claustrophobic shot. In the reverse angle, there is only Adrian's point-of-view perspective of Rocky without any distinctive framing, thus leaving the shot wide open. Filmed from a low angle, Rocky is enlarged and clearly dominates the scene.

Despite Rocky's supposed sensitivity (it is a quiet conversation, not a loud fight), this scene showcases the film's unease regarding the advances made by women in the wake of the feminist movement and comprises one of the visual and textual markers that seek to confirm what Elmwood describes as a "climate of compromised masculinity."[40] This becomes especially clear when viewed together with a previous scene in which Rocky tells Adrian that he does not want her to go back to work because he is supposed to be the provider. When Adrian eventually does go back to work, she promptly suffers a premature birth and falls into a coma—and is thus effectively punished for taking on the role of provider when Rocky fails to get a job. With this crisis in his private life, Rocky must now prove his masculinity once more in the ring, rectifying his failings as a husband and provider—the dream now rests on his boxing abilities. Yet he cannot achieve his goal without his woman: without Adrian's support Rocky does not train properly, and only when she eventually gives him her blessing does he train in earnest. With traditional gender roles thus reaffirmed and unchallenged for the rest of the film, the scene is set for the complete fulfillment of the American dream, in line with the increasingly conservative social atmosphere of 1980s America.

While gender politics throughout the *Rocky* series remains consistent in its conservatism, the racial politics in these early films is, at best, awkward. By only sometimes explicitly invoking issues of race and ethnicity, the first *Rocky* film walks what Elmwood calls "an uneasy line between dealing with the question of race and simply ignoring it. Here, race is evacuated of any particular socio-economic conditions or related material or political disadvantages and is instead invoked as a powerful symbolic tool that is historically invoked for the greater good of the boxing spectacle."[41]

In *Rocky II* not much has changed: if anything, the anxiety over the upwardly mobile black man has increased, and it is implied to be at the expense of the upward mobility of the ethnic white man as demonstrated by Rocky failing in his attempts to secure a "job sittin' down," that is, a white-collar job, at the beginning of the film. Yet, with Rocky winning the heavyweight title from Apollo in the end, this apparent misbalance is rectified.

The relationship between these two fighters remains central to two more films, *Rocky III* and *Rocky IV*. While Rocky has always respected Apollo as a fighter, in *Rocky III* this respect turns into a deep friendship. Meanwhile, Rocky's new adversary, Clubber Lang (Mr. T), is also black, but he symbolizes all that Rocky and Apollo are not. Essentially *Rocky III* is about Rocky having become too civilized, even effeminized, to fight properly—a condition that one could argue had befallen Apollo in the first film as a direct effect of the wealth and fame acquired by means of his boxing success. At the beginning of the third film a montage of Rocky's boxing and commercial achievements paints a different picture of the American dream fulfilled than *Rocky II*. Rocky has now managed to overcome his lack of education and poor publicity skills and is both a successful athlete and a bona fide advertising super star. At the same time, we are introduced to the lower-ranked fighter Clubber Lang, who is steadily climbing up the ranks and openly challenges Rocky to a title bout. Clubber is characterized as vicious, mean, and decidedly uncivilized. He trains alone in his basement with the bare essentials and has an almost tribal, savage look accented by his Mohawk and feather earrings.[42]

Rocky's training, by contrast, represents more of a show than actual physical training—while Clubber grunts and sweats alone in his basement, Rocky poses for the public in a rented hotel ballroom and receives kisses from random female fans (see fig. 4). Whereas Rocky's scenes have a cheery, colorful atmosphere, Clubber's are grim and dark. The similarities of these respective training strategies, compared to those seen in the first *Rocky*, are striking: just as Apollo Creed did not take the fight seriously and concentrated instead on his financial endeavors, Rocky now seems more intent on putting on a show and making money by selling buttons and other memorabilia than actually working hard to retain his title. In contrast, Clubber Lang resembles Rocky at the start of his boxing career, training mostly by himself, either in a grubby gym or in his basement. He has minimal support, but this is countered by his sheer determination.

Yet while their circumstances may be similar, their visual representation and subsequent narrative trajectories differ considerably. While Rocky's run-down apartment in the original film was romanticized, Clubber's grimy basement apartment is demonized in *Rocky III*; this approach contrasts legitimate and questionable versions of masculinity through the representation of the men's environment. Rocky and Clubber are further polarized by being represented as civilized and uncivilized characters, respectively. This is demonstrated in an early scene, in which Clubber repeatedly challenges Rocky to a fight, but Rocky only agrees after Clubber makes lewd comments to Adrian: "Bring your pretty little self to my apartment tonight, and I'll show you a real man." This clearly invokes the stereotype of the sexually

4. *Rocky III*: Rocky (Sylvester Stallone) and Clubber (Mr. T) training with different intensity and purpose. *Rocky III*. Metro-Goldwyn-Mayer: Sylvester Stallone (1982).

aggressive, even predatory, black man that is also at odds with the character of Apollo Creed, the intelligent and educated upper-middleclass gentleman, who is now included in the film's spectrum of acceptable proponents of 1980s American masculinities. While Clubber is grunting and sweating in his grungy basement, Rocky hardly even breaks sweat, always looking clean and neat in his training camp, which is less gym and more capitalist dream, demonstrating Rocky's buying/selling power with his sophisticated training machines, American flags, memorabilia stands, and hired band. He displays no signs of true commitment to the puritan work ethic necessary to access the American dream, but only hollow, lifeless national symbols devoid of any substance—reminiscent of those drawn upon by Apollo Creed in his showy entrance to their first fight. Consequently, and again evocative of Apollo, Rocky is swiftly punished for his lack of respect for the dream. He not only loses his title by knockout in the second round but also his coach and mentor, Mickey, who dies after a short brawl between Clubber and Rocky before the fight. While Rocky still has his wealth, it has become empty and meaningless without Mickey and without the title. Once again his identity as a true American man has been shaken to the core.

It is the force of Clubber Lang's masculinity that most endangers Rocky's American dream. As Melvin Burke Donalson explains in his study of interracial buddy films, "Lang, with his Mohawk haircut and guttural voice, represents the urban savage, the brute whose offensive and sneering demeanor only inspires adversaries."[43] Clubber accuses Rocky of fighting less-than-worthy opponents, and this is later confirmed by Mickey, who describes Rocky's opponents in previous title defenses as "handpicked." To regain his sense of self, his masculinity, and thus his dream, Rocky has to beat Clubber, regain his title, and once again prove that he is a real man. The supposedly handpicked fighters are a reminder of Rocky's anxiety over the possibility of having been "carried" by Apollo in the first fight. In both instances it is Rocky's masculinity, and not just his quality as a boxer, that is in question, because for Rocky, being a boxer equates with being a man. He has effectively become feminized by fame and wealth achieved by easy wins, which emphasizes once again the view that there is more to the American dream than a simple rags-to-riches story.

In order to become remasculinized and thus regain access to the American dream, Rocky takes on Apollo Creed as his new coach and slowly begins to shed his civilized self, symbolized by discarding his elegant suits and coiffed hairstyle and moving to a grungy apartment in downtown Los Angeles. However, this remasculinization project, which involves returning to a Puritan work ethic and the associated tough pioneer form of masculinity, does not extend as far as the open savagery and predatoriness of Clubber Lang, who is "devoid of the honor worshipped by Rocky and Apollo,"[44] and thus displays a masculinity outside the acceptable boundaries necessary to access to the American dream.

In *Rocky III* everything Rocky thought he had worked for, and thus rightly deserved, is questioned, showing that realizing the American dream, as hinted at in the first film, is an ongoing process rather than an end in itself. The answer to the question first posed in *Rocky II*—what happens once the dream is achieved?—must be that it is never fully achieved, in the sense that it requires constant nurturance and attention. The fear of losing everything, which Rocky now faces up to, is the fear inherent in the American dream itself and can be traced back to what Caldwell called the "right kind of dream [that] must be promising without being a promise."[45] With regained faith and the support of Adrian and Apollo, Rocky eventually defeats Clubber Lang, showing once again that hard work and determination can lead, at least temporarily, to the fulfillment of the dream. The power here lies with the fact that both Rocky and Apollo, despite their differences, continue to chase their ongoing dreams. This is to say that regardless of fame or riches, success, however it is defined, is in the reach of everyone with virtuous motives and respect for the American dream, as exemplified by Apollo and Rocky. In its close alignment with mythic forms, the sports film is particularly responsive to the changing nature of the American dream as personified by particular individuals, such as Rocky.

The 1980s: *Rocky IV* and the Cold War

Filmed in the early 1980s, *Rocky III* deals with a threat to the American dream and American manhood from within, in the form of both Clubber Lang's excessive and Rocky's effeminized masculinity. Three years later *Rocky*

IV came at the tail end of reinvigorated Cold War rhetoric in the United States, and correspondingly the threat to the American dream in the film has become an outside force—a muscle-packed, machine-like Russian fighter called Ivan Drago (Dolph Lundgren). Drago has come to the United States to be the first professional Russian boxer on American soil and to demonstrate his power against the current champion, Rocky Balboa. However, instead of Rocky, it is Apollo who takes up the challenge and convinces Rocky to train *him* for an exhibition bout with Drago. Similar to the first Rocky-Apollo fight, the exhibition begins as an enormous Las Vegas spectacle with dancers, American flags and nationalistic paraphernalia, and James Brown singing the patriotic "Living in America." Yet, like Rocky in the first film, Drago is not there for showmanship, and thus not only does he knock Apollo out quickly, but the brutal hit kills his opponent. Having failed to stop the vicious fight as Apollo's corner man, Rocky then travels to Russia for a rematch, in order to avenge his friend and rehabilitate the reputation of American boxing. Once again Rocky goes against Adrian's explicit concerns and trains at a dilapidated farm in Siberia with minimal support. Meanwhile, Drago trains with the help of a host of scientists and the most technologically advanced equipment. After Adrian has a change of heart and follows Rocky to Siberia, his training picks up, and he fights Drago in front of the Russian politburo. He outlasts Drago, whose bleeding cut above his brow proves he is not a machine after all. Drago still cannot beat Rocky.

Rocky IV is often considered a right-wing Cold War propaganda film, and Stallone has been called Ronald Reagan's "pornographer."[46] While in the previous films national identity and the nation remained at the level of aboutness, in Mette Hjort's terms, in *Rocky IV* the nation becomes thematized through hypersaturation, most notably in the East versus West conflict that is flagged visually throughout.[47] In terms of box office success it is the most successful of the Rocky series, indicating that it resonated widely with 1980s U.S. audiences.[48] There is no question that both *Rocky* films of the 1980s (*III* and *IV*) are indebted to the conservative politics of Ronald Reagan in numerous ways.[49] In *Rocky IV* the uneasy race politics of *Rocky III* make way for a more clear-cut antagonism of "us against them"—West versus East, Democracy versus Communism. Film historian William J.

Palmer chronicles the rhetorical shift in the American-Russian relationship that came with the first of four summits between President Reagan and his Russian counterpart Gorbachev and the effect of this shift on Hollywood. While the first years of Reagan's presidency were characterized by an increase in "distrust and belligerence," the years following the summit in Geneva in 1985 showed an "unlikely mediating spirit of cooperation."[50] *Rocky IV*, Palmer argues, is part of the early to mid-1980s "*rightist militarist*" cycle of films that also included, for example, *Red Dawn* (Milius, 1984), *White Nights* (Hackford, 1985), and *Top Gun* (Scott, 1986): "By mid-decade, films like *Rocky IV* and *White Nights* had taken up the Reagan 'evil empire' patriotic jingoism that emphasized the differences between the two societies, especially the dehumanized power of the totalitarian Soviet State."[51] On the other hand, later films such as *Little Nikita* (Benjamin, 1988) and *Red Heat* (Hill, 1988) reduced the emphasis on cultural differences between the two societies and moved away from presenting Russian villains as grotesque. After thirty years of Cold War politics, *Rocky IV* came at the moment of a surprising change in international relations and was subsequently criticized for its "anti-Soviet feelings in a post-Geneva time of thawing cold war sentiment," and, indeed, "cold war iconography virtually trumpets from the screen."[52] Countless visual and textual cues reiterate the film's embeddedness in Cold War propaganda, from soundtrack songs that explicitly thematize the East-West conflict and celebrate "Living in America" to an endless supply of American flags.

What is at stake in *Rocky IV* is nothing less than the American way of life, with its basis in the American dream. This is evidenced particularly by the thematization of a technological/pastoral divide, which equates the East, that is, Communist ideology, with a subservience to technological progress in the service of the state, which leads to a dehumanized future. The West, meanwhile, represented by America, is anchored in its deep connection to a simpler, pastoral heritage with its idealized, pioneer form of masculinity. This entails a rejection of the excessive capitalist and free market mentality, represented by the Apollo-Drago spectacle early in the film as a suitable defense against such a bleak future. Instead, *Rocky IV* harks back to a mythical past, strongly aligning itself with the time of birth of the American dream—the time of the Puritans, the frontier, and, of course, the Declaration of Independence, resulting in the emphatic assertion that free will and humanist individualism will persevere in the end.

The glorification of pastoral America forms a trajectory with its roots in the first film, where Rocky eagerly drinks raw eggs and trains in Mickey's run-down gym with minimal equipment, invoking the rugged individualism of the yeoman farmer. In *Rocky II* he chases a chicken to improve his reflexes, and finally in *Rocky III* he ditches his luxurious surroundings and fancy gym equipment in favor of Apollo's grungy old gym in downtown Los Angeles, reinforcing the image of the "lone, self-reliant boxer [who] is thus an updated and remodeled version of the pioneer situated in the urban jungle, a stand-in figure for the old frontier."[53] The propensity of the *Rocky* films for lovingly invoking frontier history connects their vision of America with that of President Reagan, who "envisioned a restoration of a glorious mythical past emanating from small-town America" with its "traditional ideals of reliance, hard work, plain talk, thrift, sacrifice, the happy family, the free market, love of country, worship of God."[54] All of these attributes are equally at home in the Rocky universe as in Reagan's "golden past, a version of an America that never actually existed."[55] It comes as no surprise, then, that Stallone and Reagan shared a friendship of sorts, with Reagan inviting Stallone to the White House in 1985 in a symbolic anti-Soviet move.[56] Ardolino argues that Reagan constructed a "vision of himself as a self-made man who exemplifies the best the American system has to offer."[57] Rocky is, of course, also such a self-made man, who grasped his once-in-a-lifetime shot and succeeded: his defeat at the hands of a Russian fighter would endanger this particular American project.

The symbolic conflict of the two systems, as represented by the technological-pastoral divide, is most obvious in the intercut training scenes of the two fighters. The pastoral scenes of Rocky's training in snow-covered Siberia clash with Drago's high-tech environment not only because of the man versus machine dichotomy but even more so because of a glorified bucolic past colliding with a deeply hostile, dehumanized future. While Drago is seen to train with the most sophisticated electronic equipment available, Rocky uses dilapidated farming equipment such as an old yoke and an abandoned ox cart. While Drago lifts weights and knocks out sparring partners, Rocky lifts rocks and fells trees. While screens flicker and LEDs light up in Drago's gym, there is only the glow of an open fire in Rocky's barn—for every machine that isolates Drago's muscle groups and helps him train, there is a more "natural" variant for Rocky (see fig. 5). Drago is linked to monitors and computers by electrodes and cables and is pumped full of steroids while a host of nameless scientists constantly measure and evaluate his development. Meanwhile, Rocky only has the support of his trainer Tony "Duke" Evers (Tony Burton), Paulie, and later Adrian to cheer him on. In the Russian gym the passing of time is visualized by the increasing numbers on the screens and the approval of the scientists, Drago's wife, and Communist Party watchdogs, whereas back at the farm, progress is indicated by the growth of Rocky's beard. By the end of the training sequence, Drago's high-tech training has made him a slave to technology and he has become a silent dehumanized fighting machine without free will, a tool in the service of the state, whereas Rocky represents a free-spirited pioneer farmer.

The man versus machine dichotomy demonstrates the appeal and superiority of Rocky's "natural" way over that of the human robot, Drago, and in this way the film rejects a future based on technological progress. This technophobia points to a deep-seated discomfort with a present that has turned its back on the "good old times" so worshipped by both Rocky and Reagan—their own imagined American nation. Indeed, Susan Jeffords argues that "in its invocation of an American heritage that seemed to leap over the 'weakness' of the recent past, Reagan imaginary offered the public a cohesive image of national strengths, accomplishments, and possibilities. And the emblem for these promises was the hard body, whether of the individual warrior or the nation itself."[58] Rocky's now hardened body, achieved by the can-do attitude of the self-made man, who eschews technological help, thus perfectly symbolizes these "national strengths, accomplishments, and possibilities."[59]

Yet Drago is not the only "robot" present in the film; Rocky's birthday present for Paulie at the beginning of the film is a household robot that is increasingly humanized. It represents an appropriate use of technology as it is mastered by the humans to whom it belongs and thus represents the

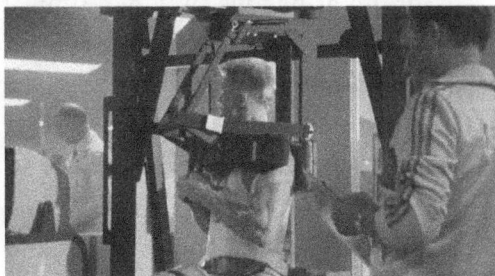

5. *Rocky IV*: Rocky (Sylvester Stallone) and Drago (Dolph Lundgren) training in different environments. *Rocky IV*. Metro-Goldwyn-Mayer: Sylvester Stallone (1985).

rapid technological changes of the 1980s in a more positive light. Drago, however, signifies an ever-present reminder of the dangers of worshipping progress for progress's sake, until at last he frees himself from the shackles of an oppressive regime. Until then Drago's masculinity is built on his impressive muscular body and his mute obedience to his wife, his trainers, and, ultimately, his country. His conformism is diametrically opposed to the values of free will and individualism championed by Rocky. Accordingly Drago's obvious physical superiority, attained as it is with the help of both technology and steroids, is no match for the power of the free spirit, as demonstrated in the fight against Rocky. However, late in the deciding fight and after a cut above his eye has proven Drago to be human after all, he rises up against his masters and declares his individuality. In effect, Rocky has rehumanized the robot by demonstrating what it means to fight with heart and soul, that is, like a real man. This, it is implied, can only be done by a free human spirit. While technology might produce a physically superior athlete, it cannot match the humanity, or heart, of a truly superior fighter and man. The opportunities technology affords are thus not only depicted as morally inferior but as incapable of leading to the ultimate goal of success. In contrast, the idealized pastoral past that Rocky represents supplies him with the necessary tools to achieve his goal—a goal that shifts initially from revenge to the morally and emotionally superior goal of human freedom leading to international peace.

In *Rocky IV*, Rocky once again comes to literally embody the American dream as he toils away in a simulated mythical past and withstands the threats of a high-tech onslaught brought on by the seemingly invincible machine-man Drago. His trials and tribulations symbolically recall the lives of the founding fathers and are a call to return to the way of life that offers the opportunity of a "life [that] should be better and richer and fuller for every man."[60]

The 1990s: *Rocky V*

Rocky V (1990) is an open rejection of the spectacle of excess of *Rocky IV*. It begins with Rocky showing signs of serious brain damage immediately after his fight with Drago. On his return to the United States he learns that his accountant has essentially bankrupted him. His ill health prevents him from undertaking any further fights to regain his wealth, and thus he opens the old gym Mickey has left to Rocky's son, Robert (Sage Stallone). Back in his old neighborhood, Rocky and his family try to adjust to the new circumstances, with Adrian assuming her old job at the pet shop again. When Rocky begins to train a young fighter called Tommy Gunn (Tommy Morrison), things begin to look up, as Rocky finds a purpose in trying to pass on his legacy to his new protégé. Yet at the same time, and unwittingly, Rocky begins to neglect his own son Robert by giving all his attention to Tommy. Tommy is eventually seduced by promises of fame and fortune to leave Rocky's humble gym and take up with seedy manager George Washington Duke (Richard Gant), who out of pure financial greed convinces Tommy to challenge Rocky. Whereas Duke is interested in the money generated by such a showdown, Tommy is manipulated into thinking he needs to beat Rocky to come into his own as a fighter. Yet, instead of a big Las Vegas fight, the film ends with a street brawl in which Rocky defeats Tommy.

The film is unusual as it rejects the formula of the previous four films that follow "a plot development from antagonism to preparation to ultimate confrontation."[61] Five years on from the excess of the conservative, capitalist smorgasbord of the mid-1980s, *Rocky V* is a comparatively introverted, emotional, and political "hang-over" film. Stallone turns away from his attempts to represent political symbolism on a grand scale and returns to a more personal story of family and personal legacy, as Ardolino concludes: "[It] primarily explores the twin themes of what merit Rocky has as a man apart from the system that rewarded him and what legacy he as a warrior-father will leave behind. By extension, the movie is raising the question of the legacy of the 1980's, the Reaganite era, through the presentation of complex father-son relationships."[62]

It is neither in international politics nor in a return to a mythical past but in the bonds of family relations that we can find traces of the American dream. What does, and does not, constitute a fuller life comes under scrutiny as Rocky eventually fights "not for money or for the boxing championship, but rather for his 'measure as a man,'" as Ardolino puts it.[63] American masculinity and the American dream become ever more intertwined as Rocky searches for new meaning in his life. The uneasiness with the rags-to-riches version of the dream displayed in the previous films is finally given center stage. A continuous conservative project that culminates in a cloying return to both moral virtue and family happiness as the definitive goals of the dream come to the fore in this much-maligned part of the saga. Wealth, fame, and greed—all prominent components of the increasingly materialistic culture of the 1980s—are categorically rejected in this film, as it seeks to reestablish a masculinity based on the values of the virtuous, hardworking pioneers. This is evidenced in Tommy Gunn's loss to Rocky as he chases fame and fortune, and in not having Rocky return to his previous wealth, but instead being happy and content with what he has in his family—love and a son to whom he can pass on his legacy. It is an American dream that dismisses the earlier rags-to-riches narratives and confirms the return to a moral version of success. While this has always been part of the saga, it becomes the focal point with *Rocky V*, which at the time was conceived of as the end of the series.

Yet, as Rocky himself says in the last film of the series that focuses on Rocky as a boxer, *Rocky Balboa* (2006), "It ain't over 'til it's over." By now Rocky runs a family-style, Italian restaurant called Adrian's, in which he tells old fight stories to his enamored guests. This scene is reminiscent of Jake LaMotta's (Robert De Niro) nightclub performances in *Raging Bull* (Scorsese, 1980), showing perhaps Stallone's ambitions as a filmmaker. At the opening of the film it is the anniversary of Adrian's death three years previously, and Rocky does his annual tour of their relationship around Philadelphia, in which he covers many of the iconic places of the first film, such as the pet shop, the gym, and the house in which they used to live. Notably absent is any reference on this tour to his wealthy and successful past. At the end of his tour he runs into "little Marie" (Geraldine Hughes) from the first film and takes an interest in her life and her son. His relationship with his own son Robert (Milo Ventimiglia) is fraught, because Robert finds it difficult to live in his father's shadow. After a much publicized virtual computer fight with current heavyweight champion Mason "The Line" Dixon (Antonio Tarver), which Rocky wins by knockout, the press jeers at the mere thought of such a result in reality. Egged on by this speculation, Rocky applies for a professional boxing license, which is granted after an impassioned speech in which he invokes no less than the Bill of Rights and the Declaration of Independence, allowing him to fight small local fights because, as he says, he has still "got some stuff in the basement." Paulie understands this "stuff" as anger and resentment at Adrian's death, and Rocky voices his frustration with life in general. Meanwhile, Mason Dixon is criticized by press and public alike for his easy fights, so when he hears about Rocky regaining his license, his managers talk him into challenging Rocky to an exhibition match to improve his image and make a fortune at the same time. Rocky derives support for this idea from Marie, but his son is firmly against it. After Rocky impresses on his son how important it is to live with the cards one is dealt, Robert turns around, and they reconcile at Adrian's grave. Rocky trains once again to the rousing Bill Conti song "Gonna Fly Now," while Mason Dixon returns to his old coach in an attempt to

6. *Rocky Balboa*: Rocky (Sylvester Stallone) and Mason (Antonio Tarver) at "home." *Rocky Balboa*. Metro-Goldwyn-Mayer: Sylvester Stallone (2006).

redeem himself, after public criticism that he has "no heart." At the final showdown in Las Vegas, Rocky once again goes the distance and proves a serious challenge for Dixon. Yet before the result is announced (Dixon wins by split decision), Rocky has already left the arena for the last time. He has achieved his goal of going the distance one last time and in doing so has proven his dignity.

In a similar vein to *Rocky V*, *Rocky Balboa* rejects the notion of wealth and fame as suitable goals for the American dream. The scenes of Mason Dixon, who supposedly "has it all," are shot in bleak and cold colors such as white and blue to give his life a sense of sterility. This is in contrast to the scenes in Rocky's cozy restaurant, which are dominated by the warm glow of orange and red (see fig. 6). This final film thus reinforces the previous installment's discomfort with the American dream interpreted as a simple rags-to-riches story.

Yet, despite Rocky's life being seemingly in order and his apparent sense of personal success and happiness, he feels compelled to enter the ring once again. In a crucial scene after his application for a boxing license is denied, despite having passed all of the relevant medical tests, Rocky defends his right to box despite his age, or any other concerns the Philadelphia boxing commission might have, with an impassioned speech that goes to the heart of American national identity:

ROCKY: Yo, don't I got some rights?

BOXING COMMISSION JUDGE #1: What rights do you think you're referring to?

ROCKY: Rights, like they wrote in that official paper down the street there.

BOXING COMMISSION JUDGE #1: That's the Bill of Rights.

ROCKY: Yeah, yeah, the Bill of Rights. Don't it say something about goin' after what makes you happy?

BOXING COMMISSION JUDGE #1: No, that's the Pursuit of Happiness. But what's your point?

ROCKY: My point is I'm pursuin' somethin' and nobody looks too happy about it.

BOXING COMMISSION JUDGE #1: But we're just looking out for your interests.

ROCKY: I appreciate that, but maybe you're lookin' out for your interests just a little bit more. I mean, you shouldn't be askin' people to come down here and pay the freight on somethin', they pay, they still ain't good enough. I mean, you think that's right? I mean, maybe you're doin' your job, but why you gotta stop me doin' mine? Cause if you're willin' to go through all the battlin' you gotta get through to get to where you wanna get, who's got the right to stop you? I mean, maybe some of you guys got something you never finished, something you really wanna do, something you never said to somebody—something! And you're told no, even after you pay your dues. Who's got the right to tell you that? Who? Nobody! It's your right to listen to your gut. It ain't nobody's right to say no after you earned the right to be what you wanna be and to do what you wanna do!

In quoting the Bill of Rights and the Declaration of Independence, Rocky directly invokes the American dream, or at least Stallone's particular interpretation thereof.[64] As Rocky sees it, it should be his decision as to whether he should enter the ring after he has passed the compulsory medical tests. His response is a criticism of an overly interfering, bureaucratic government, something quite far from Reagan's laissez-faire approach to governmental control and bureaucracy.[65] Once again the rugged individualism of the pioneers, who certainly did not have to suffer from such interference, is invoked in this scene. In a powerful symbolic move, that is, by pointing to the "old papers" that are the bedrock of the nation, Rocky calls on the core of American self-conception, reaffirming the understanding of what life in America means and offers: that if one is willing to fight on despite the hardships, then everyone can achieve their dream, regardless of what disadvantage they might have. Indeed, in a post-9/11 America led by George W. Bush, these values became ever more important, leading to a new surge of films celebrating hyperwhite and hypermasculine heroism, bravery, and aggression. As Kyle W. Kusz argues, in "new millennium America (but especially after September 11) a conservative remasculinization project was revitalized mainly through the celebration of a new figure in American culture—a conventionally masculine, yet unprivileged, white everyman figure."[66]

If the original *Rocky* was seen as a push back on the achievements of the civil rights movement of the 1960s and 1970s, *Rocky Balboa* is arguably a reaction to the perceived losses to manhood and masculinity of the 1990s, as exemplified by *Rocky V*, and part of an effort to "re-fortify the socio-cultural position of American white men following the terrorist attacks executed on September 11, 2001."[67] This can also be seen in the resurgence of predominantly white super heroes—from Captain America to Batman—who have dominated the box office for the last fifteen years. In these, the traditional institutions of law and order have been fully discredited, and the fate of the United States instead lies once again in the hands of heroic, white, masculinized individual heroes. These new hypermasculine heroes, however, have also seen an offshoot in the ageing hypermasculine hero, with a number of films resurrecting the "hard-bodied" movie stars of the 1980s, including Dolph Lundgren and Arnold Schwarzenegger, in films such as *The Expendables* (Stallone, 2010) and *Red* (Schwentke, 2010).

The representation of aging masculinity in cinema has recently become of interest to scholars.[68] Standing in for any number of social disadvantages, it is Rocky's age that makes this exploration of rights so powerful, as it opens up access to the American dream to every single citizen in the United States—the message of this film is that it is never too late to pursue one's goals. Chris Holmlund notes "that men are 'permitted' to age, i.e. to have long careers in film, is taken for granted, dismissed as self-evident."[69] This, however, becomes problematic in "muscular cinema"[70] such as the *Rocky* films, in which the hero's masculinity relies in great part on his ability to fight. In contrast to, for example, the Western, where loose clothing helps to conceal the aging body of the hero,[71] the boxer is not afforded such privacy: his body is always there for all to see. Yvonne Tasker argues that this is in fact an integral part of the film: "The visual spectacle of the male body that is central to muscular movies puts into play the two contradictory terms of *restraint* and *excess*. While the hero and the various villains of the genre tend to share an excessive physical strength, the hero is also defined by his restraint in putting his strength to the test. And it is the *body* of the male hero which provides the space in which a tension between restraint and excess is articulated."[72]

His aging body further challenges the hero, as the tension increases between restraint, as expressed in the discipline of the training, and excess, as visualized in the violence of the fights. In *Rocky Balboa*, this tension is comically resolved at the beginning of Rocky's training when his trainer lists all his ailments and frailties:

> To beat this guy, you need speed. You don't have it. And your knees can't take the poundin', so hard running is out. And you got arthritis in your neck, and you've got calcium deposits on most of your joints, so sparring is out. . . . So what we'll be calling on is good, old-fashioned blunt force trauma. Horse power. Heavy duty, cast iron, power driving punches that will have to hurt so much they'll rattle his ancestors. Every time you hit him with a shot, he's gotta feel like he tried kissin' the express train. Yeah, let's start building some hurtin' bombs.

Once magnificent, Rocky's aging body has now become just another hurdle in the long line of obstacles on the way to the American dream. Rocky's "win" over his own body and the process of aging, which generally is "experienced and regarded as deformation, disintegration, and fragmentation rather than, more neutrally, as transformation," symbolically re-instates his masculinity, or in Tasker's terms, his "musculinity."[73] Emasculated and left without agency after Adrian's death, Rocky's newly built-up body solves the problem through the discipline of training: it demonstrates Rocky's utter determination to achieve the American dream once more.

Shortly after the scene with the boxing commission, Rocky discusses with Marie his doubts about whether to participate in the exhibition fight against Dixon. Marie encourages him to seize the opportunity and fight once more as not everyone gets another chance to pursue their dreams. This scene not only represents the stereotype of the supportive woman standing by her man (a role that Marie has inherited from Adrian); it also represents an appeal to audiences to cherish the American dream—to believe in it, heed its call, and thus make it happen. The film firmly establishes that the responsibility for achieving one's dreams lies with each and every individual, quashing any accusation of inaccessibility due to social structural inequality. This view is further cemented when Rocky tells his son that "when things got hard you went lookin' for somethin' to blame," thus not taking responsibility for his own life. Taking responsibility for oneself rather than relying on a welfare state is in line with the ethos of the conservative climate in the United States under President George W. Bush under which the film was released. In essence *Rocky Balboa* is continuing in the tradition of what Andrew Britton called "Reaganite entertainment," described by Ardolino as follows: "The importance of the father as the head of the nuclear family; the marginality of women; the achievement of the American dream through continued struggle; the power of might to achieve goals; opposition to government bureaucracy; a retreat into an idealized past."[74]

All of these elements are present in *Rocky Balboa* and prefigure a return to neoconservatism in a post-Clinton, post-9/11 era. It is notable that whereas in the first films of the series, and particularly *Rocky III*, Adrian had been able to talk tough and criticize Rocky, by *Rocky IV* she retreats, instead of speaking her mind. In the latest installment Marie has taken her place, but rather than presenting a strong-minded single mother, she welcomes Rocky after some token resistance as a "knight in shining armor" who takes her son under his wing and provides her with a job. As far as gender politics is concerned, not much has changed in Rocky's world. As he himself points out to his son, "Only the clothes is different."

Having stretched the believability of the aging boxer in *Rocky Balboa*, but not quite ready to say good-bye to the character of Rocky, Sylvester Stallone introduced a new fighter to the franchise: Adonis Creed (Michael B. Jordan), illegitimate son of his former adversary turned best friend, Apollo Creed. Despite handing over the boxing mantle to the younger fighter, the overall story arch remains remarkably similar and shows particular resemblance to the first installment. A young, inexperienced fighter, hungry for success, is plucked out of obscurity by the reigning champion "Pretty" Ricky Conlan (Tony Bellew) to be his opponent in the champion's final fight. Rather than winning the fight, Adonis earns the respect of his opponent and is offered the glimpse of a future as a boxing champ. A parallel story, however, turns

Rocky himself into a fighter once again. This time, however, not in the boxing ring, but in the hospital as he battles cancer.

Creed, while not officially part of the *Rocky* franchise, is also inseparable from it. It continues to champion the same virtues and values discussed thus far, from rugged masculinity to individual self-reliance, from hegemonic masculinity to (somewhat less) dubious race politics. Indeed, Stallone entrusts this newest offshoot of the franchise to Ryan Coogler, who had only made one film before *Creed*, the highly praised *Fruitvale Station* (2013), a biographical film about the last day of a young black man's life before his death at the hands of a BART officer in 2009. The original events sparked widespread protest against police brutality against black men. The choice of Coogler as director and the handing over of the main storyline to a black character can be seen as a shrewd move on Stallone's part to counter the racist accusations against his previous films. However, Adonis's inexplicable rage and tendency toward masochism—after stints in foster care and youth facilities he is taken in by Apollo's wife and leads a privileged life from there on—plays into stereotypes of "angry young black men" who are dealing with absent fathers and a lack of suitable male role models. Rocky eventually becomes this father figure and role model, although the film carefully sidesteps the "white savior" trope by turning Adonis into Rocky's savior as he convinces him to undergo cancer treatment.

The American dream in *Creed* is defined in similar ways to the rest of the film series, as one that is achieved by hard work and self-reliance, regardless of the obstacles, be they institutional as in *Rocky Balboa* or personal as in *Creed*. Indeed, the obstacles in *Creed* range from self-inflicted—Adonis's chip on his shoulder about his father's fame and absence—to health issues in the form of Rocky's cancer. As with any other *Rocky* film, though, it is not about the obstacles; it is about the individual's response to them—will Rocky take the fight to his cancer or will he give up? Will Adonis overcome his demons or will he let them win? In effectively having two fighters succeeding in their dreams—survival and becoming a boxer—the film opens up the American dream beyond Rocky himself.[75] In handing the mantle to Adonis in a virtual parallel story to the first *Rocky* film, *Creed* invites black viewers to finally partake in the Rocky mythos and believe in the achievability of the American dream. In a time in which the Black Lives Matter movement is protesting violence and systemic racism against black people, this is at best a double-edged sword. On the one hand it offers a positive representation of black masculinity in a complex character who can overcome his limitations, but on the other hand it contributes to the myth of the achievability of the American dream despite systemic disadvantages for black people, as well as putting responsibility solely into the hands of the individual, thus ignoring institutional, class, and gender disadvantages. Much like the first film, as Seán Crosson points out, the "opportunity [to achieve the American dream] is in reality available to very few, and in most cases, skewed by the inequalities in American life itself."[76] It is perhaps above all this insistence on the individual's responsibility for himself or herself that binds all the films together.

Taken as a whole, the repetitiveness of the *Rocky* saga opens up the possibility of seeing what has *changed* within the formula of this grouping of sports films. Ardolino comments on this pattern of repetition for the series up to and including *Rocky V*: "The *Rocky* saga concerns a fighter's struggle to redo his deadbeat past by creating a new one which will lead to a successful present and the promise of a secure future. When Rocky progresses beyond his humble origins, he discovers that he must recapture the spirit of his striving past in order to move forward again. In this way, he uses the strongest aspects of his past to revivify his faltering present and continue his success into the future."[77]

Not only does Rocky use the "strongest aspects of his past"; he also, as I argue here, invokes the values that he perceives as belonging to a better past—that of American pioneer history. In his continuous struggle to succeed not only does Rocky embody the American dream, but beginning with the first film and continuing through to the very last, he also affirms a particular vision of this dream. This vision, as represented in the *Rocky* saga, is that the American dream never dies—the heroic individual is one who continuously reinvents himself in order to pursue throughout his life this impossible, yet all-important, quest. It is not the attainment of this mythical dream that counts, but its constant pursuit.

Furthermore this chapter has argued that the American dream as represented in the *Rocky* franchise is a constantly evolving myth of national identity. In examining the evolution of the American dream in the series, I show that its representation is explored from three perspectives in relation to the sextet. *Rocky* in 1976 and *Rocky II* in 1979 take up the question of the validity and definition of success, as the American dream is first interpreted as a modified goal (going the distance) and subsequently as an outright win accompanied by financial success (the World Heavyweight Champion title). This early part of the *Rocky* series seeks to stabilize some of the many incarnations of the mythical American dream. *Rocky III* (1982) and *IV* (1985) take up the idea of defending this stabilized vision of the dream against its aggressors: first a threat from within, in the form of the uncivilized Clubber Lang, and then from the outside, as represented by the Russian fighter Drago. These films mark the boundaries around who does, and who does not, have access to the American dream, thereby creating templates for acceptable American manhood (*Rocky III*) and rejecting inappropriate political affiliations (*Rocky IV*).

Finally, the last two dedicated *Rocky* films, from 1991 and 2006, respectively, return to a more modest idea of the dream and display more and more visibly a deep-seated suspicion of the rags-to-riches ideal of the American dream. Hints of this skepticism had begun to show as early as the first two films, which foreshadowed the more conservative and materialistic culture of the 1980s. By the time of *Rocky III*, however, the series was entirely in accordance with Reaganite conservatism. *Rocky V* came at the dawn of a more liberal era heralded by Bill Clinton's election, and its conservatism was consequently out of touch with a shifting sociopolitical climate. Even so the film still manages to personalize the American dream as rooted in the quintessential American family. Not surprisingly, the final chapter did not come into being until the occurrence of another sociopolitical shift brought on by George W. Bush and a turn toward neoconservative politics. *Creed* extends the American dream into the next decade, reflecting once more changes in the sociocultural and political landscapes with its shift in racial politics as embodied by the young black boxer Adonis Creed.

Despite its ability to evolve to suit changing political circumstances, the

American dream as represented in the *Rocky* series also remains surprisingly stable in its invocation of familiar American ideals of a Puritan work ethic and the importance of rugged individualism. These films consistently reference the symbolic and literal imagery of the Old West, bringing values and virtues from that era into play to act as catalysts for the achievement of Rocky's American dream. This is a nostalgic, even masochistic view of the world: the idea that life is not fair and that each individual must prove his or her worth by pursuing the impossible dream and by demonstrating how much they can take and still move forward. Once again we see that the narrative structures of the sports film create a space to imagine different and evolving versions of national identity. The *Rocky* films depict a shifting vision of the American dream over time and against changing political circumstances, but without forgoing that fundamental commitment to its underpinnings. Whereas the American dream throughout the *Rocky* series appears to be urban, it has its roots firmly in the American small town as mythologized by frontier history. Small-town sports films, as I discuss in the next chapter, take this localization even further by presenting the small town as the only valid locus for the achievement of the American dream.

CHAPTER 4

SMALL TOWNS, BIG DREAMS

American Pastoral, Race, and the Sports Film

> In Virginia, high school football's a way of life.
> It's bigger than Christmas day.
>
> Sheryl Yoast in *Remember the Titans* (2000)

From the national pastime of baseball to the gridiron field of football and the barn door hoops of basketball—sports as represented by Hollywood are integral to small-town communities. Hollywood, indeed, has made a magical world of small-town sports. Whereas the previous chapter discusses the nature and evolution of the American dream as represented in the *Rocky* series, this chapter focuses on how the small town is constructed as the "real" America, a mythical pastoral site that is at the heart of the American dream. In films depicted as set in predominantly rural areas the characters of high school or college sports films, such as *Hoosiers* (Anspaugh, 1986), *The Final Season* (Evans, 2007), and *McFarland, USA* (Caro, 2015), take great pride in their small town-ness and their distinct regional or local identity. This small town-ness constructed by the films is defined by a distinct sense of *place* and *community* that is characterized as absent in representations of urban environments located in cities. This can be seen as a simple critique of modernity, in which the "urban city" is pitted against its polar opposite, the "rural small town"; however, I argue that in these films team sports symbolize a small-town culture—a pastoral ideal—which elevates this small town-ness as the exclusive vehicle through which national identity is expressed. Here the small-town communities and the sports that they play maintain a nostalgic version of the American dream—a pastoral vision of a mythical golden age of an "authentic" America. I examine these workings of American national identity in relation to mainstream films engaging with two sports regularly considered to be at the very heart of the U.S. social organization—basketball and football—while the "national pastime" of baseball comes into focus in chapter 5.

Although most small-town films naturalize this conception of America, some films criticize the fanaticism surrounding sports, which much of the mythology facilitates and supports. In contrast high school sports films set in urban environments have in recent times transposed the small-town ethics and community feel to inner-city communities, proposing them as equally appropriate loci for the realization of American dreams. For example, *Hoosiers* celebrates the centrality of sports in small-town communities, while *Varsity Blues* (Robbins, 1999), set in small-town Texas, criticizes this centrality and the abuse of the privileges it fosters. Sometimes the small towns are presented as oppressive and limiting, as in *Varsity Blues* and *Friday Night Lights* (Berg, 2004); at other times they are depicted as idyllic loci of opportunity and growing tolerance, as in *Hoosiers* (outsiders) and *Remember the Titans* (racial integration). Yet regardless of whether the portrayal of the small town is positive or negative, in each instance it forms an integral part of the protagonists' identity. Clearly the importance of sports to small-town communities cannot be overestimated. As John C. Allen and Don A. Dillman confirm in their sociological study of community life in a small town called Bremer: "Specific rituals have been developed over time to reinforce the community identity of Bremerites. One ritual is mandatory participation at athletic events. . . . They [local residents] speak of the players as representatives of Bremer and the values that Bremerites hold."[1]

Further insight into the strong ties between the individual and the small town can be gained by examining and extending upon Joanne P. Sharp's argument concerning the repetitively constructed nature of national identities, which is in turn informed by Judith Butler's theory of gender performativity and Michael Billig's notion of banal nationalism:

Following Butler, the boundary of one nation-state and the next is not the innocent marker of the spatial extents of different cultural groupings but is instead integral to the construction of the identities it nominally illustrates. International relations, then, is not so much about protecting an identity which already exists, but about constantly creating and recreating identities. Through the repeated insistence that those outside the national boundary—those who occupy other spaces—are different or other, national identity can be reproduced as a coherent and universal form. National identity, rather than something that is retrieved from the past or protected from modernity, is in fact the effect of the modern practice of national rituals of reading newspapers, singing national songs, waving flags at sports events and so on.[2]

Like national identity, the construction of small-town identity is built on the boundaries around the town and its markers, such as town signs, as well as on the performance of a particular town identity that, following Billig, is unconsciously maintained. Intense identification with the local sports team is facilitated through the seemingly never-ending repetition of local sports rituals, such as the Friday night football game, the dissection of the team's performance over coffee, the high school trophy cupboards, and homecoming games. Team identity is directly performed through varsity team jackets, game and player statistics, newspaper stories, and the endless reciting of the glorious deeds on the sporting field by former players—who are often relatives of the contemporary ones.[3] To use Mette Hjort's terms, the team's existence is constantly flagged through a "strategy of hyper-saturation,"[4] thereby establishing dominant models of identification and behavior—for example, in the form of an active supporter off the field or an active player on the field. Deviation from this norm will often result in the person being regarded as an outsider to the community, as is illustrated, for example, in *Varsity Blues*, in which the main character's disinterest in the cult of football clearly sets him apart from his family and friends. Small-town sports films are a central part of these identity-forming processes, simultaneously representing and re-creating small-town culture in a self-perpetuating cycle.

The central focus of this chapter is the *construction* of the small town as the "real America" in a select group of films, and how this small town-ness is adapted, transposed, and reappropriated into a modern context in order to open up accessibility to the American dream. This filmic construction of small town-ness is often divorced from the actual towns in question, which more accurately might be considered cities in real life. This chapter does not purport to analyze the full range of issues (e.g., authoritarianism, class, realism) present in or connections between the films, such as the figure of the authoritarian coach. It focuses instead squarely on the representation of national identity as constructed by the pervasive myth of a "golden past." Thus the first section demonstrates, using the example of *Hoosiers*, how the small town is visually and narratively constructed and coupled with a strong sense of nostalgia for a "golden past." In the second section I argue that these concepts are modernized to enable a more progressive and future-oriented version of the small town in *Remember the Titans*, where the city of Alexandria becomes hybridized: while essentially a city, it is constructed in the film as a small town, thus enabling it to still be represented as the "real" America. Finally, I examine how in a more recent wave of films small town-ness is decoupled from the actual geographical small town and transposed onto an urban cityscape to further open up access to the American dream. These films powerfully illustrate how the idea of the small town, while transformed and modernized, lies at the heart of national identity and remains the ideal locus for the American dream.

The Small Town as the "Real" America

This section examines how the small town is constructed as the "real" America in popular American sports films. While referring to a range of films, my main focus is on *Hoosiers*, an immensely successful 1980s film set in tiny Hickory, Indiana, in which a disgraced former college basketball coach is offered a last chance at his career through coaching the high school basketball team. Seeking redemption for his former failings, Coach Dale leads the Hickory Huskers to the state championship. In this and other films like it, the small town is constructed as the real America by establishing a strong sense of place and (local) community and by evoking a strong sense of nostalgia for a mythical golden age of America, which is inherently associated with the Puritan settlers, agricultural life, and, by extension, the birth of the American dream.

SENSE OF PLACE AND COMMUNITY

Sports geographers have been influential in affirming the importance of sports in small-town communities, particularly in connection with notions of topophilia, which can be defined as "situations where sentiment is coupled with place and characterized by an intense identification between people and place."[5] In his influential article "The Place of 'Place' in Cultural Studies of Sport" John Bale surveys the development of sports geography and reviews the central features of a humanistic approach to this field, focusing on questions of topophilia. His insistence on the importance of "place" and, to a lesser degree, "landscape" for sports can be used to shed light on the values of the communities represented in the sports films in question here.[6]

First, Bale argues that the main aspects of sports-related topophilia are "place-bonding" or "place-attachment," and "place boosterism."[7] In the case of place bonding or place attachment, sport is understood to reflect the strong identification of a place with its people, as the above-mentioned example of Bremer shows.[8] The intense identification with the small town—and the sports team that represents it—helps foster a sense of community in Bremer. Place boosterism, on the other hand, attests to the sporting prowess of the town and can be used as a positive marker of place as exemplified by town signs that list the local team's achievements. Conversely, these signs, usually found at the entrance of the town and clearly visible in many small-town sports films, also have the potential to invoke topophobia in the opposing team, which is, in essence, to invoke a fear of place in visitors and, in particular, visiting sports teams from other towns.[9] It thus further demarcates the imaginary boundaries around the town to highlight the difference between "us" and "them" in a process of othering.

The title sequence of the small-town sports film is often a crucial tool in establishing the town's identity and its boundaries, and therefore, its sense of place. These opening scenes visually characterize the various towns and, in doing so, establish the distinctive link between place and narrative through the mise-en-scène. For example, the title sequence in *Hoosiers* starts with a languid thirty-second shot of a car driving on a long, straight road just before dawn accompanied by a slow, nostalgic, and romantic score. The sequence then unfolds at a leisurely pace, entirely in sync with the slowness of the few people on the screen, with most shots lasting eight seconds or longer and framed by the opening thirty-second shot and a closing twenty-five-second shot that acts as a transition to the seemingly hectic rhythm of four seconds a shot in the following sequence at the local high school. The car in this opening sequence is being driven by Coach Dale on his way to Hickory, a rural town in Indiana that is "so small it doesn't even appear on most state maps." As the sun rises, the scenery of wheat fields and country roads is bathed in pale sunshine growing increasingly golden and warm. The closer Dale gets to Hickory, the closer he gets to the "real" America—an America characterized by barns, clapboard houses and churches, fields, narrow bridges and long straight country roads, American flags, (white) country folk in cowboy boots, and boys shooting hoops before their morning farm chores. It is a very serene and wholesome setting that is only disturbed by the swirling autumn leaves the car leaves in its wake. This sequence clearly establishes the importance of Hickory as a place with a particular character rooted in agriculture and a place invested with utopianism and nostalgia for the past.

Another example for topophilia can be found in the opening sequence of *Varsity Blues* (1999), a more recent film about the life of high school football stars in a small town in Texas. In contrast to *Hoosiers*, this film initially criticizes small-town high school football as an oppressive, out-of-control machinery resulting in undue hero worship and fanaticism, before it neatly restores both the sport and the town to their innocent roots in a nostalgia-inducing finale. *Varsity Blues* initially presents the small town of West Canaan as an oppressive environment by using similar visual techniques to establish a strong sense of place. The film starts with a gently billowing Texan flag filling the screen, which is immediately followed by three increasingly intense sunset shots, with the first including a rundown shack at the entrance of the town. This shot also features the town sign in the shape of a football that reads "Now Entering West Canaan—Home of the Coyotes" and lists the Coyotes' achievements. This is exactly the kind of sign that Bale points out as a positive marker for place boosting.[10] Further fostering this sense of place is the following shot of a glowing sunset behind a silhouetted oil rig—an iconic shot that clearly denotes "Texas." As the elegiac, yet rousing score makes way for the voice-over of the main character, Jonathan "Mox" Moxon, played by then teen idol James van der Beek, we see highly stylized shots of a football stadium and referees in action at night: "In West Canaan, Texas, there's another society that has its own laws: Football is a way of life." Football and the town of West Canaan are thus inextricably linked right from the start, yet the somber score also indicates that something is being mourned—the loss of football's innocence in West Canaan, which Mox will restore by the end of the film.

These two examples, typical of a great number of small-town sports films including *Glory Road* (Gartner, 2006), *We Are Marshall* (McG, 2006), *The Final Season*, *Remember the Titans*, *Friday Night Lights*, and *The Rookie* (Hancock, 2002), show how by the end of the opening credits the films have already established a clear sense of place that, over the course of the film, will be further strengthened and linked to a distinct sense of community. In using very recognizable, if not clichéd, shots such as those of the oil rig, Main Street, wheat fields, and barns, the small town is heavily imbued with nostalgia.

Like a strong sense of place, a sense of community is represented in these films as both exclusive to small towns at the expense of the city and by extension also representative of the nation—regardless of the realities of the population distribution in the United States, in which 81 percent of the population live in urban areas.[11] As political scientist Tom Brass shows in his book *Peasants, Populism, and Postmodernism: The Return of the Agrarian Myth*, this representation of community draws on agrarian myths about the land as the essence of the nation: "A potent form of ruralism with roots in romantic and conservative notions of an organic society, the agrarian myth is an essentialist ideology which in most contexts is defended with reference to a mutually reinforcing set of arguments to do with the innate aspects of 'peasant-ness,' national identity and culture."[12]

Brass situates his discussion within European history and, in particular, the rise of modernity, and he argues that this set of arguments revolves around three major discourses: economics, politics, and culture, of which the first and last are most pertinent here, as they illustrate not only the enduring power of the agrarian myth but also its centrality to the films in question. In economic terms Brass's argument highlights the importance of farmers for the national economy and the defense of the nation: "The first of these [arguments] was about economics, and entailed a discourse ('peasants-as-the-backbone-of-the-nation') in which agriculture was presented as the historical and continuing basis of social organization, peasant farming as the source of national food self-sufficiency, and the peasantry as the source of military personnel—and thus the defence of the nation."[13]

The rural communities in the small-town sports films often either imply the importance of their rural nature or supplant an agricultural community with a small-town community that has its roots in the agricultural tradition. In a film such as *Hoosiers* we get a glimpse at the life of the "backbone-of-the-nation" and their plight to preserve their dignity and way of life in a nation that has continually devalued farm labor since modernity, and whose population has moved increasingly to the cities. This is expressed through the sports team, which in a double synecdoche represents first the town and secondly the nation (team-as-town and then town-as-nation). Hence a win over a favored city team has great symbolic power. The films thus both feed off and reinforce the tradition of understanding agriculture as the "basis of social organization" in the United States.[14]

Both *Hoosiers* and *Remember the Titans* can be seen to function in this way and are typical for the narrative trajectory of American sports films. In both films the team comes together to rise to the occasion and, with a triumphal final game, wins the state championship after overcoming various debilitating obstacles and losses. *Hoosiers* in particular clearly employs the team-as-town trope. The film is set in 1954 with Gene Hackman playing Coach Norman Dale, a former college coach with a lot of credentials but also a shady past concerning his treatment of the players. He arrives in Hickory, Indiana, as the new basketball coach—his last chance to revive his coaching career and ultimately achieve redemption for his prior misconduct while a celebrated college basketball coach. Dale's work is scrutinized from the beginning, as the townspeople identify so strongly with the basketball team, the Hickory Huskers, that they have an intense interest in the team and its progress. Immediately Dale's unusual training methods, with their emphasis on conditioning and fundamentals, present an unwelcome change to the routine. His work is not helped by vice-principal Myra Fleener (Barbara Hershey), who sees basketball as obstructing the students' potential for upward mobility through academic study. Soon, however, she not only becomes enamored of the coach but also begins to understand the value of basketball as a character-building tool. After a few early losses the town comes together to vote on Dale's dismissal, but the return to the team of former star player Jimmy Chitwood (Maris Valainis), who comes to Dale's defense, saves his job. From then on the Hickory Huskers win every game and finally even the state championship against a more highly regarded, all-black city team, thus further cementing the blatant city/country dichotomy present in the film while also celebrating whiteness.

There is a particular emphasis in *Hoosiers* on Hickory as a place, as indicated in the above discussion of the film's opening sequence, and on the community linked to this place. Shots of car processions behind the tour bus and "Go Huskers" signs in shop windows and on barn doors signify the town's strong identification with this team, and this identification is rooted in the specificities of Hickory as a small town in the rural south of Indiana. The location is of particular importance here for two reasons: first, the title of the film, *Hoosiers*, is a term used to describe persons coming from Indiana, and secondly, the state has a long and celebrated tradition of basketball as Paul Christesen, for example, describes: "High school basketball for much of the twentieth century represented an enormously important part of the social fabric in the state of Indiana, and the annual tournament brought passion for high school basketball to a fever pitch."[15] Richard B. Bierce argues, "why basketball means so much to Indiana residents is unclear, but the game has become central to the identity of many of the state's residents."[16] Phillip M. Hoose offers a convincing answer, pointing to a mix of (lack of) opportunity, class, economics, and natural environment as the main reasons for Indiana's obsession with basketball:

Basketball was indeed made for Indiana. It was a game to play in the winter, something between harvest and planting, something to do besides euchre and the lodge and church and repairing equipment. . . . Most towns were too small to send enough players for a football team and too poor to buy all the pads and helmets anyway. But it was easy enough to nail a hoop to a pole or a barn, and you could just shoot around by yourself if there wasn't anybody else, just to see how many in a row you could make.[17]

"Hoosiers" thus denotes both a place (Indiana) and a practice (basketball) that are inextricably linked, and this is especially so in Hickory.

The community is depicted as strong and tight-knit—the people of Hickory are highly protective of their own and deeply suspicious of outsiders. This is illustrated in a scene in which Coach Dale is "welcomed" by the men of Hickory at an informal meeting at the barbershop. He is immediately accosted by several men about the type of defense he plans to use (zone or man-to-man): "We've always played zone." Not only does this scene demonstrate the townsmen's skepticism toward change ("This town doesn't like change, so we thought we'd get together and show you how we do things here"), but it also isolates Coach Dale, both visually and in a narrative sense, from the rest of the town. The shots of the townsmen are crowded and from a slightly lower angle, just enough to give the scene a claustrophobic and threatening atmosphere. Coach Dale, on the other hand, is placed awkwardly at the side or in the center of the frame with visible distance from any of the other men in the room. This scene makes clear that in order to succeed the coach will need determination and self-reliance—two character traits that are strongly linked with the agrarian culture of the frontier and thus also the time of the Puritans and the birth of the American dream as discussed in the previous chapter.[18] Once the basketball team starts winning and moving toward the fulfillment of their shared (American) dream of winning the state championship, the whole town comes together to celebrate and eventually also to embrace the change that Coach Dale has brought.

Paradoxically the film simultaneously romanticizes, criticizes, and seeks to transcend the limitations of small-town life. The tight-knit community regards both outsiders and people who leave the town with the utmost suspicion—it seems to "work" only if everyone sticks together and the status quo of the town is not questioned. When the team plays away games, the team bus is followed by a parade of cars from Hickory, demonstrating the unity of the town, which is based on its extraordinary homogeneity. There appear to be only white farmers and working-class men living in Hickory—the only female character of note is vice-principal Fleener, who is doubly ostracized because of her gender and because her aspirations for a better life had led her out of town to college and thus the city. Her return to Hickory, and thus her failure to escape the small town, serve to discredit both the necessity for change within the town and education as a means of upward (or outward—that is to say, out of Hickory) mobility.

Indeed, the only permissible change is that introduced by Coach Dale, and it is not notably one of progress, but instead a return to old values and traditions: fundamentals, discipline, and teamwork.[19] At the same time, reintroducing the players to these concepts works to remind the whole town of them, and as the team comes together to play as one, so does the town. Myra Fleener's symbolically charged change, from categorically opposing basketball to wholeheartedly supporting it, embodies the strong hold the agricultural tradition has on the national imagination. The Hickory Huskers, then, function like the town itself, as Coach Dale drills into his players that the team is everything, not individual talent or glory, and thus the team breaks after each time-out with the chant "Team!" Only if the team plays as one do they have a chance of winning against the city team, and in this sense they stand symbolically for the whole town, which can only survive if the townspeople stick together and return to the basic principles of the agricultural tradition.

SENSE OF NOSTALGIA

As noted above, the community in *Hoosiers* is seemingly made up of farmers, farmers' sons, and a few workmen, but there is a notable absence of any kind of race, class, or gender consciousness. As Ron Briley points out in his analysis of the racial politics of *Hoosiers*, the absence of black players on the opposing teams until the final game is simply "historically inaccurate."[20] Such absences and inaccuracies feed into a nostalgia for a past that never was, as 1950s America is envisioned as innocent, still untouched by the civil rights movement, and devoid of the complicating issues of race, class, and gender. In concentrating on small-town Hickory, the film positions the values of this innocent and mythical American Garden of Eden in opposition to the progressive, "black urban centers which threaten not only the homogeneity of the small town but also white control of a sport such as basketball."[21] The whiteness of this community even extends to the way they play sport, for as David J. Leonard points out, the different styles of play in basketball—where textbook or formal equals white, and street or vernacular equals black—eventually inform the Huskers' win at the final: "Hickory is successful because of its discipline, teamwork, and ability to master the textbook style of ball—at its core of meaning, they win because of their white working class (rural) masculinity."[22]

The 1980s saw a particular wave of nostalgic sports films, at a time when the American cultural atmosphere was heavily influenced by President Reagan's social and cultural politics and his invocation of a mythical bucolic past. As Marjorie D. Kibby has argued: "The past recreated in the eighties' cinema was not a lived, or remembered past, although it was authenticated by reference to actual events and by objects and images of the past. The history revisited in the cinema was a restructured history. The past of the cinema was the mythical past of a desired future, sidestepping the present. It was a construction of the sort of past that would have guaranteed a preferred future."[23]

It is this mythical/nostalgic past and projection of a desired future that persists in small-town films, even beyond the conservative 1980s. Kibby's notion of a "restructured history" is not dissimilar to what Fredric Jameson describes as the postmodern nostalgia film, which is "a consumable set of images, marked very often by music, fashion, hairstyles and vehicles," where the focus is on the aesthetic, and not on any conceivable actual past.[24] Yet unlike Jameson, Kibby considers nostalgia to be a "response to a fear of change, either actual or impending."[25] Considering that most of the films discussed in this chapter assert that they are "based on a true story" and therefore most often set in the (recent) past, they are working to actively reconstruct a supposedly authentic past that is imbued with nostalgia.

Alison Landsberg's notion of "prosthetic memories," as discussed in more detail in chapter 2, is useful in conceptualizing this construction of nostalgia in the small-town sports film. Through the emotional experience of film viewing, Landsberg argues, it is possible for spectators to "gain" memories that they never actually experienced in their own lives: "Prosthetic memories circulate publicly, and although they are not organically based, they are nevertheless experienced with a person's body as a result of an engagement with a wide range of cultural technologies. Prosthetic memories thus become part of one's personal archive of experience."[26]

Spectators can thus experience nostalgia for a romanticized past that may or may not have been, and that was certainly never directly their own. A poignant example is the baseball field built for the enormously successful film *Field of Dreams* (Robinson, 1989). The field depicted in the film has become both a tourist attraction and social mythology in its own right, despite the fact that the film is not based on true events. It has been incorporated into American cultural mythology in a similar way to the run up the "Rocky steps" in Philadelphia. In contrast to the Philadelphia Art Museum, however, the field in Iowa refers to the widespread yearning for a "mythical 'Golden Age'" and the American dream associated with it.[27] This is also emphasized by Brass's last argument for the persistence of the agrarian myth: "The last and perhaps most powerful component of this discourse was about culture: this entailed a critique of industrialisation, urbanization and modernity based on nostalgia for a vanishing way-of-life, linked in turn to perceptions of an idyllic/harmonious/folkloric village existence as an unchanging/unchangeable 'natural' community and *thus the repository of a similarly immutable national identity.* Linked to the latter was the view of the countryside generally as the locus of myths/legends, spiritual/sacred attributes, non-commercial values, and traditional virtue."[28]

As the (winning) sports team literally embodies the unity of the town by way of the athletes, it comes to represent the *entire* small-town community, which in turn is symbolic of the nation. In celebrating the towns and their success, the films, as cultural texts, reinforce the view of the small town as the "real" America.

THE AMERICAN DREAM IN THE SMALL TOWN

The concept of the American dream is central to the cinematic evocation of a nostalgic past and desired future. Within the genre of the sports film, not only do sports themselves hold significant potential to invoke the success narrative of the American dream, but they also function on another level as a symbol or metaphor for the dreams of the protagonists. Usually winning the game also means "winning"—that is, achieving—one's dreams. These dreams can vary from personal dreams such as getting a football scholarship to a university as the basis for a better life, as seen in *All the Right Moves* (Chapman, 1983), or ambitious societal dreams such as overcoming racism as in *Remember the Titans*. Thus in the small towns represented by Hollywood films sport either is the American dream or the means to achieve the American dream. For example, in *Hoosiers* the dream is fulfilled because the basketball team from the tiny town of Hickory wins the state title against a heavily favored big city team of more talented players. In contrast, in *All the Right Moves* Stef Djordjevic (Tom Cruise) is on track to achieve his dream by leaving the dreary steel mill town of Ampipe with a football scholarship to a prestigious college. While his dream to become an engineer and make a better life for himself and his family is not fully achieved by the end of the film, the fact that he does manage to get a scholarship to a college with a good engineering program leads the audience to believe that the rest of his dream will follow as well. In *Remember the Titans* the American dream is not one of achievement beyond natural talents, of hard work and its rewards, but rather of what Walter Fisher called "the myth of brotherhood," that is, an idealistic, even moralistic, dream of equality.[29] Yet in different ways each film ultimately affirms the possibilities afforded through the American dream, however that dream may be envisioned, not least by insisting on the importance of place and community.

Apart from the different versions of the American dream that these films portray, they also highlight questions of individualism and community. *Hoosiers* is very much about community and a sense of togetherness, both of which are ultimately represented as the motor of success, whereas *All the Right Moves* is about the dream of a single person and the obstacles he alone must overcome to achieve it (albeit within the framework of the

128 | SMALL TOWNS, BIG DREAMS

team). *Remember the Titans*, which is discussed in more detail below, is much less straightforward than these two films, as the primary dream seems to be the winning of the state title, yet at the same time the film actually seeks to affirm a much larger dream of overcoming racial differences and ending racism. It is blatantly nostalgic, as is *Hoosiers*, whereas *All the Right Moves* aims for a realistic portrayal of small-town sports.

Yet another strand within the Hollywood small-town sports film genre, albeit even less popular than the realistic one, is that of deep-seated disillusion and cynicism as portrayed in *Varsity Blues*. Yet despite their differences— personal versus communal dreams, nostalgic versus realistic versus cynic modes of representation—all of these films rely on a strong sense of place, be that positive or negative: the small town is constructed as the "real" America.[30] It is important to note that even if the focus is on an individual player, small-town sports films almost always depict team sports, such as football, basketball, and baseball. This is because of the importance of place: whereas team sports reflect the centrality of community in small towns, the anonymity of the city more easily engenders individualistic narratives such as boxing, as seen, for example, in the *Rocky* films.

Thus the narrative of underdog small-town boys winning over the heavily favored big-city boys in *Hoosiers* not only celebrates their way of life but goes even further, validating their very existence and that of their communities by referring back to a pastoral ideal of living off the land. In *Hoosiers* agrarian life nostalgically invokes the time of pioneers and early settlers, of hard work and self-reliance. In harking back to this mythical, nostalgic past, *Hoosiers* strongly aligns itself with the time of the Puritan exodus from Europe and thus the birth of America and the American dream.[31] Symbolically, then, a win for the Huskers is a win for the American dream—and not just any American dream, but a pure, original, and white version of the American past. The Huskers have the "credible and present opportunities" that Wilber W. Caldwell cites as central to the achievement of the American dream,[32] both in spite of their hometown (because the film shows that even people with humble backgrounds and average talent can rise above and beyond their wildest dreams) and because of their hometown (because they can only do it together, as a team that is fostered by their understanding of community and hard work, which are in turn part of their distinct small-town heritage and identity). Their success is a triumph not only for themselves but for the whole town, their way of life, and their collective dream of success.

Small-town sports films thus use their setting and a strong sense of place to summon a particular past, most often a mythical, nostalgic golden past that slips onto the spectator like a prosthetic memory: an experience that never was. Nevertheless, it is an emotionally powerful misremembered memory that often evokes the time of the birth of the American dream. These films bank on the inherent ambiguity of both the American dream and of sports—one never knows whether one will win—to drive their narratives and find an affirmative happy ending. In turn, these narratives serve to legitimize and reaffirm the myth and the power of the American dream: that one can achieve one's desires through hard work and moral integrity despite all obstacles. Whether this dream is to rise above all expectations or to overcome racism, whether it is a personal dream or a collective one—its power lies in the struggle, in the potential for failure and, in these films, ultimately, in its achievement. By consciously creating a distinct sense of place, films such as *Hoosiers* irrevocably fuse this achievement to the heart of the nostalgic construction of the "true" America—the small town.

Bigger Towns, Bigger Dreams: Hybridizing Small Town-ness in *Remember the Titans*

The established framework of the small town as the "real" America is sometimes adapted in order to construct a small or medium-sized city as a small town. *Remember the Titans* (2000) is an example of such a film that continues to nostalgically invoke the golden past associated with the small town, but at the same time it updates the concept to a different place and time. I argue that the film transposes the construction of a distinct sense of place as exemplified by the small town and looks not only to the past but also to the future, thus effectively fusing the small town with the city and the past with the future, creating a new, hybridized locus for the American dream.

Remember the Titans illustrates the potency of the trope of the small town as the authentic America as well as a slow shift in terms of racial politics away from the whiteness of the small town as constructed in films such as *Hoosiers*. As the result of the *Brown vs. the Board of Education of Topeka* decision, which in 1954 found that school segregation was unconstitutional, the black and white high schools of Alexandria, Virginia, are merged in *Remember the Titans*, and so is the football team.[33] This racial integration project is capped by the appointment of a new black coach (Herman Boone, played by Denzel Washington), who replaces a very successful and adored white coach. Despite racial friction within and outside the team, Coach Boone leads the town's first integrated team to an undefeated season and the state championship. Whereas in *Hoosiers* the homogeneity of Hickory serves to represent a particularly conservative image of the small town, the "small" town in *Remember the Titans* is represented by a rather more diverse group of characters. Yet while this town is by no means as small as Hickory, the people of Alexandria also care greatly for their prize-winning high school football team, and many of them could not agree less with the appointment of the new black coach, especially as he is replacing their beloved and successful white coach, Bill Yoast (Will Patton). The problem Boone faces is trying to get his players to cross the racial divide and respect each other so that they can once again form a winning team. This he achieves with unorthodox methods during a training camp, including a midnight run to the battlefield of Gettysburg and enforced sharing of rooms, until finally the two leaders of the divided team, white Gerry Bertier (Ryan Hurst) and black Julius Campbell (Wood Harris), lead the team to some form of unity. The Titans then go on to win every game of the regular season, despite racial taunts and game manipulations seeking to bring down Boone and his mixed-race team.

While basketball is a particular source of identity and pride for Indiana, football holds special significance for the entire country, as O. Hugo Benavides points out, "football reflects what America was and is." The importance of football to the communities represented in *Remember the Titans* bears important parallels with Benavides's argument that "early in most American lives, football is linked to country and family. . . . It is the game of high-school reunions and homecoming, often the game shared with one's earliest friends. It is also the most intense of college sports creating a habit and a culture of competition and loyalty to place. This culture does not exclude non-players. Through the media, particularly television and the Internet, it permeates living rooms and language, and even the holidays of every fan. Footballers are national heroes, role models, and even guests at Thanksgiving dinner."[34]

Football serves various functions in the film: first, as in many sports films (including *Hoosiers*), the value of sports as an educational tool is highlighted and validated. The players become better human beings because of their participation in the sport, an idea that occurs repeatedly throughout sports history, from ancient Greece to the mission statement of the modern Olympic Games. Secondly, the football team functions as a microcosm of the people of Alexandria: it features a much more diverse cross-section of the population than the team in *Hoosiers*, from self-proclaimed white trash to black middle-class boys, from machos to effeminate New Age guys, and correspondingly the problems of the team reflect those of the town and, by extension, 1970s American society at large. In contrast to *Hoosiers* it is precisely the team's diversity that brings about a form of change that is not regressive but rather affirms the importance of sports as an educational tool for the players and for the whole town.

Remember the Titans builds on the framework of films such as *Hoosiers* to construct Alexandria, a city of roughly ninety thousand inhabitants in the mid-1960s, as a small-town community. As in the opening sequences described above, the film opens with shots of golden autumn maple leaves gently floating to the ground in a serene small-town graveyard while the mournful minor score further fosters a sense of loss and nostalgia. That the turbulent story of racial integration at a Virginian high school could be a source of nostalgia might be surprising, yet it is obviously not the turbulent times and the injustice of institutionalized racism that are imbued with nostalgia, but rather the innocence and spirit of a football team that will ultimately overcome these obstacles in a small Virginian town. Alexandria is a place where football still rules the community, much like basketball does in Hickory, but the city and its community are on the verge of breaking. While predominantly set in 1971, the film's opening scene begins at a funeral ten years later, which is attended by a harmonious group of black and white former football players—Alexandria's first integrated football team, the T. C. Williams Titans. Bathed in the golden afternoon sun, these first few shots of pastoral unity visualize where the film is headed: a harmonious small-town existence. The funeral scene ends with a group shot of the Titans, the peacefulness of which is disrupted by the following flashback, which takes the audience to much more urban scenes of a race riot with the police barely keeping blacks and whites apart. In juxtaposing these two shots—the mixed team in a saturated afternoon glow and the clearly separated groups of rioters in harsh daylight—the film foreshadows the resolution of this conflict and immediately associates this resolution with the golden light of the countryside.

The first few scenes of the flashback illustrate the racial tensions by continuing to carefully keep white and black characters separated within the frame. The scenes of rioting and later scenes of further conflict indicate a certain city-ness in Alexandria that is linked to civil unrest, urban street-scapes, and the black people that inhabit these streetscapes. In contrast, markers of the rural are mostly associated with white people, such as Coach Yoast's rough pickup truck and farm, both of which signify the closeness to the agrarian tradition, as well as tree-lined streets with picket fences. With Coach Boone moving onto one of these "white" streets, the potential for (segregated) Alexandria to remain an idyllic and harmonious small town is at first disrupted, and Alexandria (as opposed to Hickory in *Hoosiers*) seems to be close to losing its innocence: the ugly scenes of the riot herald the onset of Alexandria turning from a small town into a city. By the end of the film, however, this change will have been halted as Alexandria once again becomes an idyllic, but now racially integrated, small town.

EDUCATION THROUGH SPORT

The trope of sports as an educational tool is of particular importance in this film, as in the black urban films discussed below, as it is diametrically opposed to today's professionalized sports characterized by greed and doping scandals, sports heroes in conflict with the law, and erratic star behavior: the rising salaries and transfer moneys paid for professional athletes, the fall from grace of Tour de France star Lance Armstrong, or the many former

Olympic medalists forced to return their medals due to doping charges, Mike Tyson's jailing for rape, to name just a few examples. In contrast, in this film organized sports are still a meritocracy where talent and hard work, rather than wealth or race, count. This not only eliminates class or race as an issue—Coach Boone insists that the best players regardless of their race will be on the field—but also decisively places the responsibility for the achievement of success on the individual. As the players' personalities clash, their mutual prejudices are slowly eroded. They learn respect for each other through the lens of football, as this is their primary means of identification. In an attempt to help this process along and encourage dialogue between the black and the white players, Coach Boone makes them share bedrooms and family histories for the duration of the training camp. In keeping with the stereotype of the tough coach, on-field drills verge on the sadistic and culminate in a grueling midnight run to the nearby Civil War battlefield of Gettysburg. Here he conflates ideas of respect, humanity, and football when he declares: "I don't care if you like each other or not, but you will respect each other."

The scene is emotionally powerful as it evokes another bygone era—that of the American Civil War. When the boys start their run, most of them are dressed in pristine white singlets or T-shirts and pants, and it is completely dark. As the run progresses, accompanied by a Leon Russell version of Bob Dylan's song "A Hard Rain's a-Gonna Fall,"[35] the players grunt and moan as if in battle, and indeed, when they finish the run at the Gettysburg cemetery, they are dirty and marked as if they had fought through the night. The morning fog partly obscuring the graves adds to the eerie atmosphere, and Coach Boone delivers his central speech, accompanied by a now rousing soundtrack, with his back partly turned toward the team, looking instead into the mist as if to call on the ghosts of the soldiers:

> This is where they fought the battle of Gettysburg. Fifty thousand men died right here on this field, fighting the same fight that we are still fighting among ourselves today. This green field right here, painted red, bubblin' with the blood of young boys. Smoke and hot lead pouring right through their bodies. Listen to their souls, men. I killed my brother

with malice in my heart. Hatred destroyed my family. You listen, and you take a lesson from the dead. If we don't come together right now on this hallowed ground, we too will be destroyed, just like they were.

Gettysburg is, of course, a particularly potent symbol to invoke as it was one of the most devastating and bloody battles of the American Civil War.[36] The battle of Gettysburg marked a turn in favor of the Northern abolitionist states, and the cemetery became the site of one of Abraham Lincoln's most famous speeches, the Gettysburg Address. Invoking the Declaration of Independence, Lincoln announced that "all men are created equal" and that "this nation, under God, shall have a new birth of freedom."[37] It is this powerful American national legacy, for which Gettysburg has become a nostalgic, patriotic symbol to which Coach Boone refers in his motivational speech, with all its implications for racial integration and harmony. This scene sparks the eventual reconciliation between the players and is therefore of utmost importance to the narrative trajectory, yet despite the film's otherwise sincere attempts at authenticity, it is historically entirely inaccurate.[38] This fabrication stands out because it serves to present a coherent and patriotic American national identity shared by all.

It is through football that the players finally express the implementation of the concepts alluded to in Coach Boone's own personal Gettysburg address. The scene following Boone's motivational speech is another training sequence in which white leader Gerry Bertier for the first time berates another white player, who has not been blocking effectively for a black teammate. Subsequently, black player Julius Campbell tackles a black teammate more aggressively than before. The play in question had also been part of a scene just before the midnight run in which Gerry and Julius argue over being soft on players of their own race. When Gerry berates the bigoted Ray, he gives Julius a reason to play for the team rather than only looking out for his own interests. Thus the two leading defensive players conjure a truce and lead the way for the coming together of the team. Yet even within the sugar-coated world of the film, it is notable that it is the white leader Gerry who listens to Julius's complaints about Ray not blocking for the black players, and it is Gerry who initiates the truce and thus shows his insight and enlightenment, whereas Julius remains the angry young black man. As a result, even with the best of intentions, the film remains awkwardly skewed in its quest to put racism aside.

The second important function of football is that the team's makeup allows the filmmakers to depict a diverse mix of players that represent a wide variety of Alexandrians and, by extension, Americans. The team's overcoming of prejudice and segregation likewise foreshadows that of the whole town, which eventually rallies behind the integrated team and its coaches. In doing so, the film continues to equate a unified community with small town-ness, a connection well established in films such as *Hoosiers*. In *Remember the Titans* it is the power of football that unites people and communities across the lines of racial divides, and in ending with a thus unified community the film reinstates the small town as the ideal site for the fulfillment of the American dream. Yet it is important to note that there is a significant shift away from the typical small-town dream exemplified by *Hoosiers* (winning the state championship). Indeed, it is precisely the content of the dream in *Remember the Titans* that sets it apart from earlier films, and that helps modernize and open it up for the much more diverse community that is depicted. While the primary dream of winning the state championship still exists at first, the underlying dream of erasing racism comes to the fore the moment the school board tells Coach Boone that he will be fired if he loses one single game. It becomes even clearer when Coach Yoast, now the assistant coach, notices that the state championship semifinal has been fixed and is being called against the Titans. Yoast risks and loses his Hall of Fame induction when he tells the referee not to fix the game. Aaron Baker notes of this scene that "it portrays the successful integration of blacks and whites as requiring something from both sides."[39] This betrays a much more progressive outlook that is in stark contrast to the otherwise nostalgic reverence with which the film portrays the small town. Thus it is not surprising that the film does not end with a looking back to the golden past but a look to the future: captions during the end titles reveal what became of the various key players and praises their success, suggesting the larger success of racial integration at this critical historical moment.

Having established a sense of place early on, and reasserting it with

Boone's Gettysburg address, the film binds this shiny ideal of unity and success to the location of the small town, the real America, where dreams come true. The hybridization of the narrative effectively adapts the concept of the small town as the "real" America and appropriate locus for the American dream to a bigger city. Yet in casting Alexandria as a small town, the film goes beyond simply revalidating this concept to intervene in its meanings: the small-town model in *Remember the Titans* is modernized and diversified in ways that make it more progressive, accessible, and future oriented than its predecessors, and that points toward a recent wave of black urban films that take this process even further.

Transposing Small Town-ness: Basketball and Education in Inner-Urban Black Communities

Although, as discussed above, small-town films assert the status of the small town as the "real" America, inner-city sports films set within black communities such as *Coach Carter*, *Above the Rim* (Pollack, 1994) and, to a lesser extent, *Finding Forrester* (van Sant, 2000) and *He Got Game* (Lee, 1998) more recently have transposed this concept of small town-ness to suit drastically different circumstances of place, race, and social circumstances. Indeed, Spike Lee effectively visualizes this shift in the opening sequence of his film *He Got Game*, in which the camera performs a virtual journey from white midwestern farm boys shooting hoops on barn doors through small towns and trailer parks to ever more urban locations including the Chicago Bulls Stadium and the Greenwich Village cages famous for their pickup games. It is as much homage to the beauty of basketball as it is a comment on its history and change from a white game to a black one.[40] While establishing a similar framework of a clear sense of place and community as that of the small-town films, these inner-city films reappropriate small town-ness to enable much broader access to the American dream, going not only beyond the white rural masculinity of *Hoosiers* or *Varsity Blues* but also beyond the hybridized, yet ultimately reaffirmed small-town masculinity of *Remember the Titans*. Paula J. Massood highlights the potential of urban locations to serve a variety of functions in African American cinema: "The city often plays dual roles in African American film: it is a celebratory site enabling and signifying African American progress, yet it is also a place of despair and literal and psychological imprisonment. In its many permutations, African American urban cinema records and revises the role of the city in black life."[41]

The transposition of small town-ness to urban locations is accompanied by a modification of the American dream itself. As a result, rather than high school sports representing the pinnacle of one's success (that is, the "big game," the state championship, etc.), success in sports is revised to become the means to a better future. This is most often achieved in these films by giving equal or greater attention to the students' academic success than to their prowess on the basketball court, either by highlighting the importance of college education or emphasizing players' academic achievements. For example, in *Coach Carter*, the coach has the student athletes sign contracts that specify the need to maintain a grade average higher than what the official student athlete policy requires. When some of the students fail this requirement, he locks the gym and forfeits games until the students have lifted their grades. Indeed, *Coach Carter* is perhaps the most exemplary of this transposition of the small-town sports film narrative to the urban black setting and as such forms the primary focus of this final section of the analysis.[42]

In the film local sports store owner Ken Carter (Samuel L. Jackson) is persuaded to coach the varsity basketball team of his alma mater, Richmond High School, where his sporting records from the 1970s are still unbroken. The Richmond Oilers are playing as badly on the court as the high school performs academically: barely 50 percent of its students graduate successfully from Richmond High. With this in mind Coach Carter requires the team to sign the individual contracts noted above that include mostly basketball-unrelated requirements: apart from maintaining a certain GPA, players must wear ties and jackets on game day and sit in the front row of their classes. His rather dictatorial training style—"If you are late, you will run. If you give me attitude, you will do pushups. So you can pushup or shut up"—and his insistence on discipline is initially unwelcomed by the players, but this changes eventually as they come to realize the chances afforded to them by adhering to his rules. When his players fail to uphold the academic standard he requires, he locks the entire team out of the gym, thus forfeiting games, and organizes intensive tutoring in the library until the failing students show improvement. During the lockout and the resulting tutoring they begin to understand that his actions are meant to instill in them responsibility and a respect for consequences, and they continue the lockout voluntarily after it has been officially ended by the school board and Coach Carter has resigned. On seeing this, Coach Carter revokes his resignation, and the team continues its run all the way to the state championship, where they lose in the first round—the traditional "big game" of the sports movie—but are celebrated in their community nevertheless. The film ends with captions that detail various players' successes after high school, such as college scholarships and college degrees, further emphasizing the film's larger focus on educational rather than sporting achievement.

In line with generic conventions, *Coach Carter* establishes a clear sense of place through the opening sequence, but instead of fields and barns the audience sees rundown streetscapes intercut with a rough high school basketball game accompanied by the thumping bass of hip-hop music. A security guard at the entrance of the gym and the team's infighting and brawling with the St. Francis players immediately convey a drastically different environment to that of the small-town films. In Richmond, teen pregnancies, drugs, and violence are daily occurrences, and thus the film deliberately presents a less than wholesome image of this inner-urban town, which is yet to become a "community" in the sense of the small-town framework. The exposition of the film clearly references the wholesome opening scenes of films such as *Hoosiers* but at the same time reverses them: where country life is slow and idyllic, city life is fast and rough; white boys shooting hoops on barn doors are replaced by athletic black boys slam-dunking the ball with attitude; and the tiny country school with barely enough basketball players is replaced with a rundown city campus with metal detectors and security guards at the entrance.

Furthermore, Richmond High is introduced in contrast to the preppy private school, St. Francis. The game of the opening sequence not only serves to showcase the general roughness of the area and the Oilers' deficiencies on the court but also introduces their class and racial "other." The St. Francis team is trained by a white coach and has numerous white players, both their fans and their uniforms are classier, and the school clearly has the money to recruit top student athletes such as Ty Crane, who is hailed as "the next LeBron James" by a local TV reporter. At the end of the game Carter visits the Richmond coach in the locker room and is offered the rather thankless job of replacing him, while the Oilers brawl over whose fault the loss was. When Carter later talks through the offer with his girl-friend, he only sees problems: very little money, angry rough boys, a major time commitment, a losing team. Despite his reservations, he takes the job because of his own identification with the school as a successful alumnus and his desire to help those struggling boys. In constructing a strong sense of place and identification with this place through the figure of Coach Carter, the film uses topophilia just like the small-town films. In essence, the film employs the framework that has previously been established in a whole series of rural-oriented sports films to denote small town-ness to transport it to the city. It might well be a different kind of place, but the identification with this place ultimately proves to be just as strong as with places such as Hickory and Alexandria.

The many playing and training sequences further help make the film recognizable as a "small-town film in disguise." During the film it becomes clear that the playing styles differ drastically: *Hoosiers'* textbook-style pass-ing game with a layup or jump shot as its conclusion is gone,[43] and in its place is a fast, dynamic, and variable style of play that Coach Carter defines by invoking the names of his (many) sisters: the defensive play "Diane" is "straight man-to-man pressure defense," whereas "Delilah" is the "trap defense," and "Linda" is the "pick-and-roll offense." This, of course, continues the common trend of portraying women as useful for nothing other than helping men achieve their success (or, in some cases, the need to overcome their active opposition, as seen with Myra Fleener in *Hoosiers* or the players' moms in this film, discussed below). Yet while the playing style is different, the training methods are not. Carter is another strict disciplinarian and bully in a long line of hard-nosed, almost sadistic coaches. The training sessions, in fact, reveal a surprising similarity with those of the small-town films, further helping to instill small town-ness into the urban setting. These shared characteristics include a heavy emphasis on conditioning off the ball, particular training drills (e.g., "suicides") and the insistence on discipline and the importance of the team. All of these can also be found, for example, in both *Hoosiers* and *Remember the Titans*. Arguably *Hoosiers* and *Coach Carter* share a lot of the training sessions because they both deal with basketball. But there is a noticeable similarity that goes beyond common training techniques, because while the emphases and drills are similar, the filming of these is not, and yet there is distinct feeling of sameness about these sequences. It is the values and beliefs that are behind these drills that are fundamentally the same: hard work, discipline, and the belief in fundamentals and teamwork—a set of values that have previously been used to denote white, rural, working-class masculinity.[44] This is here blended successfully with the spectacular games footage that also highlights the individual style and playfulness of the not-textbook or vernacular playing style that is usually coded as black. However, playfulness is only permitted up to point—when the players start prancing and trash-talking on the field they are subjected to disciplinary action by the coach. Indeed, it is precisely the hybridization of the two playing styles that enables the successful transfer of "small town-ness" to the urban film.

The transposition of a particular sense of community works in similar ways. At first Richmond is portrayed as a community that is fragmented and powerless in the face of a failing school system and a society that has very little expectations of its kids. Initially there seems to be little interest in the team from the community; however, this changes dramatically as soon as the team starts to have an unbeaten run, which is subsequently interrupted by Carter's decision to lock the gym. Amid a media frenzy, the previously absent parents and disinterested community members suddenly turn out in support of their team and against Coach Carter. So while the team brings the town together—as in countless other sports films, this is represented by more and more cheering fans in the school, in the stands, and in the community—the team's coach divides the community much like Coach Dale does in Hickory, or Coach Boone in Alexandria. Indeed, the coach as a controversial figure could be said to have become a well-worn stereotype, yet what differentiates Coach Carter from his peers is that it is neither his credentials (*Hoosiers, We Are Marshall, The Final Season,*

Glory Road), his training or playing style (*Hoosiers, Remember the Titans, We Are Marshall, Glory Road*), or his race or race politics (*Remember the Titans, Glory Road*), that is controversial—it is his interest in the athletes as students, that is, their academic performance, that sets him apart from other coaches and enrages the community. Thus while the framework of the coach as a controversial figure stays intact and sustains the familiarity of the small-town sports films, the changes to what is controversial about him—that is, the content of the framework—functions as the marker of the adaptation to the inner-urban setting.

The coach is mystified by this development, as is the audience—shouldn't a community in these circumstances embrace a coach who tries to improve his players' grades?[45] Much like the way academic success or ambition is feminized, and thus devalued, in *Hoosiers* through the figure of Myra Fleener and her lone support for student Jimmy Chitwood's academic pursuits over basketball, Richmond's community fails to recognize the importance of education. Interestingly, though, it is above all the mothers who are most vocal in their rejection of Carter's educational plans, which is at least in part highlighting the further issue of absent fathers.[46] Rather than education being feminized here, the mothers are characterized as overambitious, greedy sports moms, for whom their sons are not much more than future providers of income playing in the NBA. Because it is the players' *own* decision, and directly opposed to their mothers' wishes, to continue the lockout and to keep studying, their becoming adults and making their own decisions suddenly also becomes an issue of gender. In contrast to the hysteria of their mothers, the players model a morally virtuous, realistic—in the sense of being realistic about their NBA chances—and stoic manhood.

It is precisely in this insistence upon education that the reconfiguration of the underlying American dream story in *Coach Carter* becomes obvious. Whereas films such as *Hoosiers, The Final Season, We Are Marshall,* and even *Varsity Blues* celebrate the win of the big, climactic game at the end of the film as the achievement of the dream (that is, the state or district championship, the first win of the season after a disaster, etc.), *Coach Carter* directly criticizes this narrow-minded understanding of success in a scene in which the coach and headmistress Garrison argue about the lockout:

GARRISON: Your intentions are good, Mr. Carter, but your methods are a bit extreme.

CARTER: You painted an extreme picture. No one expects them to graduate, no one expects them to go to college.

GARRISON: So you take away basketball, the one area of their lives where they have some success?

CARTER: Yes, Ma'am.

GARRISON: And you challenge them academically?

CARTER: Yes, Ma'am.

GARRISON: And what if they fail?

CARTER: Then we failed.

GARRISON: Unfortunately, Mr. Carter, both you and I know that for some of the kids, this basketball season will be the *highlight of their lives* [emphasis added].

CARTER: Well, I think that's the problem, don't you?

Coach Carter considers this idea of winning the game as the "highlight of their lives" to be undermining the greater goal of helping the students into a better future—a future that is not defined by a game they played when they were sixteen. He believes that constructing the basketball games as the pinnacle of success is detrimental to the students' development and severely underestimates their potential as human beings. The achievements that are prioritized by Coach Carter, and thus the film, are academic success that leads to college, which in turn leads to a better life away from the inner-urban ghetto in which the kids find themselves at the beginning of the film. Consequently, when the team loses the final game at the end as well as the state championship, this serves to highlight the players' other, by implication more worthy, achievements. In his postgame pep talk, Coach Carter first debunks the importance of the fairy tale ending and instead lists the players' less obvious accomplishments:

Well, not quite your storybook ending, huh? Not for us, anyway. But you men played like champions. You never gave up. And champions hold their heads high. What you achieved goes way beyond the win-loss column or what's gonna be written on the front page of the sports section tomorrow. You've achieved something that some people spend their whole lives trying to find. What you achieved is that ever-elusive victory within. And gentlemen, I am so proud of you. Four months ago, when I took the job at Richmond, I had a plan. That plan failed. I came to coach basketball players, and you became students. I came to teach boys, and you became men. And for that, I thank you.

On exiting the locker room the team is surprised by a large number of fans, family members, and teachers who are waiting for them and who applaud and cheer for them despite their loss. The effect of this is twofold: not only is the threat of losing de-escalated, but the sport itself is de-emphasized, while the other achievements take precedence as freeze frames of the individual players with superimposed captions of their future success end the film, and the values of good sportsmanship are emphasized (see fig. 7).

This positive reinforcement of the values of education are made clear as a deviation from previous models of success and, in consequence, in making this new kind of success achievable in the unlikeliest of places. In other words, defining education as success in an inner-urban school with the lowest of academic performance scores—headmistress Garrison mentions the "Academic Performance Index" to Coach Carter during one of their arguments about the team and points out that Richmond High School has a rank of 1, with the best being 10—marks a decisive shift in what is considered an American dream and who has access to it. While previous films often suggested that the American dream is only achievable by rural white small-town folk, this new kind of film opens it up to inner-urban black kids celebrating the values of civic humanism. By reappropriating small town-ness and reimagining the American dream, inner-urban black communities are shown to be equally legitimate loci for success even beyond sports.

In this chapter I argue that within the realm of small-town sports films the small town is constructed as the "real" America and thus the prime— and indeed, in cases such as *Hoosiers*, the only—locus for the successful fulfillment of American dreams. The small-town sports films often look

7. *Coach Carter*: Validating "success." *Coach Carter*. Paramount Pictures: Thomas Carter (2005).

back nostalgically to a romanticized agrarian past that is decidedly pre–civil rights movement. The communities depicted are set apart from their urban counterparts by their intense identification with the local sports team, which becomes emblematic for the entire town. This distinct sense of place and community is presented as the prerequisite to the achievement of the American dream.

In the last decade a new crop of films such as *Coach Carter* and *Remember the Titans* have shown that this sense of place and community—once exclusive to the mythical rural small town—can be modernized and transposed onto other settings, such as black, inner-urban neighborhoods. These films deviate from the earlier ones in that they have future-oriented, progressive tendencies that enable more complex and racially inclusive American dreams to emerge. Redefining success, they open up new loci for the cornerstone of American self-perception that is the American dream. This progressiveness, however, has its limits, as is demonstrated by my examination, in the following chapter, of sports films featuring female or homosexual athletes, who push against the established boundaries of national identity to imagine a more inclusive nation.

CHAPTER 5

GENDERING THE NATION

The "Hero Other" in Sports Films

> Every girl in this league is going to be a lady.
>
> Ira Lowenstein in *A League of Their Own* (1992)

This line from Penny Marshall's 1992 film *A League of Their Own*, which depicts the inaugural season of the All-American Girls Professional Baseball League (AAGPBL) in 1940s USA, points to one of the more thorny problems in professional sports—that of the female athlete. It illustrates the tension thrown up by the very idea of this figure, who may be athletic, talented, and physically powerful, but who above all else has to be a lady. But why would a female athlete be considered a problem, and how would her being a lady solve it? Put simply, the attributes of the successful athlete—for example, strength of mind and body, competitiveness, a certain degree of selfishness—stand in stark contrast to traditional conceptions of an "ideal" womanliness that often revolve around such issues as beauty, caregiving as mothers and homemakers, and selflessness. At a broader level, the role of women within the project of the nation has often been envisioned as that of guardians of morality, upholders of values, and symbols of virtue and modesty through their primary role as mothers. Unsurprisingly, the female athlete becomes a problematic figure not only in the world of sports but even more so when sports converge with visions of the nation in films.

Similarly problematic, and sometimes overlapping with the figure of the female athlete, is another unwelcomed figure in the sports world, the homosexual athlete. Interestingly the homosexual athlete appears to threaten the dominant norms of both genders, but for entirely different reasons. While the lesbian athlete allegedly endangers the dominant ideals of womanhood and femininity by deviating too far from these, repudiating the idea of women's essential weakness and inferiority to men, the gay male athlete jeopardizes the stability of ideal manhood and masculinity by being too similar to his heterosexual counterpart, therefore rejecting the notion of homosexual men as weak and degenerate. The depiction of women outside the normative roles of housewives and mothers, or of gay men outside of the stereotypes of weak and effeminate "queens," threatens to destabilize a national identity dependent upon the ideals of strong, active masculinity and frail, passive femininity. Indeed, it is precisely in this myth of essentialist gender identities, and the disruption of this myth by the physical and mental strength embodied by the athlete protagonist, that we find barely concealed fissures in the national fabric. The important issue that arises is how the representation of mythical notions of the nation absorbs these contradictions.

Maintaining a stable national identity in mainstream sports films, as discussed in the previous chapters, is a project that is fraught with tension. The overwhelming majority of mainstream sports films are about men and characterized by displays of hegemonic masculinity. As Deborah V. Tudor explains, "Introducing a female character who possesses overt signs of 'feminism,' such as independence and subjectivity, introduces problems into films that represent a social institution still conceptualized as a male preserve."[1] Writing in 2013, Katharina Lindner observed that "there has been a notable increase in female sports films over the last 20 years," and so too has the scholarship increased on the topic, with Lindner herself, Nicholas Chare, and Viridiana Lieberman leading the field.[2] The distinguishing characteristic of the baseball players in *A League of Their Own* is their gender, which produces anxiety not only for the makers of the new women's professional baseball league in the film but for the filmmakers and the audience as well. The term "sports" usually comes in one of two forms: as "sports" or as "women's sports." This distinction marks women's sports as Other, as requiring a qualifier, and homosexual athletes are similarly "othered" by being marked as "gay" or "lesbian athletes." Female, gay, or lesbian athletes are thus linguistically placed in opposition to athletes who do not need a qualifier and are usually conceptualized as being hetero-sexual, male, and most often white. (This hegemonic understanding and construction of sports does not necessarily reflect the reality of some of the most popular sports leagues in the world, such as the NFL and NBA, which have predominantly black athletes.) Gender and sexuality become conflated in representations of athletic performance and essentialized within heterosexual masculinity, the constructed nature of which becomes visible when the athlete is of a different gender or sexuality.

These differences, and the way they impact upon and destabilize notions of national identity, are the subject of this chapter. I argue that sports films with female or homosexual athletes present a challenge to the representation of a stable national identity by virtue of their being Other to the dominant perception of men and women in modern society. When the main characters are female or homosexual, or what I call "hero Others"—a deliberately awk-ward term in order to denote its inherent contradictions—they threaten the organization of social roles in relation to dominant masculinity. This chap-ter thus sheds light on how sports films—as representatives of hegemonic national culture—cope with incorporating non-male, non-heterosexual citizens into the national fabric through the lens of the sports film.

Nation, Gender, Sexuality, and Sports

In order to untangle the mesh of gender, sexuality, and nation as represented in sports films, it is necessary to briefly examine how these discourses are separate from, yet interact with, each other. Various scholars have examined the connections between gender, sexuality, and the nation. The editors of the collection *Nationalisms and Sexualities*, for example, argue that "where the heterosexual family played such a central role in the nation's public imaginings that motherhood could be viewed as a national service, female nonreproductive sexuality and female-female eroticism were constrained."[3] Jyotri Puri similarly contends that "gender and sexuality are central, not incidental, to the origins, meaning, and implications of nationalism."[4] In his influential study *Nationalism and Sexuality*, George L. Mosse shows how the development of a concept of "ideal manliness"—and the importance of respectability in the maintenance of such an ideal manliness—at the time of the rise of the modern nation-state functioned as a stabilizing force for the nation, while at the same time, women, "gypsies," and homosexuals came to be positioned as destabilizing Other.[5] Mosse asserts that the rise of the nation-state not only coincided with but also found a natural ally in the establishment of bourgeois or middle-class respectability, which in turn produced a variety of norms that still govern society today. This concept of respectability "was based on a consistent attitude toward the human body, its sensuous qualities and its sexual functions" and is thus inextricably linked with gender and sexual norms.[6]

With the advent of modernity, and the ensuing political, cultural, and economic changes, the middle classes sought to distance themselves from the lower classes, as well as the aristocracy, in order to maintain control during a time of upheaval. As Mosse observes, the fight for control found its expression in norms that governed the normal and abnormal, distinguished insiders from outsiders, and absorbed challenges to masculinity during the shift from an agrarian to an industrialized society. The "ideal manliness" that resulted from this process was characterized by virility, "freedom from sexual passion," restraint, and self-control. The family unit became "the policeman on the beat, an indispensable agent of sexual control as directed by physicians . . . , educators, and the nation itself," and "any threat to its survival endangered the nation's future."[7] Together, ideal manliness and respectability became ideological forces that ensured the stability of the nation itself: "nationalism and respectability assigned everyone his place in life, man and woman, normal and abnormal, native and foreigner; any confusion between these categories threatened chaos and loss of control."[8] While Mosse's argument is concerned with quite different historical contexts than this chapter, in particular the rise of Nazism, I argue that it can be usefully applied to the thorny problem engendered by female or homosexual protagonists within the genre of the sports film, for it is precisely these anxieties over the individual's place in life and society that sports films with female or homosexual athletes bring to the fore.

Female athletes have long been a contentious site for the negotiation of gender boundaries. They inhabit a space in-between the seemingly clear lines historically drawn between the sexes based on the assumption of an essential difference between masculinity and femininity. In her study of U.S. women's sports, Susan K. Cahn argues that "the controversies surrounding female athleticism broached fundamental questions about the content and definition of American woman- and manhood."[9] Examining early generations of female athletes and the debates that surrounded them, Jennifer Hargreaves similarly notes the reactions against women who appeared to be acting outside of their prescribed gender: "The small numbers of women who took part in aggressive, muscular, traditional male sports had their sexuality denied, were labelled 'mannish' or 'freakish,' presented as androgynous or, more usually, as 'super-feminine.' There was always a feminizing code—as Tuttle . . . puts it—'to neutralize the effect of the transgressive act.'"[10]

That such a "feminizing code" was not extinct by the 1940s can be seen clearly in *A League of Their Own*, where, as the quote from Ira Lowenstein indicates, the main characters have to conform to certain ideals of femininity in order to be allowed to play in the AAGPBL. Such a code represents one of the cultural strategies of controlling women's engagement in sports, in order to uphold the gender difference that equates men and masculinity with power and thus ensures the continuation of structural patriarchy, or, as David Whitson puts it, "in embodying power themselves, they challenge one of the fundamental sources of male power, the ideological equation of physical power itself with masculinity."[11] It is this equation that is deconstructed in sports films featuring female and/or homosexual hero Others, for these films narrate and visualize the challenge to (heterosexual) male hegemony.

Similar issues to those raised by the transgressive sporting bodies of female athletes can be found in discussions of the "steely" women of 1980s action cinema. In her analysis of muscular and androgynous heroines such as Ripley (Sigourney Weaver) of the *Alien* series or Sarah Connor (Linda Hamilton) of the *Terminator* franchise, Yvonne Tasker coins the term "musculinity" to define the shape and make of action bodies that had been exclusively associated with masculinity but were now also transferable to female action stars.[12] She argues that in producing such "built" bodies—that is, bodies trained to muscular perfection—the very idea of a naturalized muscular masculinity is called into question, as the muscular body is anything but natural—it is shown to be manufactured. Furthermore, the muscled bodies of action heroines, who claim agency and are therefore able to "command the narrative,"[13] dissolve any attempts at a neat gender dichotomy and thus threaten social stability in similar ways to the sporting bodies of female athletes. Discussing the "impossible bodies" of the male and female body builders in the *Pumping Iron* documentaries, Chris Holmlund further underlines the different significance of muscularity for men and women, asserting that "the association of muscularity with men poses no conflict between sex and gender: muscular men are seen as 'natural.'"[14] Quite to the contrary, she continues: "Images of muscular women . . . are disconcerting, even threatening. They disrupt the equation of men with strength and women with weakness that underpins gender roles and power relations, and that has by now come to seem familiar and comforting . . . to both women and men."[15] Furthermore, strong, muscular female bodies, in their "acquisition" of "masculinity," have frequently been seen to cross other social boundaries and, in particular, have often been conflated with the concept of the "mannish lesbian" of early sporting history.

The specter of lesbianism has become a constant companion to female athletes, producing significant representational difficulties for sports films featuring female athletic heroines. As indicated above, the very existence of the homosexual and/or female athlete destabilizes the (national) gender equilibrium, on which larger social structures and identities are based. Lesbians and gay men, as Mosse points out, "menaced the division between the sexes and thus struck at the very roots of society. Indeed, lesbians threatened society, if possible, to an even greater degree than homosexuals, given women's role as patron saints and mothers of the family and the nation."[16]

Cahn further emphasizes just how menacing the perceived threat of the lesbian athlete is: "As a powerful representation of deviance her significance reached far beyond the world of sport. She announced to all women that competitiveness, strength, independence, aggression, and same-sex physical intimacy were privileged features of manhood or, conversely, the mark of unacceptable womanhood. She represented the border that must not be crossed, reminding all women to toe the line of heterosexual femininity or risk falling into a despised and liminal category of mannish (not-women) women."[17] Unsurprisingly, then, the lesbian athlete, on the wrong end of the scale of acceptable womanhood, has become an enduring "negative symbol of female social and sexual independence."[18]

Sports films with female and/or homosexual athlete protagonists are thus concerned with challenges not only to gender roles and heteronormativity but also to hegemonic conceptions of national identity. It is with the seeming impossibility of a successful, positive, strong female or gay hero Other that this chapter is concerned, as I examine how mainstream films deal with the tension that emerges between a stabilizing "manly ideal" and the Other encroaching on his territory. Considering the "double" threat that homosexual athletes represent, it comes as no surprise that very few sports films with gay or lesbian main characters have been made. Notable exclusions to this trend are the films *Personal Best* (Towne, 1982), about lesbian/bisexual pentathletes, and *Summer Storm* (Kreuzpaintner, 2004), which I discuss briefly at the end of this chapter.

For the most part I discuss two films—*A League of Their Own* and *Bend It Like Beckham*—two films that deal with the threat of a destabilized national identity in quite different ways, which are in turn typical of broader patterns within the genre of the sports film. *A League of Their Own* marshals a range of narrative and representational strategies to tell the story of two female hero Others, sisters Dottie (Geena Davis) and Kit (Lori Petty), in the All-American Girls Professional Baseball League, but it ultimately diffuses the threat posed by female athleticism by channeling these professional sporting females back into normative roles as housewives and non-athletes. In *Bend It Like Beckham*, meanwhile, the hero Others are young female star soccer players, and one of them is of South Asian descent, doubly marking her as Other. I argue that the film, rather than containing or displacing this threat, subtly creates a changed vision of British national identity, allowing the Other to become part of the norm by expanding this "norm" to include a greater range of gendered, sexual, and ethnic identifications.

A League of Their Own: Restoring the Natural Order

The name of the league prominently features the term "All-American," which refers to outstanding college or high school athletes who are voted the best of their year in their sport and who therefore become part of the All-American team. However, All-American is also used to describe the wholesome image of the archetypal American, envisioned as clean-cut, respectable, and middle class. This is further emphasized by the official song of the league:

> We are the members of the All-American League.
> We come from cities near and far.
> We've got Canadians, Irishmen and Swedes,
> We're all for one, we're one for all,
> We're All-Americans![19]

Considering that the AAGPBL emerged in the 1940s as a professional league, the importance of the term "All-American," both in the sense of an exceptional athlete and a respectable American in the form of the girl-next-door, cannot be underestimated. It binds the league to an American tradition of honoring sportsmanship and reinforces the belief in meritocracy so crucial to the idea of the American dream. As such, the various nationalities listed (Canadian, Irish, Swedish) are less a sign of otherness than a reminder of America's multicultural roots.

Baseball has often been described as the quintessential American game—the national pastime, as the editors of *Reel Baseball* emphasize in the preface to their collection on baseball films: "Baseball has been more than just a game in this country; it has been the source of many national heroes, a reluctant but undeniable leader in forging new territory on issues of race and labor relations, and a historical marker of many of America's pivotal moments."[20]

Although baseball has been losing favor with American audiences in recent times, it is still very much considered part of American mythology.[21] As Tom Robson argues, baseball often, and never more so than in the baseball films of the 1980s and early 1990s, has been used to "support dominant U.S. economic and social norms."[22] Robson further concludes:

"Coming out of the Civil War, as the United States transitioned from an agrarian nation to an industrial one, baseball served as a unifying element in national identity. Those uncertain about what this shift in national cultural priorities portended found comfort and stability in this game that seemed to embody most of the basic values of the nation."[23]

This deep-seated connection of baseball with American national identity is what makes the threat of an active, unruly femininity in the form of the female ballplayer so unsettling, especially in light of Robson's assertion that "the U.S. baseball film reinforces and re-inscribes conservative ideology."[24] How, then, can a baseball film, with this inherent basis in conservative ideology, bridge the gap from traditional women's roles to incorporate the paradox that is the hero Other—the decidedly unconservative female professional athlete, with all the individual agency and economic freedom this figure represents?

This underlying threat to the stability of national identity and gender roles is palpable in *A League of Their Own*, and to counter this, the film employs three key strategies to resolve this threat. First, the use of a flash-back structure ensures that it is clear from the beginning that the league is long defunct and therefore was only a momentary challenge to the status quo. Secondly, the film presents a model of ideal femininity in the main character, Dottie, who first becomes a hero Other as a star ballplayer but eventually eschews her professional baseball career in favor of returning to the farm with her husband in order to "start a family." And lastly, the film visually demonstrates the disrupting potential of female agency, thus giving credence to the perceived danger and legitimizing its swift defusal. Instead it offers limited agency that does not interfere with gender boundaries.

A League of Their Own is about the premier season of the All-American Girls Professional Baseball League, which came into being to fill the gap left by the disbanding of Major League Baseball (MLB) due to World War II. Young women were scouted from farm leagues and urban softball leagues all over the country to play baseball for a living for the first time in the sport's history. The AAGPBL was relatively short-lived, in part because, with the return of soldiers after the end of the war and the subsequent reinstatement of MLB, the popularity of the women's league plummeted. Nevertheless, the twelve years of the AAGPBL left their mark in sports history, as the league provided women athletes with the opportunity to pursue their sport professionally and earn a wage that was well above that of factory workers.

The historical league was founded by Philip K. Wrigley, owner of the Chicago Cubs baseball franchise, who saw an opportunity to both capitalize on the rise of women's softball and keep Wrigley Field occupied by providing wholesome, patriotic entertainment for the masses, tapping into America's favorite pastime. In an attempt to distinguish his league from softball's somewhat tarnished reputation as a game for rough, mannish, working-class women, he instituted a detailed code of conduct, ensuring that his players maintained a feminine, "girl-next-door" charm.[25] The importance of adhering to traditional notions of femininity is highlighted by the first two rules of conduct:

1. ALWAYS appear in feminine attire when not actively engaged in practice or playing ball. This regulation continues through the playoffs for all, even though your team is not participating. AT NO TIME MAY A PLAYER APPEAR IN THE STANDS IN HER UNIFORM, OR WEAR SLACKS OR SHORTS IN PUBLIC.
2. Boyish bobs are not permissible and in general your hair should be well groomed at all times with longer hair preferable to short hair cuts. Lipstick should always be on.[26]

Further to the strict rules of conduct the league management included a beauty and charm school during spring training as well as a charm school guide that outlined beauty routines and included clothing guidelines and a section on etiquette.[27] That a player could be fired for a boyish haircut demonstrates how serious the league management was about adhering to the prescribed femininity.[28] Yet despite the league's early success and popularity it did not last, and its eventual decline is often attributed to a combination of mismanagement, competing entertainment options such as television, and a more conservative postwar social atmosphere ushering women back to home and hearth.[29]

The film tells the story of star player Dottie and her little sister Kit as they join the Rockford Peaches and the league in its inaugural season and adjust to life on the road under the supervision of a team chaperone. Amid growing sibling rivalry, which ends with Kit being traded to the Racine Belles, the Rockford Peaches advance to the championship series. They end up playing against the Belles, pitting the sisters directly against each other. In the climactic championship game Kit scores the winning run and for once outshines her big sister. Dottie, meanwhile, leaves the Rockford Peaches at the end of the season to return to life on the farm with her recently returned war veteran husband, leaving behind a promising baseball career. While the main story is set in the 1940s, it is framed by a contemporary backstory on the occasion of the induction of the AAGPBL into the Baseball Hall of Fame and the team reunion this occasion facilitates. Starting the film in this way forges a contemporary connection with the film's 1990s viewing audiences, as a reluctant Dottie is urged by her daughter to attend the reunion. When she arrives at Coopertown's Doubleday Field, the vision of women playing baseball takes her back to the beginnings of the league.

Almost all sports films about female athletes feature various storylines that both explicitly and implicitly deal with ideas of appropriate and inappropriate behavior for women. In *A League of Their Own* these include the need for the women to be beautiful and wear dress-like baseball "uniforms," to be supervised by a team chaperone, to attend the aforementioned beauty and charm classes, and Dottie's insistence on her life goal consisting of moving back to the farm with her husband to start a family. In such ways the film repeatedly gives prominence to women's status as the objects of male desire, as wives, and as mothers. The few players who are not obviously marked as married or engaged either get married during the film or are cast as either loose women or potential lesbians. *A League of Their Own* thus follows a strategy that clarifies from the beginning of the film that the challenge of the hero Others depicted was only a momentary abnormality that was quickly corrected.

The film begins in the early 1990s with an elderly Dottie contemplating whether she should attend the induction of the AAGPBL into the Baseball Hall of Fame. At the end of the film the story returns to the events at the induction, including Dottie's reunion with her former teammates and sister, and the opening of an exhibition about the AAGPBL. With the film drawing attention to the fact that the league is now but a blip in the annals of sports history, it becomes obvious that these women represented only a temporary challenge to the status quo. As the film takes the audience back in time and then safely returns it to the here and now of the film's production, it is clear that the women's baseball league is long defunct and the "natural" gender order (both within and outside of baseball) has been reinstated.

As the flashback ends and the audience is returned to Dottie at the Hall of Fame, there is further reassurance of the restored gender status quo, for when Dottie meets the other players for the first time in more than forty years, their conservation is all about their marital status:

DOTTIE: Mae? All-the-way-Mae?

MAE: Gee, no one's called me that since . . .

DORIS: Last night?

MAE: Oh, come on! I'm a married woman now.

DOTTIE: Oh, Ellen Sue—you haven't changed one bit!

ELLEN SUE: Dottie, I married a plastic surgeon.

In this brief scene the heteronormative gender equilibrium is firmly reestablished, as seemingly all players have landed in the safe haven of marriage after their turn as professional athletes. One single player, Helen (Anne Ramsay), who became a medical doctor later in life, is the only concession to the impact of the league in opening up women's lives. This one player seems an allowable abnormality, a single deviation from the norm of the otherwise successful reintegration as wives and mothers. Dottie's sister Kit, who continues to play baseball instead of returning home at the end of the first season, is also positioned as somewhat of a counterpart to Dottie. Yet rather than positioning Kit's choice to remain independent and continue to play baseball as offering a permanently different life trajectory—such as that of Helen—the film shows this independence to be short-lived. When the apparently estranged Dottie and Kit finally meet again at the reunion, it becomes clear that Kit has also become a wife and mother, just like Dottie. The flashback structure thus allows the film to highlight the reestablishment of hegemonic social and gender structures.

This structure also provides an opportunity for some romanticizing nostalgia, while at the same time allowing for some gentle ridiculing of some of the more obvious differences of women's roles in the past, such as the "need" for the athletes to attend a charm and beauty school. In playing these differences for laughs, and thus assuming a shared knowledge of the changes in women's lives in the decades since the league's inception, the film panders to the expectations of a modern, post–civil rights, and second-wave feminism audience. Yet this feminism remains at the surface, a "look how far we've come" gesture, but underneath it resides a deeply regressive current of conservatism, which resolves the threat to gender boundaries by reestablishing the traditional values of home and family.

The second and main strategy for warding off the threat of the female athlete to the stability of American national identity can be found in the storyline of main character Dottie. Not only are her life choices, particularly post-league, exemplary of the regressiveness described above, but she is heralded as a role model for appropriate American womanhood. Although scholars such as Lisa Taylor have argued that the film can be seen as being part of a feminist quest to unearth women's history, Dottie's embodiment of a very conservative version of femininity does not challenge or stretch the boundaries of these gender roles.[30] Quite in contrast, it seems to not only encourage but also strengthen the currency of traditional gender roles.

The parameters of appropriate and inappropriate behavior and social comportment for women are set early on in the film. Once in the league, Dottie displays a knack for leadership as she fills in for the frequently drunk coach Jimmy Dugan (Tom Hanks), leading the Rockford Peaches from win to win and demonstrating her love and commitment to baseball as she helps keep the league alive with spectacular displays of athleticism. In doing so she has taken on a man's job and has well and truly made it her own, and the success of the Rockford Peaches validates her ability to do so. With soldiers either in the field or returning from war deeply traumatized and women mobilized to join the workforce during their absence, there was considerable anxiety in the 1940s over whether women would be willing to give up their newfound financial and social independence to return to the family home, a situation that had already been played out in post–World War I Europe and America when the New (working) Woman unsettled gender relations.[31] One scene in particular speaks directly to these concerns of women "taking over," in ways that also acknowledge the position of the contemporary viewer.

In a high-octane baseball sequence of Dottie, Kit, and the other players at the tryouts, the baseball action is intercut and overlaid with a voice-over of a "social commentary" radio broadcast read by a concerned elderly woman, which both mocks such conservative concerns and gives them a voice:

> And now, from Chicago, The Mutual presents another social commentary by Miss Maida Gillespie: Careers and higher education are leading to the masculinization of women with enormously dangerous consequences to the home, the children, and our country. When our boys come home from war, what kind of girls will they be coming home to? And now the most disgusting example of this sexual confusion. Mr. Walter Harvey of Harvey Bars is presenting us with women's baseball. Right here in Chicago young girls, plucked from their families, are gathered at Harvey Field to see which one of them can be the most masculine. Mr. Harvey, like your candy bars, you are completely nuts.

Here humor papers over the seriousness and hard-fought nature of the maintenance of gender roles, as these women in their masculine baseball outfits run, throw, and hit with aplomb, sliding and tackling without any regard for the physical consequences either to themselves or the other players. While the players are not consciously trying to be masculine, they do play baseball like athletes—at a time when athletes were usually male. This points to the ambivalent position maintained by the film as it tackles the issue; on the one hand making a caricature of the "old biddy"[32] on the radio through her overly enunciated speech and comical facial expressions, yet on the other validating the content of the speech by visual means.

Dottie's relationship with coach Jimmy Dugan further illustrates these anxieties and in particular those around broken masculinity and new, empowered femininity in postwar U.S. society. Together Jimmy and Dottie embody these social fears about how soldiers coming home to completely changed roles for women might react. Although Jimmy is not a traumatized war veteran, his own loss of masculinity is amplified by his inability to join the armed forces because of a knee injury. This results in deeply felt guilt and shame over not being able to fulfill his manly, patriotic duties, as evident from his despairing question to Dottie: "How did I get so useless so fast?" His shame is manifested in his drunkenness and disinterest in the team as well as his lack of respect for the female athletes in the first half of the film. Disenchanted with their coach, the team members quickly learn to ignore him, and Dottie fills the gap, much like Rosie the Riveter encouraged women to fill the gaps left by the servicemen in the factories. Without hesitation Dottie assumes responsibility for and authority over the team, managing their training and strategy during the matches and thus demonstrating her capabilities in what was officially a man's job. She personifies the threat of "women taking over," not only because she is able to do so, but because in taking over she makes Dugan redundant. Yet Dottie's claiming of such power, which poses a legitimate threat to hegemonic masculinity, is soon resolved in a key scene.

For most of the season Coach Dugan is drunk and disorderly, taking refuge in the dugout while Dottie manages the team. At the first game of the season, during which he is not drunk, he nonetheless demonstrates his active disinterest by reading the paper and ignoring Dottie's coaching. After a while, however, he begins watching the game, hinting at an impending shift in power and agency in the team. As Dottie gives the sign for a squeeze bunt to the Peaches' best hitter, Marla (Megan Cavanagh)—a play that would potentially sacrifice Marla in order for the player on third base to reach home and score—Jimmy looks up and challenges Dottie's call. Although Dottie is suggesting a perfectly sound strategy, Jimmy intervenes and gives an opposing sign to Marla, telling her to swing at the ball to produce a big hit. As the scene progresses, Jimmy moves from inside the dugout in the bottom left-hand corner of the frame toward the middle, where Dottie is perched in typical coaching pose. As he moves ever further into Dottie's space, they both continue furiously signing opposing strategies at the confused Marla. Finally Jimmy erupts with, "Hey, who is the goddamn manager here?" To which Dottie replies, "Then act like it, you big lush," and retreats into the background to the approving mutterings of her teammates. This leaves Jimmy in exactly the position previously occupied by Dottie in the frame, suggesting that her coaching days are over. She is now left sulking in the dugout in much the same way Jimmy was before, showing them to have effectively swapped both their places and their roles in relation to the team (see fig. 8). Marla then scores a big hit, bringing home the runner on third base, thus implying that Jimmy's strategy was correct.

The scene is played for laughs, thus reducing the resentment Dottie feels toward Jimmy for suddenly reclaiming his duties to girlish sulking rather than justified anger at literally being put back into her place, after having carried out these duties quite successfully. As the "signing battle" for authority begins, the scene is suddenly accompanied by an upbeat, jazzy score that underlines its humorous side. This segues seamlessly into a more somber tone as Dottie steps down, and finishes in a rousing finale suggesting the winning of the match. This sound-over directs the emotional response of the audience in a much more subtle and affective way than the relatively sparse dialogue. Together with the visuals of the furious signing and Dottie's departure, the scene is a powerful representation of the reclaiming of masculine power and makes it clear that such authority, if given at all to the hero Other, can only be temporary.

This scene foreshadows the rest of Dottie's storyline. Close to the end of the season—the Peaches have just made it to the World Series—Dottie's husband Bob returns injured from the war to take Dottie home. Jimmy tries to convince her to stay, even telling her that "baseball is what gets inside you. It lights you up. You can't deny that." Rather than denying that baseball means something to her, she feebly replies, "It just got too hard." Overtly this refers to the growing tension between her and her sister Kit, which has led to Kit being traded to another team, and also the death of a teammate's husband. However, with Dottie having taken on various responsibilities up to this point, some of which lie firmly in the male domain, her quitting the team like this is unusual and can be read in different ways. It might suggest that to be a "real" ballplayer is simply "too hard" for a woman. In a more positive reading, Dottie's "too hard" might refer to her having to give up the extra (masculine) responsibilities, such as the coaching, as soon as the men return. However, both readings have in common that in the end Dottie does what is expected of her as a woman

8. *A League of Their Own*: Coach Dugan (Tom Hanks) reclaiming his place as coach from Dottie (Geena Davis). *A League of Their Own*. Columbia Pictures: Penny Marshall (1992).

in postwar U.S. society: she returns to her place rather than insisting on the freedom and independence that were granted to her during the brief period of the war.

Moreover, she is not forced back into her place by the men around her at this stage but returns willingly, and this presents the ideal solution to the radio announcer's question, "What kind of girls will they be coming home to?" In *A League of Their Own* the answer to this question is the kind of girls who subject their own desires and needs to the greater good by devoting themselves to family and homemaking, and thus who willingly accept a safely contained, normative heterosexual life. By exposing how Dottie is constructed as a role model of ideal womanhood, the inner workings of how traditional gender roles are maintained are laid bare.

Disrupting this central narrative tendency that preferences Dottie's model of ideal womanhood over that of Kit and the other team members, however, are scenes in which the women assume collective agency, with varying results. The film depicts these moments of agency only to subsequently contain them, in what constitutes another strategy to rein in the threat of the hero Other. The first such scene depicts the women conspiring to sneak out of their residence to go to a roadhouse for some dancing and fun. The scene is visually marked as different from the rest of the film in that it is characterized by fast-paced editing mixed with handheld and moving camera shots. As a result it becomes quite literally a whirlwind of women and men swing dancing, flirting, drinking, and kissing seemingly random partners. While "All-the-Way-Mae" dances with two partners, suggesting indecisiveness at best and promiscuity at worst, her best friend Doris flips her male dance partner instead of being flipped. At the end of the dance Mae lands in Doris's arms instead of those of either of the two men with whom she has been dancing, leaving further room for speculation by raising the specter of lesbianism that has long been associated with female athletes in general, but with softball and baseball players in the United States in particular.[33]

This scene depicts a wildness and freedom otherwise absent in the film and thus demonstrates the consequences of "setting women loose" and freeing them of their gendered responsibilities as wives, mothers, and caregivers (they leave the sick chaperone in the care of men), as moral compasses and upholders of values (they engage in wild dancing, careless drinking, and flirting with both sexes), and as homemakers (they leave the home behind). What is visualized in this scene is precisely the kind of moral and social threat to society that needs to be reined in throughout the entire film. In this instance the danger is quickly defused by the arrival of Dottie, who represents the still-functioning moral compass of the team.

With Dottie's entrance, the mood and music changes from jitterbug elation to a somber blues, as Marla wails a drunken rendition of "It Had to Be You" to Nelson, her entranced new admirer. This dalliance, forged by a break into freedom, is later validated by their marriage, transforming Marla from an ugly duckling, ferocious hitter into a respected and loyal wife, who, in another showcase of domesticated femininity, chooses to skip the league finals for her honeymoon. However, it is Dottie who represents the most sensible and morally righteous choice in this scene, by not going to the bar in the first place and coming only in order to rescue her teammates from certain expulsion from the league should they be discovered. Her display of team spirit and care for her fellow players saves her from becoming a respectable bore who always obeys the rules, yet it still sets her apart from the other players, who took to their evening of freedom with abandon. Women taking agency over their lives, even if it is just for an evening at a dance hall, are thus presented as a danger to society, foreshadowing social upheaval and moral degeneration.

The second scene in which the women take control follows shortly after and presents a more positive brand of agency—that is, agency within the boundaries of "play." It is sparked by Ira Lowenstein, who has been acting as the general manager of the league, telling the women that the league is in danger if they cannot raise attendance levels. In order to raise awareness of the league, he has brought along reporters and photographers from *Life* magazine. The team reacts with frustration, outrage, and fear, but the players' fighting spirit is kindled when Doris voices a call to arms: "We'll show them how we play." As Lowenstein leaves, he encourages them to "give it everything you got," to which the women defiantly reply, "we always do." Grasping the moment more quickly than anyone else, Dottie understands this as a barely veiled call for spectacle, which she promptly delivers by catching a ball while doing the splits. In the following montage that chronicles both the league's and the Peaches' increasing success, the women are seen performing flashy catches, daredevil slides, and outrageous hits to ever more enticed, mostly male, audiences. Instead of launching direct action against the men who wield power over the league, such as a strike, the women stay within the rules of the game and pander to the (male) audience's expectations and demands.

One publicity stunt, for example, advertises "Catch a foul—get a kiss," and promptly the former Miss Georgia is shown to kiss a member of the audience. In another shot, men from the audience call out "slide!" and when the player does so with her skirt riding up, they answer with a smirk and a sly "thank you." Essentially the women give the audience what they want without much concern for the physical or moral consequences, but they do so because of their own commitment to the league. They claim agency within the fragile realm of women's early professional baseball, the one realm in which they have been granted a small slice of freedom. Staying within the boundaries of this realm marks this agency as positive, as it does not threaten to unhinge moral, social, and cultural conventions in the way the dance hall scene does. Further legitimizing this limited freedom is the eventual return of Kit and the other team members to marriage and motherhood as presented in the reunion scenes.

The only person who is allowed to voice open concern for the women is the "marketing mastermind" Ira Lowenstein, who first came up with the idea of the league for Mr. Harvey of Harvey Bars. In a scene in which Harvey informs Lowenstein that the league will be shut down as the war is coming to an end and the men are returning, Lowenstein angrily chastises the startled Harvey: "This is what it's gonna be like in the factories, too, I suppose, isn't it? Men are back. Rosie, turn in your rivets. First we told them it was their patriotic duty to get out of the kitchen to work, and now when the men come back, we'll send them back to the kitchen."

Thus even voicing indignation remains the privilege of men, who ultimately wield power over every aspect of the league, from designing feminine uniforms unsuitable to the sport to selecting only pretty players and requiring attendance at the charm school. Those in power ensure that while a certain degree of freedom might come with being a professional female athlete, this agency can only be exercised within severely curtailed limits.

In *A League of Their Own* the threat to U.S. society of having professional women athletes is dispersed in various ways, but most significantly in the way that Dottie emerges as the moral heroine after having given up her spot as the best player in the league to return to a conventional, domestic life with her husband. In doing so without a fight, she represents the ideal outcome for postwar U.S. society. Holmlund comments in referring to *Personal Best* that "a lesbian, and especially a femme, is *not* a lesbian when there's a man around";[34] similarly we could say of Dottie that a female athlete is not an athlete when there is a husband to take her home. Through its flashback structure, the film frames the league as a short-term opportunity for independence and self-determination for women, without any real changes to their traditional life trajectories. The flashback reassures viewers that almost all of the players eventually did turn into—as prophesied by the makers of the league and quoted in the epigraph—beautiful, charming "ladies," who were steered into the safe haven of marriage either during their active sporting career (like Marla) or afterward (like Kit). As the moral linchpin of this film, Dottie personifies the idealized woman who has done her patriotic duty but who ultimately rejects being a hero Other in order to obediently return to her husband, and the film celebrates these actions in a way that helps ensure a stable society of American men and women clear about their appropriate gender roles.

Bend It Like Beckham: Stretching the Boundaries

Bend It Like Beckham is the coming-of-age story of Jesminder "Jess" Bhamra, a second-generation immigrant of Indian descent who lives in the suburbs of London and who comes into conflict with her cultural heritage when she gets a chance to play soccer on an all-girls team, the Hounslow Harriers. Soccer is seen as an improper activity for a girl in the eyes of her conservative immigrant parents, as Mr. Bhamra (Anupam Kher) points out: "You must start behaving like a proper woman, okay?!" Jess, however, encouraged by her teammate and best friend Juliette "Jules" Paxton (Kiera Knightley), continues to defy her parents' wishes and is determined to find her own way in life. Soccer proves to be the catalyst for such self-determination, symbolizing a way out of the constrictions imposed on Jess by social conventions, while also raising questions of racism, gender propriety, and the consequences of "not fitting in."

The film is split between the South Asian London community of the Bhamra family and the predominantly white Anglo-Saxon community of the Paxton family and the Hounslow Harriers soccer club. It thus offers two diverging representations of contemporary British experience: that of the "new" or "hybridized" Britons and the associated conflicts that come with the idea of a multicultural society, and that of the Anglo-Saxon Britons, who are rarely touched by these conflicts.[35] *Bend It Like Beckham* is part of a small wave of films starting in the 1990s, such as *Young Soul Rebels* (Julien,

1991), *Bhaji on the Beach* (Chadha, 1993), *My Son the Fanatic* (Prasad, 1997), or *East Is East* (O'Donnell, 1999), that sought to capture and express the nonwhite, non-Western experience of life in Britain.[36] Formally *Bend It Like Beckham* incorporates many of Bollywood's staple features: the love interest, lively dance sequences, overwrought emotions, and bright color schemes. It has been described as being part of "Bollylite"—a westernized version of Bollywood that eschews much of the "original" Bollywood's social critique. It follows the first internationally successful Bollywood sports film, *Lagaan* (Gowariker, 2001), and in the wake of both films there has been a spate of successful, both domestically and internationally, Bollywood sports films such as *Chak De! India* (Amin, 2007) and *Patiala House* (Advani, 2011).[37] However, the Bollywood influences are somewhat skin deep in *Bend It Like Beckham*—it owes much more to the American sports film such as the previously discussed *A League of Their Own* and to postfeminist neoliberalism in the British context of New Labour.

There is an underlying tension between the (sub)cultural groups the film depicts, for as much as *Bend It Like Beckham* depicts white Britain as welcoming of the South Asian community, its members feel misunderstood, criticized, and disturbed in the everyday activities of living their lives. This is depicted particularly through Jess's parents, who are shown to live mostly as if they were still in India—following the same customs, eating the same food, and socializing only with people of their own community. The interaction between the two communities is shown to be limited, at least for the older generation, suggesting that the Bhamras and their community are living a somewhat insular life, even if their South Asian roots are tempered by British social norms and customs.

In contrast, Jess, who has grown up in Britain, chooses to step outside of this restrictive experience, much to the distaste and fear of her parents, and much of the film's conflict derives from this decision by a doubly marginalized hero Other. Playing soccer and thus venturing outside her own community appears both improper and unwise in the eyes of her family, as it will not guarantee Jess the kind of secure future her parents envision. Jess ignores her family's concerns and continues to play for the Hounslow Harriers, in a move that places the film squarely within the classic coming-of-age genre. Yet when her deception leads to a misunderstanding with dire consequences for her sister Pinky (Archie Panjabi), whose upcoming wedding is canceled, Jess realizes that her playing soccer is about more than a game. Her identity as a British woman and an Indian woman and as an athlete produces a conflict without an easy solution.

Bend It Like Beckham deals with the threat of the female athlete in an altogether more progressive way than *A League of Their Own*. The film deflects the destabilizing threat of the female athlete and hero Other away from national identity and onto Jess's ethnic identity, so that it is her cultural heritage that becomes the site of contestation. Furthermore, the narrative includes a subplot heightening the potential for subversiveness by briefly suggesting that the main characters are lesbians, which serves to diminish the original threat of the female athlete in the face of a far scarier prospect. Having deflected the threat of the female hero Other onto these other discourses of ethnicity and homosexuality, the film then subtly stretches the boundaries of British national identity to open up a space for female athletes, which is subsequently validated and sanctified by men. Thus instead of defusing or dissolving the threat of the female athlete, as seen in *A League of Their Own*, this figure becomes an asset who is incorporated into the fabric of British identity, which in turn becomes more flexible and tolerant.

The first means by which this more inclusive British national identity is created in *Bend It Like Beckham* involves denying and deflecting the female athlete's destabilizing potential. The opening scene masterfully sets up this deflection strategy by presenting England as a nation unthreatened by women athletes. This, however, is not the "real" England, but an England envisioned by the teenage Jess as she daydreams about her success as a Manchester United player alongside her idol David Beckham, scoring the winning goal off Beckham's cross in a Champions League match. The footage of the match has clearly been digitally enhanced to include Jess, thus marking it as her daydream, but gains authenticity by being commentated by a lineup that includes well-known BBC soccer commentator John Motson, former soccer great Gary Lineker, now host of the BBC's premier soccer program *Match of the Day*, and two further real-life soccer stars and commentators, Alan Hansen and John Barnes. The four men discuss Jess's abilities as a soccer player just as they would those of any male player on *Match of the Day*, thus providing a framework of authenticity for this imaginary but inclusive view of English sports.

Jess is praised by all four commentators as they predict a bright future for her and the possibility that England's national team might "relive their World Cup glory from '66," until a guest commentator destroys this vision— Jess's mother, Mrs. Bhamra (Shaheen Khan). Instead of being proud of her daughter, as Gary Lineker suggests she must be, Mrs. Bhamra criticizes Jess for "running around with all these men showing her bare legs to seventy thousand people" and "bringing shame on the family." It is in this instance that the threat of the female athlete is transferred from the national arena represented by Manchester United and the discussion of the British soccer legends to the private ethnic and cultural context of the Bhamra family. Despite the first part of the scene being a utopian daydream, it is nonetheless a powerful statement of how Jess sees England—a place of endless possibilities. This optimistic opening foreshadows the film's subsequent trajectory, with Jess's vision confirmed, albeit with some adjustments, by the end of the film.

Interfering with this vision of a national identity that can accommodate female athletes of Indian heritage into its fabric at the highest level, Mrs. Bhamra returns Jess to brutal reality by insisting that she go sari shopping with her sister Pinky, who is fully consumed by her impending wedding. This wedding symbolizes Jess's reality, the careful balancing act of the second-generation immigrant, who is caught between the customs of British Asianness as expressed by her parents and the integration of this cultural heritage into her "new" British circumstances. It is this conflict that the film ultimately blames for the incompatibility of "female" and "athlete," as women soccer players are almost exclusively vilified within the South Asian community inhabited by the Bhamras.[38] In contrast, the Anglo-Saxon Jules and the rest of the team appear to encounter very little resistance to their own athleticism, marking this particular problem as that of the South Asian minority rather than that of England at large. Jules's mother is the only other person to show some objection to girls' sports, always trying to push Jules toward more "feminine" endeavors such as chasing boys, but even she is won over and becomes supportive of her daughter's passion for soccer much earlier than the Bhamra family. This difference is crucial, as it eventually delineates the new boundaries around the acceptable female athlete.

After this transference of the threat to the stability of the national gender order onto the British South Asian community, the film expresses Jess's conflict through two contrasting "ideal femininities," represented by Jess's sister Pinky and her English teammate Jules. These figures are offered as relatively unproblematic ideals within their respective communities and are, for the most part, portrayed positively. Furthermore, both remain valid options for successful, positive femininity beyond the film's conclusion, as neither is devalued in the course of the narrative. Pinky is presented as a likable, if somewhat ditzy, "girly" girl, who is mostly interested in clothes and planning her wedding to her fiancé Teetu (Kulvinder Ghir). Apart from sneaking out to dates with Teetu, Pinky's desires and ambitions are completely in line with what her parents have in mind for her: a decent job at nearby Heathrow airport until she finds a suitable husband, to whom she will be a good wife, and becomes a mother. Just how impossible the idea of a female athlete is within the South Asian community depicted in the film is exemplified by the contrast between Pinky and Jess, who is good at school and somewhat of a tomboy, and whose main interest is in soccer and sports clothes. The two sisters have diametrically opposed ideas about the implications of their cultural heritage. These different worldviews come to a head when Mrs. Bhamra finds Jess dressed in her new soccer uniform and playing with boys in the park, during which one of the boys picks up Jess and throws her over his shoulder when he cannot outplay her.

The Bhamras' standards of behavior are marked as the product of their ethnicity, conflating religion, manners, and reputation into a moral way of life that is clearly in opposition to both Jess's needs and desires as well as her English surroundings. Mary Ann Chacko in her discussion of *Bend It Like Beckham* as a tool for the multicultural classroom points out that "no single identity can sufficiently articulate the concept of self as each individual occupies multiple subject positions or identities simultaneously."[39]

This scene thematizes what is and is not proper for a British Indian girl, and here the emphasis must lie on both "Indian" and "girl"—the multiple subject positions to which Chacko refers—for it is, of course, not improper for the bare-chested Indian boys to play soccer in the park "half-naked," as Mrs. Bhamra describes it, whereas it is considered unacceptable for Jess to wear a soccer uniform with shorts. In contrast, the much more fashionable and sexualized Pinky symbolizes her parents' ideal of a nice Indian girl, marrying a nice Indian boy from a good family. While Pinky is staying within the cultural limits of an Indian community within Britain, Jess is pushing against those same limits, defined not only by her ethnic identity but also and especially by her gender. Jess thus finds herself in a position of not fitting in with her peers as defined by her cultural heritage, and also not quite fitting in with the "outside" community of England. Yet while the comparison between the two sisters' lives provides a continuous thread in the narrative, it is also surprisingly accommodating, in that it does not overtly value one lifestyle over the other and instead offers multiple visions of equal validity of British Asian femininity.

The differing standards between the English and the Indian communities on the question of girls and soccer is demonstrated in a training scene featuring the Hounslow Harriers, where all of the girls wear the team uniform, but some girls, notably Jules, eschew the top in favor of just a sports bra. The scene foregrounds the girls' athleticism and skill rather than their looks, desexualizing their half-nakedness in the process.[40] In contrast to Jess and Pinky, who represent different ways of being Indian in England, Jules more generally symbolizes an ideal English femininity by way of what Hjort terms "intercultural approach"—the "contrastive mobilisation of *different* national cultures [which] easily directs audience attention toward the very question of national identity and specificity."[41] Intercultural contrast uses cultural elements in a system of flagging by comparison and contrast; in this case Englishness and Indianness. Jules thus comes to represent pure English girl power, or what Angela McRobbie calls "top girls," who are "understood to be ideal subjects of female success, exemplars of the new competitive meritocracy."[42] This idea of meritocracy is often considered to be of central importance to the politics of New Labour ushered in by Tony

Blair in the mid-1990s and places responsibility for "success" squarely in the hands of the citizen in a similar way that the American dream stories of American sports films have advocated, as I show in chapters 3 and 4. Jules is thus a modern, post–Spice Girls, post–Cool Britannia, athletic, and feisty teenager, or postfeminist top girl, who displays both confidence and ambition. In her mind there is nothing that she cannot do or achieve, for as she repeatedly says: "You just can't take 'no' for an answer." She knows exactly what she wants and how she is going to get it—be that a girls' soccer team, a scholarship, or recruiting Jess to play for her team.

Whereas Jess and Pinky and their family are presented as outsiders within England, as represented by their language, their clothes, their food, and the shops they frequent, Jules, her family, and her soccer team represent mainstream England. However, this is not thematized through the flagging of Jules's Englishness, but rather by way of Jess's difference from her, so that Jess's Indianness becomes much more prominent than Jules's Englishness. This has the effect of othering Jess, while almost excessively normalizing Jules; as "being Indian" is flagged and explained, while "being English" is taken for granted. Jules stands for what it means to be English precisely because she is not flagged as special or different from the norm—she *is* the norm. She exemplifies for Jess all that is desirable in English national identity: freedom of choice, individuality, meritocracy, and equality for girls. In effect, Jess exemplifies the "hyphenated identities that occupy an in-between space,"[43] stuck between the ideal of South Asian femininity modeled by her sister Pinky and the ideal of English femininity modeled by Jules, whose athleticism appears to cause little concern within mainstream England.

The one exception to this lack of concern is Jules's mother, Mrs. Paxton, who is characterized as somewhat hysterical and overbearing. Together with Mrs. Bhamra, she serves the function of moral guardian and upholder of gender boundaries, at least initially. It is the two mothers who most object to their daughters' athletic pursuits and thus actively police these gender boundaries, in particular within what is coded as their domain—the home. "This 'home,'" as Claudia May argues, "is not just a literal place but symbolic of an ideological, cultural, religious home, where traditions upheld by a family, a community, are honoured over those of an individual whose wants challenge set gender roles, set mores."[44] Indeed, Justine Ashby goes as far as suggesting that "it is not so much social and sexual discrimination as their mothers who are the problem."[45] While the differences between the Bhamras and the Paxtons are made clear throughout the film, the mothers are seen to share some basic values, in particular, a strong concern for their daughters' happiness through traditional heteronormative channels. This is expressed via desires such as wanting their daughters to dress more femininely or learn to cook, which Ashby considers to be "coded as trivial and laughably *pre*feminist."[46] Like Dottie in *A League of Their Own*, the mothers identify with and adhere unquestioningly to traditional gender roles, but unlike Dottie, they are also shown as able to progress beyond this constricted view.

With the Paxton family representing the English community, it is important that Mrs. Paxton is the first of the two mothers to evolve to a more progressive stance, for even as she is depicted as the last of her community to embrace this newer and expanded role for women, the fact that she beats the Bhamras to the post helps cement the transference of the threat of the female athlete to the minority community. However, even Mrs. Bhamra eventually accepts Jess's desire to play soccer for an American college and thus redeems not only herself but her whole community. It is in these moments of acceptance that the stretching of the national fabric becomes visible, as the mothers delineate new borders around acceptable British femininity. These boundaries are stretched to include not only female athletes but also ones of Indian heritage, suggesting greater acceptance of the South Asian community within Britain, which in turn is depicted as evolving to incorporate westernized ideals of gender equality.

This new hybridized femininity comes at a cost, however, as new boundaries must also be defined. Once again it is Mrs. Paxton who is at the center of this process of redefinition. Misinterpreting a fight between Jess and Jules, who have fallen out over Jess nearly kissing their coach, Joe (Jonathan Rhys-Myers), Mrs. Paxton wrongly concludes that the girls have been lovers and are breaking up. She is devastated at seemingly seeing her worst fear—that Jules has become a lesbian because of soccer—come true. She drives Jules to Pinky's wedding, which is back on after Jess has cleared up the initial misunderstanding. Mrs. Paxton, by now hysterical at the prospect of a lesbian daughter, makes a scene in front of the wedding party by accusing Jess of being a lesbian. This scene marks the new borders around the expanded, more inclusive notion of acceptable British femininity suggested by the film: while it is now acceptable for a girl to play soccer, being homosexual is a step too far.

For their part the extended Bhamra family is utterly confounded by Mrs. Paxton's accusation, mistaking "lesbian" for "Lebanese," as lesbianism is represented as so far removed from the South Asian collective imagination that it is not even understood as a risk. This demonstrates once more that the minority community is represented as lagging behind in the "evolutionary" process of social progress. The Paxton family, on the other hand, illustrate a slightly more advanced position in this same process: having explained the fight about Joe to her mother, Jules declares that "being a lesbian is not that big a deal," and Mrs. Paxton, relieved by her daughter's heterosexuality, agrees: "No. No, of course it isn't. I mean I've got nothing against them." Katharina Lindner points out that "these hysterically comical moments of dialogue are symptomatic of the ways in which the film continuously flags up its 'lesbian potential' while simultaneously assuaging the threatening implications of its lesbian (sub-)text."[47] In the end the potential homosexual threat is displaced onto the minor character of Jess's best friend Tony, who comes out as gay, but his storyline is not further explored. This containment strategy ensures that while at this stage of the film the female athlete may have become an acceptable version of femininity, the homosexual athlete has most certainly not. By including the heterosexual love triangle between Jess, Jules, and the coach, the film further ensures that these boundaries are not stretched too far.

This lesbian subplot enables the film to touch on the relationship between homosexuality and female athleticism without veering too close to it. It is important, however, because with the potential for a double or even triple othering of the girls—as female athletes, as lesbian female athletes, and, for Jess, as a potential ethnic lesbian athlete—the original threat of the female athlete to a balanced and stable national identity appears diminished in comparison. Thus while lesbian athletes might be too hard to incorporate into the national fabric, at least for now, that fabric might just stretch enough to allow entry for female athletes, and British Asian female athletes at that. It is this shift in perspective, which contrasts a "bad" with an "even worse" option, that allows for an expansion of the original boundaries around socially acceptable femininity.

The task of validating this newly defined, socially acceptable female athleticism remains the privilege of those in power—the men of the film. First, and setting the tone for the film from the start, the male soccer commentators from the *Match of the Day* scene are nonplussed about a girl on the Manchester United team and indeed laud her skills—for this brief moment gender ceases to exist, albeit in a utopian fantasy. Secondly, the girls' fathers have less of a problem with their sporting endeavors than the mothers and appear unthreatened by their more masculine femininity. It is Alan Paxton (Frank Harper) who speaks up for Jules when her mother wants her to stop playing soccer, while Mr. Bhamra goes even further when he allows Jess to play the final match during her sister's wedding against his wife's wishes and eventually makes the decision as head of the family to let Jess to go to college in the United States and follow her dreams. This can be seen as a rather ambiguous kind of support, for as Ashby contends, "when each father finally puts his foot down and insists that their wives support their daughters' ambitions, the fathers strike a blow for 'girl power,' on the one hand, while reasserting their more traditional power as head of the family, on the other."[48] Thirdly, at the conclusion of the film Joe reveals that he has been offered the job of coaching the men's side, his dream job, but has turned this down in favor of continuing to train the girls' team.[49] Having previously stated that coaching the girls' side was akin to an apprenticeship or "pulling pints," this represents a significant change in his perspective and underscores the increase in respect for women's soccer by the end of the film.

These recurrent instances of male validation facilitate a more inclusive yet still stable British national identity, for neither the four wise soccer players at the beginning of the film, nor the benevolent fathers, nor indeed the enabling coach Joe are threatened by the prospect of the hero Other encroaching on their territory. As the masculinity of the men is depicted as unaffected by the advance of the female athlete, her destabilizing potential for British national identity is neutralized. *Bend It Like Beckham* thus features a range of strategies to counteract the threat to British national identity posed by the hero Others Jess and Jules. Displacing this threat onto the South Asian minority community, which is depicted as lagging behind in social progressiveness, serves to normalize female athleticism within mainstream Britain. That British identity can accommodate the expansion of female gender roles up to a certain point is demonstrated by the demarcation of new boundaries, drawn in particular by the mothers. Granted the nod of masculine approval by the various male authorities in the film, these new boundaries highlight the validity of multiple versions of femininity attainable within a new, increasingly inclusive Britain.

Queering the Nation

While Jess's soccer-playing gay friend Tony is a character on the margins in *Bend It Like Beckham*, there are films that feature gay or lesbian athletes as lead characters. Most of these still very rare sports films are independent or art films, with the 1982 feature *Personal Best* (Towne) probably the closest to what could be termed a mainstream release. In *Personal Best*, two pentathletes, Chris (Mariel Hemingway) and Tory (Patrice Donnelly), fall in and out of love as they are training for the Olympic track and field tryouts, and the emphasis is on the inappropriateness of women being either competitive or lesbian. Indeed, the film shows Chris being unable to compete against the other women, demonstrating the limits of her gender as ambition and competitiveness are coded as inherently masculine and therefore unavailable to Chris. When her coach's cruel and intimidating "motivational" techniques fail to lift Chris's performance, her newfound boyfriend suggests that she only compete against herself. This advice proves successful, as she goes on to win the competition and secure a place on the Olympic team. In *Personal Best* we see the strain in which films featuring gay or lesbian athletes find themselves, and in this case ultimately succumb to, as the film resorts to a heterosexualization of its main character, Chris. By heterosexualizing Chris and linking her subsequent performance issues with competitiveness, the film equates inappropriate female behavior with "masculine" competitiveness and lesbianism.

Films made with specifically subcultural or queer audiences in mind, on the other hand, seem to encounter fewer difficulties in representing the nexus of gender, sexuality, and nation. Queer film festival hits such as the German *Summer Storm* (Kreuzpaintner, 2004), about queer and straight youth rowers competing in a national championship, *Guys & Balls* (Hormann, 2004), about a recently outed gay goalkeeper seeking revenge on his former soccer team in West Germany's former coal-mining region, the Icelandic film *Eleven Men Out* (Douglas, 2007), also about a recently outed soccer player, and the Thai film *The Iron Ladies* (Thongkonthun, 2001), about a volleyball team of transgender, drag queen, and gay athletes winning the Thai championship, all show quite a different, less heteronormative approach to the intersection of gender roles, homosexuality, and national identity than the films discussed above. On the grounds of their own outsider status as art house or independent productions targeting a nonmainstream audience, these films find themselves in a position that allows them to claim a positive space for homosexual hero Others within the broader framework of national identity.

Summer Storm exemplifies this trend in multiple ways. It starts out in the sleepy and conservative small town of Starnberg in Bavaria, Germany, presenting teenage life as a heady mix of sexual excitement and anxiety, hormones, and sporting ambition. On the brink of finishing school, the teenagers of the local rowing club, RSC Starnberg, have only two things on their minds: rowing and sex. At first sight their identities seem quite clear-cut and stable: the jock, the macho, the sensitive guy. But soon the first cracks appear in this seemingly perfect world as misunderstandings, lies, and coincidences begin to complicate the youths' understanding of themselves and others. The pressure to win the national championship serves as a catalyst to bring the increasing tensions to boiling point and sets up a striking contest between urban homosexuals and regional heterosexuals as the teams battle for national honor.

The narrative centers on best friends and champion rowers Tobi (Robert Stadlober) and Achim (Kostja Ullmann). As Achim's relationship with his girlfriend Sandra grows more serious, Tobi inexplicably begins to feel rejected and left out. When a rower from the girls' team, Anke (Alicja Bachleda-Curus), makes advances toward Tobi, he is even further confused. Miscommunications thus begin even before the team heads off to the national championships, where they meet competing teams from all over Germany, including an all-girl Christian club from Saxony and the Queer-Strokes, a gay male team from Berlin. Tensions soon mount between and within the groups, and Tobi's confusion, anger, and pain about his own sexual identity reach breaking point during a massive summer storm the night before the finals. With the national title on the line, the narrative climax revolves around the question, which team will pull together to win the race?

Similarly to *Bend It Like Beckham*, *Summer Storm* transfers the main conflict, here the impossibility of the gay athlete, away from the nation and onto a distinct cultural group within Germany, this time the region of Bavaria. Known for its staunch Catholic conservatism, Bavaria is presented as lagging behind the times, just as the South Asian community in *Bend It Like Beckham*, in contrast to the urban progressiveness of the Berlin team. Tobi's sexual identity is questioned, and he is effectively outed during a frightful storm that not only sees both teams flee to an abandoned youth hostel but also includes vicious fights between and within the teams. At first it appears that this hero Other is forced to choose between two options, that of urban queer or Bavarian heterosexual. The difficulty of reconciling this choice with his multiple strands of identification is visualized in a scene depicting the breakfast the morning after the storm.

The atmosphere between the Bavarian and Berlin teams is frosty after the fight the evening before, and thus they sit at separate tables. The significance of this becomes apparent when Tobi, the last to enter the breakfast room, has to choose where to sit. Sitting with the Berlin QueerStrokes will out him officially and thus show him to be effectively repudiating his own team, as well as his Bavarian roots, whereas choosing his own team suggests an outright rejection of homosexuality, both his own and that of the QueerStrokes. With the teams at separate tables, Tobi's choice is visualized as an exclusionary one: there is no middle ground, no room for integrating one with the other. In this scene both sexuality and regionality are thematized, with the focus directed toward the impossibility of their fusion. As Tobi sits down next to his supposed girlfriend, Anke, and kisses her on the cheek, his choice seems to reinforce the mutually exclusionary relationship between "gay" and "Bavarian." But into the stunned silence, Tobi offers his own solution: "What, can't I kiss women anymore, just because I'm gay?" In doing so Tobi creates a middle ground for himself by boldly exploding the seeming impossibility of being both Bavarian and gay, articulating for himself a new, synthesized identity category.

The film ends with a utopian vision of the Bavarian team accepting Tobi's sexuality and one of Tobi's teammates overcoming his deep-seated homophobia to help the QueerStrokes win the national championship. Through this displaced focus on the conflict between regional and sexual identity—similar to the focus on gender and ethnicity in *Bend It Like Beckham*—national identity is able to accommodate changes with minimal attention. This kind of positive ending is characteristic of most specifically gay and lesbian sports films, where the protagonists find acceptance and respect within the wider community, thus envisioning a shift toward a more inclusive society. These films create a vision of multiple possibilities for gender and sexual configurations within the nation. It remains to be seen, however, when films with successful gay or lesbian athletes or hero Others will achieve mainstream success without having to sacrifice their protagonists' sexual otherness (as in *Personal Best*) or relegating it to minor characters (as in *Bend It Like Beckham*).

Female or homosexual athlete protagonists—which I have termed hero Others—disrupt the myth of essentialist gender identities and are therefore a threat to the stability of national identity. The films examined in this chapter showcase some of the different ways in which this threat posed by the athletic hero Other is negotiated in contemporary sports films. With the female athlete there is a long cinematic tradition of employing a strict feminizing code to ensure her return to the traditionally acceptable gender roles of heterosexual wife and mother. While this conservative strategy is evidenced particularly strongly by *A League of Their Own,* it can also be found in films as diverse as the classic Katharine Hepburn movie *Pat and*

Mike (Cukor, 1952), in which Hepburn's character needs to moderate her sporting ambition and success in order to conform to her partner's wishes, and *Personal Best*, where the return of one of the characters to heterosexuality provides the turning point to her sporting success.

The homosexual male athlete is likewise a site of cultural and national anxiety, a threat negotiated in the film *Summer Storm* by displacing the nation-sexuality conflict onto the subnational context of regional Bavaria. As a result of this strategy and the film's independent production context, it can afford to present a utopian vision of a German society growing increasingly tolerant of strong and confident hero Others. Most illuminating, however, is the complex system of contrast and displacement found in *Bend It Like Beckham*. Presenting gender and ethnicity as non-essentialized and transformable, this film heralds new possibilities for the depiction of hero Others in the context of a mainstream British film. By first acknowledging the limitations of the binary gender and ethnic roles of male/female and English/Indian, and then refuting and expanding these, the film offers a positive depiction of female athletes who can be (re)incorporated into the national fabric, even as it remains somewhat defined by the boundaries of heterosexuality.

The dual questions of female and homosexual sporting participation and their representation is one of ongoing urgency and contestation. Television coverage of women's sport continues to make up a very minor percentage of commercial broadcasting schedules, while the world still awaits the first openly homosexual male athlete in such nation-defining sports as baseball. The majority of sports films remain limited by very traditional notions of the athlete as a heterosexual male, often fighting as part of a team to defend the glory of the nation. Films such as those examined in this chapter can go some way toward changing cultural perceptions of female and homosexual athletes and their traditional exclusion from the elusive "deep, horizontal comradeship" of the imagined community that, according to Anderson, makes up the nation.[50]

CONCLUSION

> No, that's where you're wrong, it's not just an "exhibition
> bout" that doesn't mean anything. It's us against them.
> Apollo Creed in *Rocky IV* (1985)

Rather than conceptualizing national identity as fixed or monolithic, this
study has shown the ways in which sports films can provide new models for
national identification and integration in constantly shifting sociopolitical,
economic, and cultural climates. National identity pervades mainstream
contemporary sports films at various levels, from the explicit or "hot"
forms of nationalism that reside on the surface of cultural texts, as seen
in the spectacle of nationalisms in *Rocky IV*, to the subtle, and seemingly
"banal," in films such as *A League of Their Own*. I argue that films from
this frequently underestimated genre provide a powerful vehicle for the
development and maintenance of national identity, incorporating complex
matrices of racial, gendered, and sexual identities.

Sports films offer audiences a means of negotiating ideas about national
unity and community, but they also reflect the ways in which these ideas
change over time. *Chariots of Fire*, as I argue in chapter 1, is a film torn
between mourning a lost golden age of British elite society and at the same
time hailing a meritocratic future for the nation. In *The Miracle of Bern*,
the historical event of Germany's success at the 1954 World Cup serves as a

model for integration and acceptance in the present, speaking to the fissure and disorientation brought on by the reunification of the two German states. The *Rocky* films (1976–2006) showcase three decades of a changing American dream and of evolving models of "success," as what begins as a tale of an individual made good comes to encompass a story of a nation in need of defending against aggressors from within and outside the United States. Similarly the flexibility of the American dream is showcased by the beloved small-town American sports film and its successful transposition in a number of films since the 1990s onto inner-urban black communities. Recent American sports films have often favored parables of integration, such as *Remember the Titans* or *Glory Road*. These films reaffirm the validity of the American dream, in pastoral and urban contexts alike: they contribute to a vision of a contemporary America in which the American dream is open to everyone, regardless of ethnicity, location, or systemic disadvantage.

In particular, I argue across the chapters of this book that the sense of emotional authenticity established by many sports films facilitates the audience's engagement with, and ultimate acceptance of, specific versions of national identity or particular interpretations of a nation's past. This analytical lens highlights the ways in which filmmakers establish a relationship of trust and believability with their audiences, through a visual and technical framework that is built on an explicit, and at times almost excessive, attention to historical period and character detail. It opens up new ways of understanding how films use constructions of the past to cultivate a sense of historical accuracy for spectators, particularly in relation to the representation of past events—the 1924 Olympics, for example, or the 1954 World Cup—and the ways in which these are tied up with larger questions of national belonging. In the films examined here the concept of emotional authenticity works to shape the films' presentation of the nation and national identity in ways that are not always strictly bound by historical "truth." By creating an emotional connection with audiences, these films open up possibilities for redefining the boundaries of national belonging.

Such strategies are also at work beyond the immediate context of sports films: one need only look to recent Oscar contenders, all loudly declaring that they are "based on a true story," from *The Iron Lady* (Lloyd, 2011) to

The Imitation Game (Tyldum, 2014) to *The Post* (Steven Spielberg, 2017), to see that a sense of historical authenticity has become increasingly pertinent to both filmmakers and film critics in the first decades of the new millennium. The concept of emotional authenticity opens up new and fruitful ways of thinking about what constitutes historically authentic or believable representations and how these can function to underline specific versions of historical "truth." As my analyses of *Chariots of Fire* and *The Miracle of Bern* in particular show, emotional authenticity can provide a means of focusing on both the expectations of, and the effects on, the viewing audiences, rather than on just the characters and historical, national, and (sub)cultural contexts depicted. Above all, it underlines the significance of the period of reception for understanding what is "felt" as authentic, rather than limiting understandings of authenticity to the historically accurate depiction of the film's real-life precedents.

Through such strategies sports films can provide new models for national identification and integration, as well as envisioning less hierarchical gender relations or successful multiculturalism. Hero Others, who I argue form the counterpoint to the prevalent model of the white, heterosexual, male athlete protagonist, take figures conventionally marginalized not only within the worlds of sports and film but also within society generally and reconceptualize them as positive agents of change. These characters unsettle the balance of normative gender dichotomies and open up new models for embodying identities of place and nation. Whereas in *A League of Their Own* the revalidation of normative gender roles quickly repairs the perceived imbalance brought on by the hero Other in the form of the female professional baseball player in 1940s America, in *Bend It Like Beckham* the borders around acceptable British and British Asian femininities are extended to include soccer-playing female athletes. *Bend It Like Beckham* showcases the changes brought on by an increasingly multicultural society and the Blairite politics of "Cool Britannia" and displays a forward-looking, progressive stance toward national identity in contemporary British society.

The figure of the active female hero remains contentious, and more work needs to be done to expand the vision of femininity acceptable within national boundaries. It is, for example, striking to note that since *Bend*

It Like Beckham, the only other high-profile sports film featuring female athletes to be produced in any of the nations examined in this book has been the 2009 coming-of-age story *Whip It* (Barrymore) about a budding roller derby contestant. With their potential to reach beyond the realm of the sports film, hero Others offer a further productive model by which to rethink gender and its media representations.

The sports film is a genre that continues to fascinate audiences and producers alike. Although often sidelined within scholarly discussions of contemporary cinema, sports films provide a unique critical window onto contemporary society and onto the role of popular media forms in the ever-evolving task of nation building. In laying bare the processes of national identity maintenance, as well as the fissures that threaten to disrupt it, these films in fact broaden its remit: they demonstrate the ongoing importance of the nation in the contemporary imagination and the ways in which its ideological underpinnings and boundaries are continually reaffirmed and reconfigured both for and by mainstream audiences.

NOTES

INTRODUCTION

1. Eskenazi, "Miracle on Ice."
2. Zucker and Babich, *Sports Films*. This filmography focuses primarily on American films and does not reach beyond the 1980s.
3. "Report," 123–24.
4. Luke McKernan, as quoted in G. Jones, "'Down on the Floor,'" 30.
5. Crosson, *Sport and Film*, 58.
6. Tudor, *Hollywood's Vision of Team Sports*; Babington, *Sports Film*; Baker, *Contesting Identities*; Chare, *Sportswomen in Cinema*; Crosson, *Sport and Film*.
7. Bordwell and Thompson, *Film Art*, 51–52.
8. See, for example, Altman, *Film/Genre*; Grant, *Film Genre: Theory and Criticism*; Grant, *Film Genre Reader*; Grant, *Film Genre Reader II*; Grant, *Film Genre Reader III*; Steve Neale, "Questions of Genre"; Steve Neale, *Genre and Contemporary Hollywood*; Wright, *Six Guns and Society*.
9. Grant, *Film Genre: From Iconography to Ideology*, 2.
10. Jeffrey H. Wallenfeldt, as quoted in G. Jones, "'Down on the Floor,'" 31.
11. Tom Ryall, as quoted in Stephen Neale, *Genre*, 19.
12. Gledhill, "Rethinking Genre," 221. On the flexibility of genre boundaries, see also Steve Neale, *Genre and Contemporary Hollywood*.
13. Steve Neale, "Questions of Genre," 46.
14. Babington, *Sports Film*, 18.
15. J. Collins, *Architectures of Excess*, 126.
16. Roberts, Arth, and Bush, "Games in Culture," 557.
17. Wallenfeldt, as quoted in G. Jones, "'Down on the Floor,'" 31.
18. Perinbanayagam, *Games and Sport*, 28–29.

19. Mihelj, *Media Nations*, 29.

20. On this term see, for example, Bevins, "Winners and Losers of Globalization."

21. See, for example, Akkerman, de Lange, and Rooduijn, *Radical Right-Wing Populist Parties*; Mammone, Godin, and Jenkins, *Mapping the Extreme Right*; Rydgren, *Movements of Exclusion*.

22. Dissanayake, "Globalization and the Experience," 25. See also Dissanayake and Wilson, *Global/Local*; Mihelj, *Media Nations*; Roosvall, "Image-Nation."

23. Anderson, *Imagined Communities*.

24. Perinbanayagam, *Games and Sport*, 25.

25. Rowe, "If You Film It," 353.

26. Anderson, *Imagined Communities*; Billig, *Banal Nationalism*; Gellner, *Nationalism*; Hayward, "Framing National Cinemas"; Hjort, "Themes of Nation"; A. D. Smith, *National Identity*; A. D. Smith and Hutchinson, *Nationalism*.

27. Billig, *Banal Nationalism*, 8.

28. Billig, *Banal Nationalism*, 8.

29. Hayward, "Framing National Cinemas," 89.

30. Crosson, *Sport and Film*, 131.

31. Hayward, "Framing National Cinemas," 101.

32. Crawford, "Sport Film," 45.

33. For example, the main opponent "Pretty" Ricky Conlan in *Creed* is played by English professional boxer and light-heavyweight champion Anthony Bellew.

34. Kelso, "*Field of Dreams*."

35. David Thompson, cited in G. Jones, "'Down on the Floor,'" 33.

36. Barthes, "Reality Effect," 234.

37. Rosenstone, *Visions of the Past*, 11.

38. L. Williams, "Film Bodies"; Sobchack, "What My Fingers Knew"; Barker, *Tactile Eye*; Elsaesser, "'Where Were You When,'" 120. See also Marks, *Touch*; Marks, *Skin of the Film*.

39. Kracauer, *Theory of Film*, 158.

40. Hogan, *Gender, Race and National Identity*, 3.

41. Yuval-Davis, "Belongings," 131.

42. See, for example, Carroll, *Engaging the Moving Image*; Grodal, *Moving Pictures*; Grodal, *Embodied Visions*; Marks, *Skin of the Film*; Plantinga, *Moving Viewers*; G. M. Smith, *Film Structure*.

43. Perinbanayagam, *Games and Sport*, 29.

44. Rosenstone, *Visions of the Past*, 60.

45. Antunes, *Multisensory Film Experience*.

46. Basketball, for example, has undergone dramatic changes in playing style since the 1960s; see Boyd and Shropshire, *Basketball Jones*.

47. See, for example, Charland and Zachar, *Fact and Value in Emotion*; Salmela, "What Is Emotional Authenticity?"

48. On sports and nation: Allison, *Politics of Sport*; Allison and Monnington, "Sport, Prestige and International Relations"; Bairner, *Sport, Nationalism, and Globalization*; Baker and Boyd, *Out of Bounds*; Brownell, *Beijing's Games*; Cahn, *Coming on Strong*; Ernest Cashmore, *Making Sense of Sports*; Hargreaves, *Heroines of Sport*; Miller et al., *Globalization and Sport*; Pope, *New American Sport History*; Tomlinson and Young, *National Identity and Global Sports Events*. On national cinemas: Ashby and Higson, *British Cinema*; Bergfelder, "National, Transnational or Supranational Cinema?"; Bhabha, *Nation and Narration*; Celli, *National Identity*; Collins and Davis, *Australian Cinema after Mabo*; Cook, *Fashioning the Nation*; Cooke, *Representing East Germany*; Hake, *German National Cinema*; Hayward, "Framing National Cinemas"; Hjort and MacKenzie, *Cinema and Nation*; Rings, "Questions of Identity." The following are examples of some of the many studies of media and sports in which sports films figure, at most, in a peripheral fashion: Whannel, *Media Sport Stars*; Blain and Bernstein, *Sport, Media, Culture*; Blain, Boyle, and O'Donnell, *Sport and National Identity*; Brookes, *Representing Sport*. Of the few studies focusing on the sports films, many have sprung from special journal issues or conferences: Briley, Schoenecke, and Carmichael, *All-Stars & Movie Stars*; Poulton and Roderick, *Sport in Film*; S. C. Wood and Pincus, *Reel Baseball*; King and Leonard, *Visual Economies*; Bonzel and Chare, *Representations of Sports Coaches*.

49. See, for example, Baker, "Sports Films"; Giardina, "'Bending It Like Beckham'"; Crawford, "Sport Film"; Heinrich, "1954 Soccer World Cup"; Briley, "Basketball's Great White Hope"; Rowe, "If You Film It"; G. Jones, "'Down on the Floor'"; Elmwood, "'Just Some Bum'"; Motley, "Fighting for Manhood"; Kwauk, "*Goal! The Dream Begins*"; T. Williams, "'I Could've Been a Contender'"; Ardolino, "*Rocky* Times Four"; Paino, "Hoosiers in a Different Light"; Solomon, "Villain-less Quest"; Ellis Cashmore, "*Chariots of Fire*"; Caudwell, "*Girlfight*"; Robson, "Field of American Dreams"; Baker, "Hoop Dreams." Furthermore, much of the scholarship produced to date has often been in anthologies or journals with a different primary focus, such as sports sociology or national cinema; see Boyd and Shropshire, *Basketball Jones*; Ernest Cashmore, *Making Sense of Sports*; F. Collins and Davis, *Australian Cinema after Mabo*; Leach, *British Film*.

50. Babington's book *Sports Film*, published in Wallflower Press's "Short Cuts" series, is designed to be an introduction into the world of sports films and covers an impressive range of films from around the world despite its brevity. The effect is a somewhat eclectic mix of film choices that reveals much about the scope of issues and narrative complexities of the genre, although with less sustained critical focus than Seán Crosson's 2013 *Sport and Film*, which examines the sports film

as a lens through which wider cultural values and ideological processes can be unveiled. Crosson provides an excellent historical overview of the development of the genre as well as an insightful introduction to the visual and theoretical analysis of (sports) films, before focusing on particular recurring themes including gender, race, and national identity. With a focus on American cultural history, Crosson argues that sports films "play a crucial role in sustaining and affirming the myth of achieving the American Dream," taking up my own arguments in a previous article on the connection of "emotional authenticity" with representations of the American dream in Disney sports films of the new millennium. Crosson, *Sport and Film*, 164. See also Bonzel, "Reviving the American Dream."

51. See especially chapter 2, "Images of the Athletic Hero in Films," and chapter 3, "Gender, the Family and Sports," in Tudor, *Hollywood's Vision of Team Sports*.

52. Baker, *Contesting Identities*.

53. See, for example, J. Hill, *British Cinema in the 1980s*; Leach, *British Film*; Higson, *English Heritage, English Cinema*; Wollen, "Over Our Shoulders."

54. Deleuze, *Cinema 1*; Deleuze, *Cinema 2*.

55. Martin-Jones, *Deleuze, Cinema and National Identity*.

56. Landsberg, *Prosthetic Memory*.

57. See, for example, Ardolino, "*Rocky* Times Four"; Elmwood, "'Just Some Bum'"; Leab, "Blue Collar Ethnic"; Motley, "Fighting for Manhood"; Schubart, "Birth of a Hero."

58. *Creed II* was not released until this book was in the final production stages and so does not form part of the analysis in chapter 3.

59. Leonard and King, "Screening the Social," 3.

60. Chare, *Sportswomen in Cinema*; Lindner, "Fighting for Subjectivity"; Lindner, "'There Is a Reason'"; Lindner, "Bodies in Action"; Lieberman, *Sports Heroines on Film*. See also Bisin et al., "*Bend It Like Beckham*"; Caudwell, "*Girlfight*"; Caudwell, "*Girlfight* and *Bend It Like Beckham*"; May, "What's Love Got to Do." My own research into female sports coaches investigates the implications of the power relations inherent in coaches and how these change when put in the hands of women. See Bonzel, "Mind the Gap."

61. Holmlund, *Impossible Bodies*; Tasker, *Spectacular Bodies*.

62. Chare, *Sportswomen in Cinema*.

63. Mosse, *Nationalism and Sexuality*.

1. "LET US PRAISE FAMOUS MEN"

1. Reilly, "Bumbling Mr Bean."

2. Purves, "*Chariots of Fire*," 10; British Film Institute, "BFI Celebrates." Additionally, a new biography of Harold Abrahams was published prior to the London Olympics; see Ryan, *Running with Fire*.

3. "Eric Liddell Sports Scholarships Launched"; Hamilton, *For the Glory*. Liddell also received coverage in the *Times* (London) in the lead-up to the 2016 Rio Olympics; see Broadbent, "Runner Who Only Stopped."

4. Deleuze, *Cinema 1*; Deleuze, *Cinema 2*; Martin-Jones, *Deleuze, Cinema and National Identity*.

5. For an in-depth analysis of the heritage film and the debates surrounding it, see Vidal, *Heritage Film*. Some key texts for the discussion of *Chariots of Fire* in this way include, but are not limited to, Auty and Roddick, *British Cinema*; Chapman, *Past and Present*; Hall, "Wrong Sort of Cinema"; Higson, "Re-Presenting the National Past"; J. Hill, *British Cinema in the 1980s*; Johnston, "Charioteers and Ploughmen"; Leach, *British Film*; Street, *British National Cinema*; Street, *Transatlantic Crossings*; Wollen, "Over Our Shoulders."

6. Hall, "Wrong Sort of Cinema," 46.

7. Hall, "Wrong Sort of Cinema," 46.

8. Higson, "Re-Presenting the National Past," 91.

9. It is perhaps noteworthy, though, that while film scholars were quick to point out a host of inaccuracies in the film—see, for example, Carter, "*Chariots of Fire*"— sports scholars have more recently turned their attention toward this aspect of the film. See Dee, "'Too Semitic'"; Jefferys, "Lord Burghley"; Kebric, "London 2012."

10. While Abrahams was considered to be the "father" of British athletics within elite sports circles, this does not rival the strong sense of nationhood and national identity tied to the event of the Miracle of Bern and all those that had a part in it. Liddell was well known in Scotland, but again, not to the degree of the "heroes" of the Miracle of Bern. See Hamilton, *For the Glory*; Ryan, *Running with Fire*.

11. On the importance of television in the establishment of the 1950s German national myth of the Miracle of Bern, see "Herberger 3:2." See also Breitmeier, "Ein Wunder," 135.

12. Radio live reportage did not start until 1927 with the incorporation of the BBC. Beforehand the BBC was only allowed limited news reportage, of which sports were considered a part, due to pressure from the Newspaper Proprietors' Association. See Crisell, *British Broadcasting*, 40–41.

13. See Carter, "*Chariots of Fire*."

14. Boxer Rocky Balboa's success in *Rocky III* (Stallone, 1982), by contrast, is measured by his appearance on the covers of popular magazines such as *Newsweek*, on television shows, and in television advertisements. See chapter 3.

15. Carter, "*Chariots of Fire*." Carter's article contains a full list of such "faults."

16. Colin Welland in the making-of DVD featurette *Wings on Their Heels* (2005).

17. David Puttnam in *Wings on Their Heels*.

18. See Higson, *English Heritage, English Cinema*; J. Hill, *British Cinema in the 1980s*; Landy, "Looking Backward"; Monk, "British Heritage-Film Debate Revisited"; Wollen, "Over Our Shoulders."

19. Higson, *English Heritage, English Cinema*, 39.

20. Higson, *English Heritage, English Cinema*, 38.

21. Mulvey, "Visual Pleasure," 838.

22. Ecclesiasticus 44 (in the apocrypha of the Bible). It should be noted that the service appears to be Anglican, which is of course at odds with Abrahams being introduced moments later as a somewhat defensive Jew. In real life, Abrahams converted to Catholicism, which makes the Protestant service even more awkward but perhaps better suited to the vehicle of British national identity that I argue *Chariots of Fire* to be.

23. On the hero in mythology, see O. Rank, "Birth of the Hero"; Raglan, *Hero*; Campbell, *Hero with a Thousand Faces*.

24. Hjort, "Themes of Nation."

25. The poem is best known in its incarnation as the popular hymn "Jerusalem," with music by Sir Hubert Parry. It is considered to be one of Britain's most patriotic songs and a highlight every year at the *Last Night of the Proms* concert; it also featured at the opening ceremony of the 2012 London Olympics. While the poem itself possibly refers to a brief period of heaven in England during a visit by Jesus, the phrase "Chariot of Fire" appears originally in the Bible (2 Kings, 2:11), and the chariot carries the prophet Elijah into heaven. These religious references are investigated in Bowden, "Jerusalem."

26. Leach, *British Film*, 26; Andrew Sarris, quoted in Leach, *British Film*.

27. Deleuze, *Cinema 1*, 102–22.

28. Deleuze, *Cinema 1*. These two types of films have various subtypes, such as the action-images, duration-images, or perception-images, but for the purpose of this chapter, the distinction between time-images and movement-images is the one of most importance.

29. Martin-Jones, *Deleuze, Cinema and National Identity*, 3.

30. Martin-Jones, *Deleuze, Cinema and National Identity*, 4.

31. Martin-Jones, *Deleuze, Cinema and National Identity*, 4.

32. Martin-Jones, *Deleuze, Cinema and National Identity*, 4 (emphasis in original).

33. Martin-Jones, *Deleuze, Cinema and National Identity*, 5 (emphasis in original).

34. Martin-Jones, *Deleuze, Cinema and National Identity*, 4.

35. Martin-Jones, *Deleuze, Cinema and National Identity*, 85.

36. Martin-Jones, *Deleuze, Cinema and National Identity* (see in particular chapter 3).

37. Martin-Jones, *Deleuze, Cinema and National Identity*, 85.

38. Martin-Jones, *Deleuze, Cinema and National Identity*, 38 (emphasis added).
39. Martin-Jones, *Deleuze, Cinema and National Identity*, 89.
40. Martin-Jones, *Deleuze, Cinema and National Identity*, 28. Martin-Jones discusses a Freudian view of history that relies on the idea of first causes that lead on a single path to the present, rather than a Nietzschean-derived genealogical view, in which the past is examined by going backward in time without necessarily wanting to establish a certain beginning.
41. Martin-Jones, *Deleuze, Cinema and National Identity*, 28.
42. The producers may have felt that Abrahams's conversion to Catholicism did not sufficiently symbolize this acceptance and therefore altered his new faith to Anglican (Protestant), picking up on Abrahams's criticism of England as "Anglo-Saxon and Christian." The film, however, at no point explains or shows this change of faith.
43. Butler, *Gender Trouble*; Butler, *Bodies That Matter*. See, for example, chapter 3, "Performing National Identity," in Edensor, *National Identity, Popular Culture*, 69–102; D. Taylor, "Theatre of Operations"; Weber, "Performative States."
44. Edensor, *National Identity, Popular Culture*, 69.
45. Judith Butler, as quoted in Martin-Jones, *Deleuze, Cinema and National Identity*, 29 (emphasis in original).
46. Edensor, *National Identity, Popular Culture*, 71.
47. J. Hill, *British Cinema in the 1980s*, 27.
48. The lyrics of this song comically attest to Abrahams's quest for Englishness: "ALL: He is an Englishman! BOAT: He is an Englishman! For he himself has said it, And it's greatly to his credit, That he is an Englishman! ALL: That he is an Englishman! BOAT: For he might have been a Roosian, A French, or Turk, or Proosian, Or perhaps Itali-an! ALL: Or perhaps Itali-an! BOAT: But in spite of all temptations To belong to other nations, He remains an Englishman! He remains an Englishman! ALL: For in spite of all temptations to Belong to other nations, He remains an Englishman! He remains an Englishman!"
49. The pervasive influence of Gilbert and Sullivan's works within British culture is highlighted in Cannadine, "Gilbert and Sullivan."
50. Various studies of 1980s British cinema and society highlight these Thatcherite values, including Friedman, *Fires Were Started*; Higson, *Waving the Flag*; J. Hill, *British Cinema in the 1980s*; Richards, *Films and British National Identity*; Robbins, *Great Britain*.
51. Johnston, "Charioteers and Ploughmen," 104; Leach, *British Film*, 26.
52. On the concept of the heritage industry see, for example, Corner and Harvey, *Enterprise and Heritage*; De Groot, *Consuming History*; Hewison, *Heritage Industry*; Higson, *English Heritage, English Cinema*.

53. J. Hill, *British Cinema in the 1980s*, 28.

54. The element of muscular Christianity is commented on explicitly within the film and has been mentioned in several analyses, including Solomon, "Villainless Quest," 277. On the historical muscular Christianity movement see, for example, Bradstock, *Masculinity and Spirituality*; Vance, *Sinews of the Spirit*.

55. Solomon, "Villainless Quest," 277.

56. Solomon, "Villainless Quest," 277.

2. UNIFYING GERMANY

1. In order to distinguish between the historical event and the film, I refer to the event in German as the Wunder von Bern and to the film by the English title *The Miracle of Bern*. All translations are my own unless otherwise stated.

2. Delius, *Weltmeister*. Highlights of the dramatic radio commentary were sold at least until the 1980s on cassette tapes and LPs. The event has also been the source of numerous documentary films, sports history books, and soccer players' biographies. See, for example, Frei, *Finale Grande*; Heinrich, *Tooor! Toor! Tor!*; Schweer, *Der Sieg von Bern*; Walter, *3:2 Die Spiele zur Weltmeisterschaft*.

3. Koepnick, "Reframing the Past," 50. See also Patzner, "Das Wunder von Bern"; Taberner, "Philo-Semitism in Recent German Film"; Hochscherf and Laucht, "'Every Nation Needs a Legend'"; Ludewig, "'Heimat, Heimat, Über Alles'"; Uecker, "Fractured Families"; Kapczynski, "Imitation of Life"; Hagener, "*Das Wunder von Bern*."

4. Rentschler, "Cinema of Consensus," 263.

5. Cooke and Homewood, "Introduction," 8–9.

6. Frey, "Rebirth of a Nation."

7. Landsberg, *Prosthetic Memory*.

8. Landsberg, *Prosthetic Memory*, 2.

9. Landsberg, *Prosthetic Memory*, 2.

10. Cook, *Screening the Past*, 4.

11. Landsberg, *Prosthetic Memory*, 21.

12. Landsberg, *Prosthetic Memory*, 21.

13. See, for example, Larres and Panayi, *Federal Republic of Germany*.

14. Breitmeier, "Ein Wunder." See also Heinrich, "1954 Soccer World Cup."

15. Pyta, "German Football," 8. See also O'Dochartaigh, *Germany since 1945*, 37.

16. O'Dochartaigh, *Germany since 1945*, 71.

17. Von Moltke, *No Place Like Home*, 23.

18. Taberner, "Philo-Semitism in Recent German Film," 362.

19. Anderson, *Imagined Communities*, 7.

20. Moeller, "Introduction," 21.

21. See, for example, Heinrich, "1954 Soccer World Cup."
22. Hjort, "Themes of Nation," III.
23. Making-of featurette on *The Miracle of Bern* DVD.
24. Frey, "Rebirth of a Nation," 21; Hagener, "*Das Wunder von Bern*," 245–46.
25. Heinrich, "1954 Soccer World Cup," 1493.
26. The original German *Wir sind wieder wer* is notoriously difficult to translate; alternatively a less literal translation could be, "We can show our face again."
27. For more detail on the seamy sides of the win, see Heinrich, *3:2 für Deutschland*. For a collection of reactions from the international press, see "Bundestrainer Adenauer."
28. This phrase is from Higson, *English Heritage, English Cinema*, 39.
29. Cooke and Young, "Selling Sex," 191.
30. Breitmeier, "Ein Wunder," 129.
31. Heinrich, "1954 Soccer World Cup," 1494.
32. Delius, *Weltmeister*.
33. Pyta, "German Football," 17.
34. Pyta, "German Football," 13. See also Patzner, "Das Wunder von Bern."
35. Breitmeier, "Ein Wunder," 148.
36. A contemporary report in the weekly magazine *Der Spiegel* notes: "The exciting live transmissions of the soccer world championship ignited a run on television sets. Three companies (Telefunken, Saba, and Mende) sold their entire factory stock, while Philips sold 1000 television sets in fourteen days [and] the people from [TV station] NWDR declaimed: 'Now television has begun for real.'" "Herberger 3:2." See also Leinemann, "Fussball." Breitmeier also notes that only 28,000 TVs were registered before the World Championship, but by 1955 this number had risen to 170,000. Breitmeier, "Ein Wunder," 135.
37. Hagener, "*Das Wunder von Bern*," 237.
38. Landsberg, *Prosthetic Memory*, 20.
39. Landsberg, *Prosthetic Memory*, 34.
40. Cook, *Screening the Past*, 4.
41. See, for example, Heineman, "Hour of the Woman."
42. The so-called fraternizers were reviled by many for consorting with the victors and "became the symbol of Germany's moral decline." Heineman, "Hour of the Woman," 38.
43. See, for example, Cooke, *Representing East Germany*; Ludewig, "'Ostalgie' und 'Westalgie'"; Plowman, "Westalgia."
44. Cook, *Screening the Past*, 4.
45. Hjort, "Themes of Nation."
46. Hochscherf and Laucht, "'Every Nation Needs a Legend,'" 287.

47. Hochscherf and Laucht, "'Every Nation Needs a Legend,'" 289.

48. Uecker, "Fractured Families," 90.

49. Von Moltke, *No Place Like Home*.

50. Cook, *Screening the Past*, 2.

3. ANXIOUS IN AMERICA

1. Vitez, *Rocky Stories*, 1.

2. Bill Clinton, as quoted in Jillson, *Pursuing the American Dream*, 1.

3. Cullen, *American Dream*, 6.

4. Cogliano, "Baseball and American Exceptionalism," 147.

5. Cogliano, "Baseball and American Exceptionalism," 147.

6. See Campbell, *Hero with a Thousand Faces*.

7. For examples of some recent scholarship on this topic, see Bush and Bush, *Tensions in the American Dream*; Caldwell, *Cynicism and the Evolution*; Cullen, *American Dream*; Delbanco, *Real American Dream*; Graham, *Happiness for All?*; Hochschild, *Facing Up*; Jillson, *Pursuing the American Dream*; Jillson, *American Dream*; Slaughter, *Idea That Is America*; Sternheimer, *Celebrity Culture*.

8. Emphasis added.

9. As discussed in Winn, "Every Dream Has Its Price," 308.

10. Jillson, *Pursuing the American Dream*, xii.

11. See Cullen, *American Dream*; Caldwell, *Cynicism and the Evolution*.

12. Cullen, *American Dream*, 5.

13. Jensen, "Painful Collapse of Empire."

14. Most damning is perhaps Thomas Piketty's recent book on income inequality; see Piketty, *Capital in the Twenty-First Century*. See also Putnam, *Our Kids*; M. R. Rank, Hirschl, and Foster, *Chasing the American Dream*.

15. Hochschild, *Facing Up*, 72.

16. Alexis de Tocqueville, as quoted in Hochschild, *Facing Up*, 72.

17. Walter Fisher, as cited in Winn, "Every Dream Has Its Price," 308.

18. Caldwell, *Cynicism and the Evolution*, 39–41.

19. Kimmel, *Manhood in America*, 46.

20. Baker, *Contesting Identities*, 49.

21. Kimmel, *Manhood in America*, 7.

22. Kimmel, *Manhood in America*, 14.

23. Kimmel, *Manhood in America*, 18.

24. Kimmel, *Manhood in America*, 18.

25. Cullen, *American Dream*, 7.

26. See Elmwood, "'Just Some Bum.'"

27. Bodnar, *Blue-Collar Hollywood*.

28. See, for example, Leab, "Blue Collar Ethnic"; Motley, "Fighting for Manhood"; Quart and Auster, *American Film and Society*; Schubart, "Birth of a Hero."

29. See Elmwood, "'Just Some Bum'"; Leab, "Blue Collar Ethnic"; Motley, "Fighting for Manhood."

30. Leab, "Blue Collar Ethnic," 258.

31. Quart and Auster, *American Film and Society*, 125–26.

32. See, for example, Elmwood, "'Just Some Bum'"; Leab, "Blue Collar Ethnic"; Motley, "Fighting for Manhood"; Quart and Auster, *American Film and Society*.

33. For further exploration of the multiplicity of masculinities, see Connell, *Masculinities*; Whitehead, *Men and Masculinities*; Whitehead and Barrett, *Masculinities Reader*. For masculinity without men, see Halberstam, *Female Masculinity*.

34. Elmwood, "'Just Some Bum,'" 49.

35. Winn, "Every Dream Has Its Price," 309.

36. Crosson, *Sport and Film*, 97.

37. See also Elmwood and especially Williams for an analysis of the Depression-era boxer as a remodeled frontier battler. Elmwood, "'Just Some Bum,'" 52–53; T. Williams, "'I Could've Been a Contender.'"

38. Jeffords, *Hard Bodies*, 25.

39. James Truslow Adams, as quoted in Cullen, *American Dream*, 7.

40. Elmwood, "'Just Some Bum,'" 51.

41. Elmwood, "'Just Some Bum,'" 53.

42. Mr. T's Mohawk was reportedly modeled on the Mandinka hairstyle worn by warriors of an African tribe in honor of his African heritage, unlike Travis Bickle's (Robert De Niro) Mohawk in Martin Scorsese's *Taxi Driver* six years earlier. As Amy Taubin notes, this Mohawk was in reference to soldiers in the Vietnam War who were shaving their heads the day before a mission. Taubin, *Taxi Driver*, 68.

43. Donalson, *Interracial Buddy Film*, 60–61.

44. Donalson, *Interracial Buddy Film*, 61.

45. Caldwell, *Cynicism and the Evolution*, 47.

46. Ardolino, "*Rocky* Times Four," 147. For a detailed analysis of *Rocky IV* and Cold War rhetoric, see Palmer, *Films of the Eighties*, 206–8.

47. Hjort, "Themes of Nation."

48. "Rocky," Box Office Mojo, http://boxofficemojo.com/franchises/chart/?id=rocky.htm.

49. See, for example, Ardolino, "*Rocky* Times Four"; Palmer, *Films of the Eighties*; R. Wood, *Hollywood from Vietnam to Reagan*.

50. Palmer, *Films of the Eighties*, 207.

51. Palmer, *Films of the Eighties*, 209 (emphasis in original), 208.

52. Palmer, *Films of the Eighties*, 208, 19.

53. Elmwood, "'Just Some Bum,'" 52.

54. Ardolino, "*Rocky* Times Four," 149; Arthur Schlesinger, as quoted in Ardolino, "*Rocky* Times Four," 149.

55. Ardolino, "*Rocky* Times Four," 149.

56. See Palmer, *Films of the Eighties*, 206. Palmer also points out that Stallone had another anti-Soviet box office hit at the time, *Rambo II* (Cosmatos, 1985).

57. Ardolino, "*Rocky* Times Four," 149.

58. Jeffords, *Hard Bodies*, 61–62.

59. Jeffords, *Hard Bodies*, 62.

60. Adams, as quoted in Cullen, *American Dream*, 7.

61. Palmer, *Films of the Eighties*, 219.

62. Ardolino, "*Rocky* Times Four," 156.

63. Ardolino, "*Rocky* Times Four," 156.

64. One could argue that Stallone also defends his right to finish the Rocky series on his own terms, having said before that he was not happy with *Rocky V*.

65. On Reaganite politics see, for example, Ardolino, "*Rocky* Times Four," 150.

66. Kusz, "Remasculinizing American White Guys," 211.

67. Kusz, "Remasculinizing American White Guys," 210.

68. See, for example, Addison, "'Must the Players Keep Young?'"; Beugnet, "Screening the Old"; Chivers, *Silvering Screen*; Evans, "No Genre for Old Men?"; Gates, "Acting His Age?"; Holmlund, *Impossible Bodies*; Holmlund, "Celebrity, Ageing and Jackie Chan"; Elizabeth Markson, "Female Aging Body."

69. Holmlund, *Impossible Bodies*, 144.

70. Tasker, *Spectacular Bodies*, 5.

71. Holmlund, *Impossible Bodies*, 146.

72. Tasker, *Spectacular Bodies*, 9.

73. Holmlund, *Impossible Bodies*, 145; Tasker, *Spectacular Bodies*, 3.

74. Andrew Britton, as quoted in Ardolino, "*Rocky* Times Four," 147.

75. Amelie Hastie argues that there is a third fight at the center of the story paralleling the stories of the two men in the form of Bianca (Tessa Williams), Adonis's new girlfriend and an aspiring musician who suffers from progressive hearing loss. Hastie argues that the storyline surrounding Bianca's increasing success as an artist and Adonis's respect for her goes a long way to inject "subtle feminist moments" into the film. Hastie, "Ryan Coogler's *Creed*," 73.

76. Crosson, *Sport and Film*, 94.

77. Ardolino, "*Rocky* Times Four," 152.

4. SMALL TOWNS, BIG DREAMS

1. Allen and Dillman, *Against All Odds*, 156.

2. Sharp, "Patriarchal World," 475.

3. For a satirical look at this phenomenon, see Bruce Springsteen's song and video "Glory Days."

4. Hjort, "Themes of Nation," 111.

5. Bale, "Cartographic Fetishism."

6. Bale, "Place of 'Place.'" See also Bale, "Cartographic Fetishism"; Bale, *Sports Geography*. It is worth noting that since Bale's studies, the fields of cultural, social, and human geography have risen to more prominence and could be seen as continuing the trend of the humanistic approach called for by Bale. For the connection between landscapes, sport, and national identities, see Bairner, "National Sports and National Landscapes."

7. Bale, "Place of 'Place,'" 513–18.

8. Bale, "Place of 'Place,'" 513–16.

9. Bale, "Place of 'Place,'" 513–18. See also Bale, *Sports Geography*.

10. Bale, "Place of 'Place,'" 516.

11. See "Table A.1. Population of urban and rural areas at mid-year" in *World Urbanization Prospects*, 72.

12. Brass, *Peasants, Populism, and Postmodernism*, 11.

13. Brass, *Peasants, Populism, and Postmodernism*, 11.

14. Brass, *Peasants, Populism, and Postmodernism*, 11.

15. Christesen, "Dreams of Democracy," 1021–22. On the term "Hoosier" itself see, for example, Paino, "Hoosiers in a Different Light." The film was internationally released as *Best Shot*, as "Hoosiers" is not an easily recognizable term outside the United States. On the importance of basketball for Indiana, see also the many popular histories on "Hoosier Hysteria," including N. Jones, *Growing Up in Indiana*; Lawrence, *Hoosier Hysteria Road Book*; B. Williams, *Hoosier Hysteria!*

16. Pierce, "More Than a Game," 3.

17. Hoose, *Hoosiers*, 10.

18. A Puritan version of the American dream can be described as one that relies on hard work and moral integrity to enable opportunities for a better life (whatever that better life might be). For a more detailed analysis of the history of the American dream see, for example, Caldwell, *Cynicism and the Evolution*; Cullen, *American Dream*; Jillson, *Pursuing the American Dream*; Jillson, *The American Dream*.

19. Mead and Mead, "'I Love You Guys.'"

20. Briley, "American Sport in Film," 14.

21. Briley, "American Sport in Film," 15.

22. Leonard, "'Is This Heaven?,'" 180.

23. Kibby, "Nostalgia for the Masculine," 21.

24. Jameson, *Cultural Turn*, 129.

25. Kibby, "Nostalgia for the Masculine," 27.

26. Landsberg, *Prosthetic Memory*, 25–26.

27. Kibby, "Nostalgia for the Masculine," 20.

28. Brass, *Peasants, Population, and Postmodern*, 11 (emphasis added).

29. See Fisher, as quoted in Winn, "Every Dream Has Its Price," 308.

30. Tudor also points this out in relation to Hickory in *Hoosiers*, but surprisingly she does not draw a wider conclusion between this film and the many others she analyses; see Tudor, *Hollywood's Vision of Team Sports*, 153.

31. See Cullen, *American Dream*, 6–9.

32. Caldwell, *Cynicism and the Evolution*, 37.

33. See also the 1971 *Swann vs. Charlotte-Mecklenburg Board of Education* decision that allowed bussing to enforce and accelerate integration.

34. Benavides, "Football and the Nation."

35. The song is based on an old traditional English folk ballad, "Lord Randall," and in this instance it is used to reinforce a sense of the hardships of life and battle.

36. This is, of course, a very broad summary; for further reference see, for example, McPherson, *Battle Cry of Freedom*.

37. Gienapp, *This Fiery Trial*, 184.

38. See the frequently asked questions page of the Original Titans website, which discusses the accuracy of the film: http://www.71originaltitans.com/faqs.html.

39. Baker, *Contesting Identities*, 147.

40. See also McLaughlin, *Give and Go*, 197.

41. Massood, "Urban Cinema," 111.

42. For a different take on basketball films in particular, see Baker, "Hoop Dreams." On the relationship between basketball and race in general, see Boyd, *Am I Black Enough*; Boyd and Shropshire, *Basketball Jones*.

43. On the importance of the racially coded variants of playing style in *Hoosiers*, see Leonard, "'Is This Heaven?'"

44. See, for example, Leonard, "'Is This Heaven?,'" 181.

45. The film emphasizes the statistics that one in three African American males between eighteen and twenty-five in this neighborhood are expected to end up in jail.

46. The real Coach Carter noted in an interview that of the forty-five players under his tutelage, only about seven had fathers in the house. Moring, "Just Call Him 'Sir.'"

5. GENDERING THE NATION

1. Tudor, *Hollywood's Vision of Team Sports*, 80–81.

2. Lindner, "Blood, Sweat and Tears," 238; Lindner, "Bodies in Action"; Lindner, "Fighting for Subjectivity"; Lindner, "'There Is a Reason'"; Chare, *Sportswomen*

in *Cinema*; Lieberman, *Sports Heroines on Film*. See also Bonzel, "*League of Their Own*"; Caudwell, "*Girlfight* and *Bend It Like Beckham*"; Caudwell, "*Girlfight*"; Caudwell, *Sport, Sexualities and Queer/Theory*; Chacko, "*Bend It Like Beckham*"; Garratt and Piper, "Too Hot to Handle?"; S. Hill, "Ambitious Young Woman"; Rings, "Questions of Identity." More recently attention has also shifted from the representation of female athletes to female coaches, an even rarer cinematic occurrence. See the chapter "Measured and Recorded: Cinematic Female Coaches" in Lieberman, *Sports Heroines on Film*, 126–50, and Bonzel, "Mind the Gap."

3. Parker et al., *Nationalisms and Sexualities*, 4.
4. Puri, *Encountering Nationalism*, 65. See also Conrad, "Queer Treasons"; Hogan, *Gender, Race and National Identity*; Nagel, "Masculinity and Nationalism."
5. Mosse, *Nationalism and Sexuality*.
6. Mosse, *Nationalism and Sexuality*, 4.
7. Mosse, *Nationalism and Sexuality*, 13, 20.
8. Mosse, *Nationalism and Sexuality*, 16.
9. Cahn, *Coming on Strong*, 3.
10. Hargreaves, *Heroines of Sport*, 2.
11. Whitson, "Embodiment of Gender," 231.
12. Tasker, *Spectacular Bodies*, 3.
13. Tasker, *Spectacular Bodies*, 132.
14. Holmlund, *Impossible Bodies*, 19.
15. Holmlund, *Impossible Bodies*, 19.
16. Mosse, *Nationalism and Sexuality*, 105.
17. Cahn, *Coming on Strong*, 184.
18. Cahn, *Coming on Strong*, 184.
19. The song was written by two players, Lavonne "Pepper" Paire Davis and Nalda "Bird" Phillips, according to the AAGPBL website, https://www.aagpbl.org/profiles/nalda-bird-phillips-birdie/129. I would like to thank the anonymous reviewers for *Screening the Past* for their helpful comments on an earlier version of this section.
20. S. C. Wood and Pincus, *Reel Baseball*, 7.
21. On the decline in baseball's popularity see, for example, Corso, "While Gap Narrows." On the importance of baseball in the United States, see Butterworth, *Baseball and Rhetorics of Purity*; Elias, *Baseball and the American Dream*; Szymanski and Zimbalist, *National Pastime*. Similarly, Hollywood's love affair with baseball has continued throughout the years; see Good, *Diamonds in the Dark*; Grella, "Baseball Moment in American Film"; S. C. Wood and Pincus, *Reel Baseball*.
22. Robson, "Field of American Dreams."
23. Robson, "Field of American Dreams."

24. Robson, "Field of American Dreams."

25. Cahn, *Coming on Strong*, 149.

26. Emphasis in original. For the "Rules of Conduct" and the "Beauty Handbook," which was part of the "Charm School," see https://www.aagpbl.org/history/rules -of-conduct and https://www.aagpbl.org/history/charm-school.

27. For the charm and beauty guide, see https://www.aagpbl.org/history/charm-school.

28. Player Josephine D'Angelo, for example, recalls getting fired from the league for getting her hair cut in a bob. Cahn, *Coming on Strong*, 186.

29. For more detailed histories of the AAGPBL, see Gregorich, *Women at Play*; Johnson, *When Women Played Hardball*.

30. L. Taylor, "Psychoanalytic Feminism to Popular Feminism."

31. See, for example, Heilmann and Beetham, *New Woman Hybridities*; Honey, *Creating Rosie the Riveter*; Meyerowitz, *Not June Cleaver*; Sutton, *Masculine Woman in Weimar Germany*.

32. For the character name of the radio announcer in an early draft of the script, see Ganz and Mandel, "League of Their Own."

33. See especially chapter 6, "No Freaks, No Amazons, No Boyish Bobs: The All-American Girls Professional Baseball League," chapter 7, "Beauty and the Butch: The 'Mannish' Athlete and the Lesbian Threat," and chapter 8, "'Play It Don't Say It': Lesbian Identity and Community in Women's Sport," in Cahn, *Coming on Strong*.

34. Holmlund, *Impossible Bodies*, 40.

35. For a more detailed analysis of the discourse on hybridized identities within *Bend It Like Beckham*, see Giardina, "'Bending It Like Beckham'"; Guarracino, "Musical 'Contact Zones'"; Korte and Sternberg, *Bidding for the Mainstream?*

36. For further information on black and Asian British film see, for example, Bourne, *Black in the British Frame*; Desai, *Beyond Bollywood*; Korte and Sternberg, *Bidding for the Mainstream?*

37. Ransom provides an excellent overview of the development of Bollywood sports films in "Bollywood Goes to the Stadium." On the cultural politics of *Lagaan*, see Farred, "Double Temporality of *Lagaan*," 57–84. *Chak De! India* has been examined for its representation of gender politics and social identities; see, for example, Chakraborty, "Nationalist Transactions"; De, "Sporting with Gender"; Kaushik, "Exclusion in Cinematic Space."

38. The only exception is Jess's best friend Tony (Ameet Chana), who encourages and supports Jess's decision to play soccer with the Hounslow Harriers.

39. Chacko, "*Bend It Like Beckham*," 84.

40. Lindner examines the gender and sexuality politics of the film through an analysis of the (sporting) gaze—the gaze as a means of interacting within the athletic activity. See Lindner, "'There Is a Reason.'"

41. Hjort, "Themes of Nation," 111.
42. McRobbie, "Top Girls?," 718.
43. Chacko, *Bend It Like Beckham*," 84.
44. May, "What's Love Got to Do," 256–57.
45. Ashby, "Postfeminism," 130.
46. Ashby, "Postfeminism," 130.
47. Lindner, "'There Is a Reason,'" 205–6.
48. Ashby, "Postfeminism," 130.
49. For further analysis of the coach-athlete relationship in the film, see Garratt and Piper, "Too Hot to Handle?"; Jolly and Lyle, "Traditional."
50. Anderson, *Imagined Communities*, 7.

BIBLIOGRAPHY

Addison, Heather. "'Must the Players Keep Young?': Early Hollywood's Cult of Youth." *Cinema Journal* 45, no. 4 (2006): 3–25.

Akkerman, Tjitske, Sarah L. de Lange, and Matthijs Rooduijn, eds. *Radical Right-Wing Populist Parties in Western Europe: Into the Mainstream?* London: Routledge, 2016.

Allen, John C., and Don A. Dillman. *Against All Odds: Rural Community in the Information Age*. Boulder CO: Westview Press, 1994.

Allison, Lincoln. *The Politics of Sport*. Manchester: Manchester University Press, 1986.

Allison, Lincoln, and Terry Monnington. "Sport, Prestige and International Relations." *Government and Opposition* 37, no. 1 (January 2002): 106–34.

Altman, Rick. *Film/Genre*. London: BFI, 1999.

Anderson, Benedict. *Imagined Communities: Reflections on the Origin and Spread of Nationalism*. London: Verso, 1991.

Antunes, Luis Rocha. *The Multisensory Film Experience: A Cognitive Model of Experiential Film Aesthetics*. Bristol: Intellect Books, 2016.

Ardolino, Frank. "*Rocky* Times Four: Return, Resurrection, Repetition and Reaganism." *Aethlon: The Journal of Sport Literature* 11, no. 1 (1993): 147–61.

Ashby, Justine. "Postfeminism in the British Frame." *Cinema Journal* 44, no. 2 (2005): 127–33.

Ashby, Justine, and Andrew Higson, eds. *British Cinema, Past and Present*. London: Routledge, 2000.

Auty, Martyn, and Nick Roddick. *British Cinema Now*. London: BFI, 1985.

Babington, Bruce. *The Sports Film: Games People Play*. New York: Columbia University Press, 2014.

Bairner, Alan. "National Sports and National Landscapes: In Defence of Primordialism." *National Identities* 11, no. 3 (2009): 223–39.

———. *Sport, Nationalism, and Globalization: European and North American Perspectives*. Albany: State University of New York Press, 2001.

Baker, Aaron. *Contesting Identities: Sports in American Film*. Urbana: University of Illinois Press, 2003.

———. "Hoop Dreams in Black and White: Race and Basketball Movies." In *Basketball Jones: America above the Rim*, edited by Todd Boyd and Kenneth L. Shropshire, 215–39. New York: New York University Press, 2000.

———. "Sports Films, History, and Identity." *Journal of Sport History* 25, no. 2 (1998): 217–33.

Baker, Aaron, and Todd Boyd, eds. *Out of Bounds: Sports, Media, and the Politics of Identity*. Bloomington: Indiana University Press, 1997.

Bale, John. "Cartographic Fetishism to Geographical Humanism: Some Central Features of a Geography of Sports." *Innovation in Social Sciences Research* 5, no. 4 (1992): 71–88.

———. "The Place of 'Place' in Cultural Studies of Sports." *Progress in Human Geography* 12, no. 4 (1988): 507–24.

———. *Sports Geography*. 2nd ed. London; New York: Routledge, 2003.

Barker, Jennifer M. *The Tactile Eye: Touch and the Cinematic Experience*. Berkeley: University of California Press, 2009.

Barthes, Roland. "The Reality Effect." In *The Novel: An Anthology of Criticism and Theory, 1900–2000*, edited by Dorothy J. Hale. Malden MA: Blackwell, 2006.

Benavides, O. Hugo. "Football and the Nation: Producing American Culture." *Oppositional Conversations* 1, no. 1 (2013): n.p.

Bergfelder, Tim. "National, Transnational or Supranational Cinema? Rethinking European Film Studies." *Media, Culture & Society* 27, no. 3 (2005): 315–31.

Beugnet, Martine. "Screening the Old: Femininity as Old Age in Contemporary French Cinema." *Studies in the Literary Imagination* 39, no. 2 (2006): 1–20.

Bevins, Vincent. "To Understand 2016's Politics, Look at the Winners and Losers of Globalization: An Interview with Economist Branko Milanovic." *New Republic*, December 21, 2016.

Bhabha, Homi K. *Nation and Narration*. London; New York: Routledge, 1990.

Billig, Michael. *Banal Nationalism*. London: SAGE, 1995.

Bisin, Alberto, Eleonora Patacchini, Thierry Verdier, and Yves Zenou. "*Bend It Like Beckham*: Identity, Socialization and Assimilation." *CEPR Discussion Papers*, January 1, 2006, 1–40.

Blain, Neil, and Alina Bernstein. *Sport, Media, Culture: Global and Local Dimensions*. London: Frank Cass, 2003.

Blain, Neil, Raymond Boyle, and Hugh O'Donnell. *Sport and National Identity in the European Media*. Leicester: Leicester University Press, 1993.

Bodnar, John E. *Blue-Collar Hollywood: Liberalism, Democracy, and Working People in American Film*. Baltimore: Johns Hopkins University Press, 2003.

Bonzel, Katharina. "*A League of Their Own*: The Impossibility of the Female Sports Hero." *Screening the Past* 37 (2013): n.p.

———. "Mind the Gap: Female Coaches in Hollywood Sports Films." *Sports Coaching Review* 5, no. 1 (2016): 54–69.

———. "Reviving the American Dream: The World of Sports." In *Learning from Mickey, Donald and Walt: Essays on Disney's Edutainment Films*, edited by A. Bowdoin Van Riper, 201–8. Jefferson NC: McFarland, 2014.

Bonzel, Katharina, and Nicholas Chare, eds. *Representations of Sports Coaches in Film: Looking to Win*. London: Routledge, 2017.

Bordwell, David, and Kristin Thompson. *Film Art: An Introduction*. 5th ed. New York: McGraw-Hill, 1997.

Bourne, Stephen. *Black in the British Frame: The Black Experience in British Film and Television*. London: Continuum, 2001.

Bowden, Martyn J. "Jerusalem, Dover Beach, and Kings Cross: Imagined Places as Metaphors of the British Class Struggle in *Chariots of Fire*." In *Place, Power, Situation, and Spectacle: A Geography of Film*, edited by Stuart C. Aitken and Leo Zonn, 69–100. Lanham MD: Rowman & Littlefield, 1994.

Boyd, Todd. *Am I Black Enough for You? Popular Culture from the 'Hood and Beyond*. Bloomington: Indiana University Press, 1997.

Boyd, Todd, and Kenneth L. Shropshire. *Basketball Jones: America above the Rim*. New York: New York University Press, 2000.

Bradstock, Andrew. *Masculinity and Spirituality in Victorian Culture*. New York: St. Martin's Press, 2000.

Brass, Tom. *Peasants, Populism, and Postmodernism: The Return of the Agrarian Myth*. London: Frank Cass, 2000.

Breitmeier, Florian. "Ein Wunder, wie es im Drehbuch steht: Die WM 1954-Ein Deutscher Erinnerungsfilm." In *Der lange Weg zur Bundesliga: Zum Siegeszug des Fussballs in Deutschland*, edited by Wolfram Pyta, 127–50. Muenster: LIT Verlag, 2004.

Briley, Ron. "American Sport in Film, Television and History: Introduction." *Film & History* 35, no. 1 (2005): 10.

———. "Basketball's Great White Hope and Ronald Reagan's America: *Hoosiers* (1986)." *Film & History* 35, no. 1 (2005): 12–19.

Briley, Ron, Michael K. Schoenecke, and Deborah A. Carmichael, eds. *All-Stars & Movie Stars: Sports in Film & History*. Lexington: University Press of Kentucky, 2008.

British Film Institute. "BFI Celebrates the London 2012 Olympics with a Host of Activity." BFI Film Forever, April 29, 2014. http://www.bfi.org.uk/news/bfi-celebrates-london-2012-olympics-host-activity.

Broadbent, Rick. "The Runner Who Only Stopped for God: Rick Broadbent Is Impressed by the Iron Integrity and Sheer Courage of Eric Liddell." *Times* (London), May 7, 2016, 14.

Brookes, Rod. *Representing Sport*. London: Arnold, 2002.

Brownell, Susan. *Beijing's Games: What the Olympics Mean to China*. Lanham MD: Rowman & Littlefield, 2008.

"Bundestrainer Adenauer." *Der Spiegel*, July 7, 1954.

Bush, Melanie E. L., and Roderick D. Bush. *Tensions in the American Dream: Rhetoric, Reverie, or Reality*. Philadelphia: Temple University Press, 2015.

Butler, Judith. *Bodies That Matter: On the Discursive Limits of "Sex."* New York: Routledge, 1993.

———. *Gender Trouble: Feminism and the Subversion of Identity*. New York: Routledge, 1999.

Butterworth, Michael L. *Baseball and Rhetorics of Purity: The National Pastime and American Identity during the War on Terror*. Tuscaloosa: University of Alabama Press, 2010.

Cahn, Susan K. *Coming on Strong: Gender and Sexuality in Twentieth-Century Women's Sport*. New York: Free Press, 1994.

Caldwell, Wilber W. *Cynicism and the Evolution of the American Dream*. Dulles VA: Potomac, 2006.

Campbell, Joseph. *The Hero with a Thousand Faces*. 3rd ed. Novato CA: New World Library, 2008.

Cannadine, David. "Gilbert and Sullivan: The Making and Unmaking of a British Tradition." In *Myths of the English*, edited by Roy Porter, 12–32. Cambridge: Polity Press, 1992.

Carroll, Noël. *Engaging the Moving Image*. New Haven CT: Yale University Press, 2003.

Carter, Ed. "*Chariots of Fire*: Traditional Values/False History." *Jump Cut: A Review of Contemporary Media*, no. 28 (1983): 14–17. https://www.ejumpcut.org/archive/onlinessays/JC28folder/ChariotsFire.html.

Cashmore, Ellis. "*Chariots of Fire*: Bigotry, Manhood and Moral Certitude in an Age of Individualism." *Sport in Society* 11, no. 2/3 (2008): 159–73.

Cashmore, Ernest. *Making Sense of Sports*. 4th ed. New York: Routledge, 2005.

Caudwell, Jayne. "*Girlfight*: Boxing Women." *Sport in Society* 11, no. 2 (2008): 227–39.

———. "*Girlfight* and *Bend It Like Beckham*: Screening Women, Sport, and Sexuality." *Journal of Lesbian Studies* 13, no. 3 (January 1, 2009): 255–71.

———. *Sport, Sexualities and Queer/Theory*. New York: Routledge, 2006.

Celli, Carlo. *National Identity in Global Cinema: How Movies Explain the World*. New York: Palgrave Macmillan, 2011.

Chacko, Mary Ann. "*Bend It Like Beckham*: Dribbling the Self through a Cross-Cultural Space." *Multicultural Perspectives* 12, no. 2 (2010): 81–86.

Chakraborty, M. N. "Nationalist Transactions: *Chak De! India* and the Down-and-Out Sports Coach." *Continuum: Journal of Media & Cultural Studies* 26, no. 6 (2012): 845–58.

Chapman, James. *Past and Present: National Identity and the British Historical Film*. London: I. B. Tauris, 2005.

Chare, Nicholas. "Handling Pressures: Analysing Touch in American Films about Youth Sport." *Sport, Education and Society* 18, no. 5 (2013): 663–77.

———. *Sportswomen in Cinema: Film and the Frailty Myth*. London: I. B. Tauris, 2015.

Charland, Louis C., and Peter Zachar. *Fact and Value in Emotion*. Amsterdam: John Benjamins, 2008.

Chivers, Sally. *The Silvering Screen: Old Age and Disability in Cinema*. Toronto: University of Toronto Press, 2011.

Christesen, Paul. "Dreams of Democracy, or the Reasons for *Hoosiers*' Enduring Appeal." *International Journal of the History of Sport* 34, no. 11 (2017): 1020–60.

Cogliano, Francis D. "Baseball and American Exceptionalism." In *Sport and National Identity in the Post-War World*, edited by Dilwyn Porter and Adrian Smith, 145–67. New York: Taylor & Francis, 2004.

Collins, Felicity, and Therese Davis. *Australian Cinema after Mabo*. Cambridge: Cambridge University Press, 2004.

Collins, Jim. *Architectures of Excess: Cultural Life in the Information Age*. New York: Routledge, 1995.

Connell, R. W. *Masculinities*. 2nd ed. Berkeley: University of California Press, 2005.

Conrad, Kathryn. "Queer Treasons: Homosexuality and Irish National Identity." *Cultural Studies* 15, no. 1 (2001): 124–37.

Cook, Pam. *Fashioning the Nation: Costume and Identity in British Cinema*. London: British Film Institute, 1996.

———. *Screening the Past: Memory and Nostalgia in Cinema*. London: Routledge, 2005.

Cooke, Paul. *Representing East Germany since Unification: From Colonization to Nostalgia*. Oxford: Berg, 2005.

Cooke, Paul, and Chris Homewood. "Introduction: Beyond the Cinema of Consensus? New Directions in German Cinema since 2000." In *New Directions in German Cinema*, edited by Paul Cooke and Chris Homewood, 1–19. London: I. B. Tauris, 2011.

Cooke, Paul, and Christopher Young. "Selling Sex or Dealing with History? German Football in Literature and Film and the Quest to Normalize the Nation." In

German Football: History, Culture, Society, edited by Alan Tomlinson and Christopher Young, 181–203. London: Routledge, 2005.

Corner, John, and Sylvia Harvey. *Enterprise and Heritage: Crosscurrents of National Culture*. London: Routledge, 1991.

Corso, Regina. "While Gap Narrows, Professional Football Retains Lead over Baseball as Favorite Sport." Harris Poll, January 20, 2011. https://theharrispoll.com/new-york-n-y-january-20-2011-its-the-eternal-debate-among-sports-fans-football-or-baseball-most-die-hard-sports-fans-will-always-say-both-but-if-forced-to-choose-football-wins-yet-again/.

Crawford, Scott A. G. M. "The Sport Film—Its Cultural Significance." *Journal of Physical Education, Recreation & Dance* 59, no. 6 (August 1988): 45–49.

Crisell, Andrew. *An Introductory History of British Broadcasting*. 2nd ed. London: Routledge, 2002.

Crosson, Seán. *Sport and Film*. New York: Routledge, 2013.

Cullen, Jim. *The American Dream: A Short History of an Idea That Shaped a Nation*. Oxford: Oxford University Press, 2003.

De, Aparajita. "Sporting with Gender: Examining Sport and Belonging at Home and in the Diaspora through *Patiala House* & *Chak De! India*." *South Asian Popular Culture* 11, no. 3 (2013): 287–300.

Dee, David. "'Too Semitic' or 'Thoroughly Anglicised'? The Life and Career of Harold Abrahams." *International Journal of the History of Sport* 29, no. 6 (2012): 868–86.

De Groot, Jerome. *Consuming History: Historians and Heritage in Contemporary Popular Culture*. Abingdon: Routledge, 2008.

Delbanco, Andrew. *The Real American Dream: A Meditation on Hope*. Cambridge MA: Harvard University Press, 1999.

Deleuze, Gilles. *Cinema 1: The Movement-Image*. London: Athlone, 1986.

———. *Cinema 2: The Time-Image*. London: Athlone, 1989.

Delius, Friedrich Christian. *Der Sonntag, an dem ich Weltmeister wurde: Erzählung*. Reinbek bei Hamburg: Rowohlt, 1994.

Desai, Jigna. *Beyond Bollywood: The Cultural Politics of South Asian Diasporic Film*. New York: Routledge, 2004.

Dissanayake, Wimal. "Globalization and the Experience of Culture: The Resilience of Nationhood." In *Globalization, Cultural Identities, and Media Representations*, edited by Natascha Gentz and Stefan Kramer, 25–44. Albany: State University of New York Press, 2006.

Dissanayake, Wimal, and Rob Wilson, eds. *Global/Local: Cultural Production and the Transnational Imaginary*. Durham NC: Duke University Press, 1996.

Donalson, Melvin Burke. *Masculinity in the Interracial Buddy Film*. Jefferson NC: McFarland, 2006.

Edensor, Tim. *National Identity, Popular Culture and Everyday Life*. New York: Berg, 2002.

Elias, Robert. *Baseball and the American Dream: Race, Class, Gender, and the National Pastime*. Armonk NY: M. E. Sharpe, 2001.

Elmwood, Victoria A. "'Just Some Bum from the Neighborhood': The Resolution of Post–Civil Rights Tension and Heavyweight Public Sphere Discourse in *Rocky* (1976)." *Film & History* 35, no. 2 (2005): 49–59.

Elsaesser, Thomas. "'Where Were You When . . . ?'; or, 'I Phone, Therefore I Am.'" *PMLA* 118, no. 1 (2003): 120–22.

"Eric Liddell Sports Scholarships Launched." University of Edinburgh, April 13, 2016. http://www.ed.ac.uk/news/all-news/liddellscholars-190612.

Eskenazi, Gerald. "The Miracle on Ice." *New York Times*, February 10, 2010.

Evans, Nicola. "No Genre for Old Men? The Politics of Aging and the Male Action Hero." *Revue Canadienne d'Études Cinématographiques / Canadian Journal of Film Studies* 24, no. 1 (2015): 25–44.

Farred, Grant. "The Double Temporality of *Lagaan*: Cultural Struggle and Postcolonialism." In *Visual Economies of/in Motion: Sport and Film*, edited by C. Richard King and David J. Leonard, 57–84. New York: Peter Lang, 2006.

Frei, Alfred Georg. *Finale Grande: Die Rückkehr der Fussballweltmeister 1954*. Berlin: Transit, 1994.

Frey, Mattias. "Rebirth of a Nation: *Das Wunder von Bern*, the 1950s, and the Reactions to the New German Cinema." In *Postwall German Cinema: History, Film History and Cinephilia*, 19–46. New York; Oxford: Berghahn Books, 2013.

Friedman, Lester D. *Fires Were Started: British Cinema and Thatcherism*. Minneapolis: University of Minnesota Press, 1993.

Ganz, Lowell, and Babaloo Mandel. "A League of Their Own." Script draft. 1991.

Garratt, Dean, and Heather Piper. "Too Hot to Handle? A Social Semiotic Analysis of Touching in *Bend It Like Beckham*." *Sports Coaching Review* 5, no. 1 (2016): 102–15.

Gates, Philippa. "Acting His Age? The Resurrection of the '80s Action Heroes and Their Aging Stars." *Quarterly Review of Film and Video* 27, no. 4 (2010): 276–89.

Gellner, Ernest. *Nationalism*. London: Weidenfeld & Nicolson, 1997.

Giardina, Michael D. "'Bending It Like Beckham' in the Global Popular: Stylish Hybridity, Performativity, and the Politics of Representation." *Journal of Sport and Social Issues* 27, no. 1 (February 2003): 65–82.

Gienapp, William E., ed. *This Fiery Trial: The Speeches and Writings of Abraham Lincoln*. New York: Oxford University Press, 2002.

Gledhill, Christine. "Rethinking Genre." In *Reinventing Film Studies*, edited by Linda Williams and Christine Gledhill, 221–43. London: Arnold, 1999.

Good, Howard. *Diamonds in the Dark: America, Baseball, and the Movies*. Lanham MD: Scarecrow Press, 1997.

Graham, Carol. *Happiness for All? Unequal Hopes and Lives in Pursuit of the American Dream*. Princeton: Princeton University Press, 2017.

Grant, Barry Keith. *Film Genre: From Iconography to Ideology*. London; New York: Wallflower, 2007.

———. *Film Genre: Theory and Criticism*. Metuchen: Scarecrow Press, 1977.

———. *Film Genre Reader*. Austin: University of Texas Press, 1986.

———. *Film Genre Reader II*. Austin: University of Texas Press, 1995.

———. *Film Genre Reader III*. Austin: University of Texas Press, 2003.

Gregorich, Barbara. *Women at Play: The Story of Women in Baseball*. San Diego: Harcourt Brace, 1993.

Grella, George. "The Baseball Moment in American Film." *Aethlon* 14, no. 2 (1997): 7–16.

Grodal, Torben Kragh. *Embodied Visions: Evolution, Emotion, Culture, and Film*. Oxford: Oxford University Press, 2009.

———. *Moving Pictures: A New Theory of Film Genres, Feelings, and Cognition*. Oxford: Clarendon Press, 1997.

Guarracino, Serena. "Musical 'Contact Zones' in Gurinder Chadha's Cinema." *European Journal of Women's Studies* 16, no. 4 (November 1, 2009): 373–90.

Hagener, Malte. "*Das Wunder von Bern*." In *The Cinema of Germany*, edited by Joseph Garncarz and Annemone Ligensa, 237–45. London: Wallflower Press, 2012.

Hake, Sabine. *German National Cinema*. London: Routledge, 2002.

Halberstam, Judith. *Female Masculinity*. Durham NC: Duke University Press, 1998.

Hall, Sheldon. "The Wrong Sort of Cinema: Refashioning the Heritage Film Debate." In *The British Cinema Book*, edited by Robert Murphy, 46–56. London: Palgrave Macmillan on behalf of the British Film Institute, 2009.

Hamilton, Duncan. *For the Glory: Eric Liddell's Journey from Olympic Champion to Modern Martyr*. New York: Penguin, 2016.

Hargreaves, Jennifer. *Heroines of Sport: The Politics of Difference and Identity*. London: Routledge, 2000.

Hastie, Amelie. "Ryan Coogler's *Creed*: Showing the Love." *Film Quarterly* 69, no. 4 (2016): 72–77.

Hayward, Susan. "Framing National Cinemas." In Hjort and MacKenzie, *Cinema and Nation*, 88–102.

Heilmann, Ann, and Margaret Beetham. *New Woman Hybridities: Femininity, Feminism and International Consumer Culture, 1880–1930*. London: Routledge, 2004.

Heineman, Elizabeth D. "The Hour of the Woman: Memories of Germany's 'Crisis Years' and West German National Identity." In *The Miracle Years: A Cultural History of West Germany, 1949–1968*, edited by Hanna Schissler, 21–56. Princeton: Princeton University Press, 2001.

Heinrich, Arthur. "The 1954 Soccer World Cup and the Federal Republic of Germany's Self-Discovery." *American Behavioral Scientist* 46, no. 11 (July 2003): 1491–505.

————. *3:2 für Deutschland: Die Gründung der Bundesrepublik im Wankdorf-Stadion zu Bern*. Göttingen: Werkstatt, 2004.

————. *Tooor! Toor! Tor!: 40 Jahre 3:2*. Berlin: Rotbuch-Verlag, 1994.

"Herberger 3:2." *Der Spiegel*, July 7, 1954, 21–25.

Hewison, Robert. *The Heritage Industry: Britain in a Climate of Decline*. London: Methuen London, 1987.

Higson, Andrew. *English Heritage, English Cinema: Costume Drama since 1980*. Oxford: Oxford University Press, 2003.

————. "Re-presenting the National Past: Nostalgia and Pastiche in the Heritage Film." In *Fires Were Started: British Cinema and Thatcherism*, edited by Lester D. Friedman, 91–109. Minneapolis: University of Minnesota Press, 1993.

————. *Waving the Flag: Constructing a National Cinema in Britain*. Oxford: Clarendon Press, 1995.

Hill, John. *British Cinema in the 1980s: Issues and Themes*. Oxford: Oxford University Press, 1999.

Hill, Sarah. "The Ambitious Young Woman and the Contemporary British Sports Film." *Assuming Gender* 5, no. 1 (2015): 37–58.

Hjort, Mette. "Themes of Nation." In Hjort and MacKenzie, *Cinema and Nation*, 103–17.

Hjort, Mette, and Scott MacKenzie, eds. *Cinema and Nation*. London: Routledge, 2000.

Hochscherf, Tobias, and Christopher Laucht. "'Every Nation Needs a Legend': *The Miracle of Bern* and the Formation of a Postwar Foundational Myth." In *All-Stars & Movie Stars: Sports in Film & History*, edited by Ron Briley, Michael K. Schoenecke, and Deborah A. Carmichael, 279–302. Lexington: University Press of Kentucky, 2008.

Hochschild, Jennifer L. *Facing Up to the American Dream: Race, Class, and the Soul of the Nation*. Princeton NJ: Princeton University Press, 1995.

Hogan, Jackie. *Gender, Race and National Identity: Nations of Flesh and Blood*. New York: Routledge, 2009.

Holmlund, Chris. "The Aging Clint." In *Impossible Bodies: Femininity and Masculinity at the Movies*, edited by Chris Holmlund, 141–56. London: Routledge, 2002.

————. "Celebrity, Ageing and Jackie Chan: Middle-Aged Asian in Transnational Action." *Celebrity Studies* 1, no. 1 (2010): 96–112.

————. *Impossible Bodies: Femininity and Masculinity at the Movies*. London: Routledge, 2002.

Honey, Maureen. *Creating Rosie the Riveter: Class, Gender, and Propaganda during World War II*. Amherst: University of Massachusetts Press, 1984.

Hoose, Phillip M. *Hoosiers: The Fabulous Basketball Life of Indiana*. Bloomington: Indiana University Press, 2016.

Jameson, Fredric. *The Cultural Turn: Selected Writings on the Postmodern, 1983–1998*. London: Verso, 1998.

Jefferson, Thomas, and Michael Hardt. *The Declaration of Independence*. London: Verso, 2007.

Jefferys, Kevin. "Lord Burghley, *Chariots of Fire* and the Gentleman Amateur in British Athletics." *Sport in History* 33, no. 4 (2013): 445–64.

Jeffords, Susan. *Hard Bodies: Hollywood Masculinity in the Reagan Era*. New Brunswick NJ: Rutgers University Press, 1994.

Jensen, Robert. "The Painful Collapse of Empire: How the 'American Dream' and American Exceptionalism Wreck Havoc on the World." http://www.informationclearinghouse.info/article28433.htm.

Jillson, Calvin C. *The American Dream: In History, Politics, and Fiction*. Lawrence: University Press of Kansas, 2016.

———. *Pursuing the American Dream: Opportunity and Exclusion over Four Centuries*. Lawrence: University Press of Kansas, 2004.

Johnson, Susan E. *When Women Played Hardball*. Seattle: Seal Press, 1994.

Johnston, Sheila. "Charioteers and Ploughmen." In *British Cinema Now*, edited by Martyn Auty and Nick Roddick, 99–110. London: BFI, 1985.

Jolly, Sue, and John Lyle. "The Traditional, the Ideal and the Unexplored: Sport Coaches' Social Identity Constructs in Film." *Sports Coaching Review* 5, no. 1 (2016): 41–53.

Jones, Glen. "'Down on the Floor and Give Me Ten Sit-Ups': British Sports Feature Film." *Film & History* 35, no. 2 (2005): 29–40.

Jones, Norman. *Growing Up in Indiana: The Culture & Hoosier Hysteria Revisited*. Bloomington IN: AuthorHouse, 2005.

Kapczynski, Jennifer M. "Imitation of Life: The Aesthetics of Agfacolor in Recent Historical Cinema." In *The Collapse of the Conventional: German Film and Its Politics at the Turn of the Twenty-First Century*, edited by Jaimey Fisher and Brad Prager, 39–62. Detroit: Wayne State University Press, 2010.

Kaushik, Nancy. "Exclusion in Cinematic Space: A Case Study of *Chak De India*." *Innovation: International Journal of Applied Research* 1, no. 1 (2013): 27–30.

Kebric, Robert B. "London 2012, *Chariots of Fire* Resurrected and Colombes Stadium Today: Hype, History and Olympic Realities." *Sport in Society* 17, no. 5 (2013): 656–73.

Kelso, Paul. "*Field of Dreams*." *Guardian*, September 2, 2005.

Kibby, Marjorie D. "Nostalgia for the Masculine: Onward to the Past in the Sports Films of the Eighties." *Canadian Journal of Film Studies* 7, no. 1 (1998): 16–28.

Kimmel, Michael S. *Manhood in America: A Cultural History*. New York: Oxford University Press, 2006.

King, C. Richard, and David J. Leonard, eds. *Visual Economies of/in Motion: Sport and Film*. New York: Peter Lang, 2006.

Koepnick, Lutz. "Reframing the Past: Heritage Cinema and Holocaust in the 1990s." *New German Critique*, no. 87 (2002): 47–82.

Korte, Barbara , and Claudia Sternberg. *Bidding for the Mainstream? Black and Asian British Film since the 1990s*. Amsterdam: Rodopi, 2004.

Kracauer, Siegfried. *Theory of Film: The Redemption of Physical Reality*. Princeton NJ: Princeton University Press, 1997.

Kusz, Kyle W. "Remasculinizing American White Guys in/through New Millennium American Sport Films." *Sport in Society* 11, no. 2/3 (2008): 209–26.

Kwauk, Christina. "*Goal! The Dream Begins*: Globalizing an Immigrant Muscular Christianity." *Soccer & Society* 8, no. 1 (2007): 75–89.

Landsberg, Alison. *Prosthetic Memory: The Transformation of American Remembrance in the Age of Mass Culture*. New York: Columbia University Press, 2004.

Landy, Marcia. "Looking Backward: History and Thatcherism in Recent British Cinema." *Film Criticism* 15, no. 1 (1990): 17–38.

Larres, Klaus, and Panikos Panayi. *The Federal Republic of Germany since 1949: Politics, Society, and Economy before and after Unification*. London: Longman, 1996.

Lawrence, Dale. *Hoosier Hysteria Road Book: A Guide to the Byways of Indiana High School Basketball*. South Bend IN: Diamond Communications, 2001.

Leab, Daniel J. "The Blue Collar Ethnic in Bicentennial America: *Rocky* (1976)." In *American History/American Film: Interpreting the Hollywood Image*, edited by John E. O'Connor and Martina A. Jackson, 257–72. New York: Frederick Ungar, 1979.

Leach, Jim. *British Film*. Cambridge: Cambridge University Press, 2004.

Leinemann, Jürgen. "Fussball: Wie ein kleiner König (Teil 2)." *Der Spiegel*, December 30, 1996.

Leonard, David J. "'Is This Heaven?': White Sporting Masculinities and the Hollywood Imagination." In King and Leonard, *Visual Economies of/in Motion*, 164–94.

Leonard, David J., and C. Richard King. "Screening the Social: An Introduction to Sport Cinema." In King and Leonard, *Visual Economies of/in Motion*, 1–11.

Lieberman, Viridiana. *Sports Heroines on Film: A Critical Study of Cinematic Women Athletes, Coaches and Owners*. Jefferson NC: McFarland, 2015.

Lindner, Katharina. "Blood, Sweat and Tears: Women, Sport and Hollywood." In *Postfeminism and Contemporary Hollywood Cinema*, edited by Joel Gwynne and Nadine Muller, 238–55. Houndmills, Basingstoke: Palgrave Macmillan, 2013.

———. "Bodies in Action: Female Athleticism on the Cinema Screen." *Feminist Media Studies* 11, no. 3 (February 2011): 321–45.

———. "Fighting for Subjectivity: Articulations of Physicality in *Girlfight*." *Journal of International Women's Studies* 10, no. 3 (January 2009): 4–17.

―――. "'There Is a Reason Why Sporty Spice Is the Only One of Them without a Fella': The 'Lesbian Potential' of *Bend It Like Beckham*." *New Review of Film and Television Studies* 9, no. 2 (January 2011): 204–23.

Ludewig, Alexandra. "'Heimat, Heimat, Über Alles': Heimat in Two Contemporary German Films." *Studies in European Cinema* 5, no. 3 (2009): 219–32.

―――. "'Ostalgie' und 'Westalgie' als Ausdruck von Heimatsehnsüchten." In *Heimat: Konturen und Konjunkturen eines umstrittenen Konzepts*, edited by Gunther Gebhard, Oliver Geisler, and Steffen Schroeter, 141–60. Bielefeld: Transcript, 2007.

Mammone, Andrea, Emmanuel Godin, and Brian Jenkins, eds. *Mapping the Extreme Right in Contemporary Europe: From Local to Transnational*. London: Routledge, 2012.

Marks, Laura U. *The Skin of the Film: Intercultural Cinema, Embodiment, and the Senses*. Durham NC: Duke University Press, 2000.

―――. *Touch: Sensuous Theory and Multisensory Media*. Minneapolis: University of Minnesota Press, 2002.

Markson, Elizabeth. "The Female Aging Body through Film." In *Aging Bodies: Images and Everyday Experiences*, edited by Christopher Faircloth, 77–102. Walnut Creek CA: AltaMira Press, 2003.

Martin-Jones, David. *Deleuze, Cinema and National Identity: Narrative Time in National Contexts*. Edinburgh: Edinburgh University Press, 2008.

Massood, Paula J. "Urban Cinema." In *African Americans and Popular Culture: Theater, Film, and Television*, edited by Todd Boyd, 89–115. Westport CT: Praeger, 2008.

May, Claudia. "What's Love Got to Do with It? (Un)bending Identities and Conventions in Gurinda Chadha's *Bend It Like Beckham*." *Culture and Religion* 11, no. 3 (January 2010): 247–76.

McLaughlin, Thomas. *Give and Go: Basketball as a Cultural Practice*. Albany: State University of New York Press, 2008.

McPherson, James M. *Battle Cry of Freedom: The Civil War Era*. New York: Oxford University Press, 1988.

McRobbie, Angela. "Top Girls?" *Cultural Studies* 21, no. 4/5 (2007): 718–37.

Mead, Bryan, and Jason Mead. "'I Love You Guys': *Hoosiers* as a Model for Transformational and Limited Transactional Coaching." *Sports Coaching Review* 5, no. 1 (2016): 29–40.

Meyerowitz, Joanne J. *Not June Cleaver: Women and Gender in Postwar America, 1945–1960*. Philadelphia: Temple University Press, 1994.

Mihelj, Sabina. *Media Nations: Communicating Belonging and Exclusion in the Modern World*. Basingstoke: Palgrave, 2011.

Miller, Toby, Geoffrey Lawrence, Jim McKay, and David Rowe. *Globalization and Sport: Playing the World*. London: SAGE, 2001.

Moeller, Robert G. "Introduction: Writing the History of West Germany." In *West Germany under Construction: Politics, Society, and Culture in the Adenauer Era*, 1–30. Ann Arbor: University of Michigan Press, 1997.

Monk, Claire. "The British Heritage-Film Debate Revisited." In *British Historical Cinema: The History, Heritage, and Costume Film*, edited by Claire Monk and Amy Sargeant, 176–98. London: Routledge, 2002.

Moring, Mark. "Just Call Him 'Sir.'" *Christianity Today*, January 11, 2005. http://www.christianitytoday.com/ct/movies/interviews/2005/kencarter.html.

Mosse, George L. *Nationalism and Sexuality: Respectability and Abnormal Sexuality in Modern Europe*. New York: H. Fertig, 1985.

Motley, Clay. "Fighting for Manhood: *Rocky* and Turn-of-the-Century Antimodernism." *Film & History* 35, no. 2 (2005): 60–66.

Mulvey, Laura. "Visual Pleasure and Narrative Cinema." In *Film Theory and Criticism: Introductory Readings*, edited by Leo Braudy and Marshall Cohen, 833–44. New York: Oxford University Press, 1999.

Nagel, Joane. "Masculinity and Nationalism: Gender and Sexuality in the Making of Nations." *Ethnic and Racial Studies* 21, no. 2 (January 1998): 242–69.

Neale, Stephen. *Genre*. London: British Film Institute, 1980.

Neale, Steve. *Genre and Contemporary Hollywood*. London: British Film Institute, 2002.

———. "Questions of Genre and Film." *Screen* 31, no. 1 (Spring 1990): 45–66.

O'Dochartaigh, Pol. *Germany since 1945*. Hampshire: Palgrave Macmillan, 2004.

Paino, Troy D. "Hoosiers in a Different Light: Forces of Change vs. the Power of Nostalgia." *Journal of Sport History* 28, no. 1 (2001): 63–80.

Palmer, William J. *The Films of the Eighties: A Social History*. Carbondale: Southern Illinois University Press, 1993.

Parker, Andrew, Mary Russo, Doris Sommer, and Patricia Yaeger, eds. *Nationalisms & Sexualities*. New York: Routledge, 1992.

Patzner, Richard. "Das Wunder von Bern: Ein Mythos wird geboren." In *Mythen in Moderne und Postmoderne: Weltdeutung und Sinnvermittlung*, edited by Marion M. Helmes and Gabriele C. Weiher, 191–216. Berlin: Weidler, 1995.

Perinbanayagam, Robert. *Games and Sport in Everyday Life: Dialogues and Narratives of the Self*. Boulder CO: Paradigm, 2006.

Pierce, Richard B. "More Than a Game: The Political Meaning of High School Basketball in Indianapolis." *Journal of Urban History* 27, no. 1 (2000): 3–23.

Piketty, Thomas. *Capital in the Twenty-First Century*. Cambridge MA: Harvard University Press, 2014.

Plantinga, Carl R. *Moving Viewers: American Film and the Spectator's Experience*. Berkeley: University of California Press, 2009.

Plowman, Andrew. "Westalgia: Nostalgia for the Old Federal Republic in Recent German Prose." *Seminar* 40, no. 3 (2004): 249–61.

Pope, Stephen W. *The New American Sport History: Recent Approaches and Perspectives.* Urbana: University of Illinois Press, 1997.

Poulton, Emma, and Martin Roderick, eds. *Sport in Film.* London: Routledge, 2008.

Puri, Jyoti. *Encountering Nationalism.* Malden MA: Blackwell, 2004.

Purves, Libby. "*Chariots of Fire*: Theatre." *Times* (London), May 24, 2012, 10.

Putnam, Robert D. *Our Kids: The American Dream in Crisis.* New York: Simon & Schuster, 2015.

Pyta, Wolfram. "German Football: A Cultural History." In *German Football: History, Culture, Society,* edited by Alan Tomlinson and Christopher Young, 1–22. London: Routledge, 2005.

Quart, Leonard, and Albert Auster. *American Film and Society since 1945.* New York: Praeger, 1991.

Raglan, Fitzroy Richard Somerset. *The Hero: A Study in Tradition, Myth, and Drama.* Mineola NY: Dover, 2003.

Rank, Mark R., Thomas A. Hirschl, and Kirk A. Foster. *Chasing the American Dream: Understanding What Shapes Our Fortunes.* Oxford: Oxford University Press, 2014.

Rank, Otto. "Myth of the Birth of the Hero." In *In Quest of the Hero,* edited by Otto Rank, Fitzroy Richard Somerset Raglan, and Alan Dundes, 1–86. Princeton NJ: Princeton University Press, 1990.

Ransom, Amy J. "Bollywood Goes to the Stadium: Gender, National Identity, and Sport Film in Hindi." *Journal of Film and Video* 66, no. 4 (2014): 34–49.

Reilly, Jill. "Bumbling Mr Bean Brings Down the House as He Leads Orchestra in Hilarious Rendition of *Chariots of Fire.*" *Daily Mail* (London), July 28, 2012.

Rentschler, Eric. "From New German Cinema to the Post-Wall Cinema of Consensus." In Hjort and MacKenzie, *Cinema and Nation,* 260–77.

"Report." *Photographic Journal,* January 31, 1896, 123–24.

Richards, Jeffrey. *Films and British National Identity: From Dickens to Dad's Army.* Manchester: Manchester University Press, 1997.

Rings, Guido. "Questions of Identity: Cultural Encounters in Gurinder Chadha's *Bend It Like Beckham.*" *Journal of Popular Film and Television* 39, no. 3 (January 2011): 114–23.

Robbins, Keith. *Great Britain: Identities, Institutions, and the Idea of Britishness.* New York: Longman, 1997.

Roberts, J. M., M. J. Arth, and R. R. Bush. "Games in Culture." *American Anthropologist* 61, no. 4 (1959): 597–605.

Robson, Tom. "Field of American Dreams: Individualist Ideology in the U.S. Baseball Movie." *Jump Cut: A Review of Contemporary Media* 52 (2010): n.p. http://www.ejumpcut.org/archive/jc52.2010/RobsonBaseball/index.html.

Roosvall, Anna. "Image-Nation: The National, the Cultural and the Global in Foreign News Slide-Shows." In *Communicating the Nation: National Topographies of Global Media Landscapes*, edited by Anna Roosvall and Inka Salovaara-Moring, 215–36. Göteborg: Nordicom, Göteborgs Universitet, 2010.

Rosenstone, Robert A. *Visions of the Past: The Challenge of Film to Our Idea of History*. Cambridge MA: Harvard University Press, 1995.

Rowe, David. "If You Film It, Will They Come? Sports on Film." *Journal of Sport and Social Issues* 22, no. 4 (1998): 350–59.

Ryan, Mark. *Running with Fire: The Harold Abrahams Story*. London: JR Books, 2011.

Rydgren, Jens, ed. *Movements of Exclusion: Radical Right-Wing Populism in the Western World*. New York: Nova Science, 2005.

Salmela, Mikko. "What Is Emotional Authenticity?" *Journal for the Theory of Social Behaviour* 35, no. 3 (2005): 209–30.

Schubart, Rikke. "Birth of a Hero: Rocky, Stallone, and Mythical Creation." In *Stars in Our Eyes: The Star Phenomenon in the Contemporary Era*, edited by Angela Ndalianis and Charlotte Henry, 149–64. Westport CT: Praeger, 2002.

Schweer, Joachim. *Der Sieg von Bern: V. Fussball-Weltmeisterschaft 1954*. Kassel: Agon-Sportverlag, 1994.

Sharp, Joanne P. "Gender in a Political and Patriarchal World." In *Handbook of Cultural Geography*, edited by Kay Anderson, Mona Domosh, Nigel Thrift, and Steve Pile, 473–84. London: SAGE, 2003.

Slaughter, Anne-Marie. *The Idea That Is America: Keeping Faith with Our Values in a Dangerous World*. New York: Basic Books, 2007.

Smith, Anthony D. *National Identity*. London: Penguin, 1991.

Smith, Anthony D., and John Hutchinson. *Nationalism*. Oxford: Oxford University Press, 1994.

Smith, Greg M. *Film Structure and the Emotion System*. Cambridge: Cambridge University Press, 2003.

Sobchack, Vivian. "What My Fingers Knew: The Cinesthetic Subject, or Vision in the Flesh." *Senses of Cinema*, no. 5 (April 2000).

Solomon, Martha. "Villainless Quest: Myth, Metaphor, and Dream in *Chariots of Fire*." *Communication Quarterly* 31, no. 4 (1983): 274–81.

Sternheimer, Karen. *Celebrity Culture and the American Dream: Stardom and Social Mobility*. 2nd ed. New York: Routledge, 2015.

Street, Sarah. *British National Cinema*. London: Routledge, 1997.

————. *Transatlantic Crossings: British Feature Films in the United States*. New York: Continuum, 2002.

Sutton, Katie. *The Masculine Woman in Weimar Germany*. New York: Berghahn Books, 2011.

Szymanski, Stefan, and Andrew S. Zimbalist. *National Pastime: How Americans Play Baseball and the Rest of the World Plays Soccer*. Washington DC: Brookings Institution Press, 2005.

Taberner, Stuart. "Philo-Semitism in Recent German Film: *Aimee und Jaguar, Rosenstrasse* and *Das Wunder von Bern*." *German Life & Letters* 58, no. 3 (2005): 357–72.

Tasker, Yvonne. *Spectacular Bodies: Gender, Genre, and the Action Cinema*. London: Routledge, 1993.

Taubin, Amy. *Taxi Driver*. London: BFI, 2000.

Taylor, Diana. "The Theatre of Operations: Nation-Ness in the Public Sphere." In *Internationalizing Cultural Studies: An Anthology*, edited by M. A. Abbas, John Nguyet Erni, and Wimal Dissanayake, 132–44. Malden MA: Blackwell, 2005.

Taylor, Lisa. "From Psychoanalytic Feminism to Popular Feminism." In *Approaches to Popular Film*, edited by Joanne Hollows and Mark Jancovich, 151–71. Manchester: Manchester University Press, 1995.

Tomlinson, Alan, and Christopher Young, eds. *National Identity and Global Sports Events: Culture, Politics, and Spectacle in the Olympics and the Football World Cup*. Albany: State University of New York Press, 2006.

Tudor, Deborah V. *Hollywood's Vision of Team Sports: Heroes, Race, and Gender*. New York: Garland, 1997.

Uecker, Matthias. "Fractured Families—United Countries? Family, Nostalgia and Nation-Building in *Das Wunder von Bern* and *Goodbye Lenin*." *New Cinemas: Journal of Contemporary Film* 5, no. 3 (2007): 189–200.

Vance, Norman. *The Sinews of the Spirit: The Ideal of Christian Manliness in Victorian Literature and Religious Thought*. Cambridge: Cambridge University Press, 1985.

Vidal, Belén. *Heritage Film: Nation, Genre and Representation*. New York: Columbia University Press, 2012.

Vitez, Michael. *Rocky Stories: Tales of Love, Hope, and Happiness at America's Most Famous Steps*. Photographs by Tom Gralish. Philadelphia: Paul Dry Books, 2006.

Von Moltke, Johannes. *No Place Like Home: Locations of Heimat in German Cinema*. Berkeley: University of California Press, 2005.

Walter, Fritz. *3:2 Die Spiele zur Weltmeisterschaft; Erinnerungen eines Fussball-Idols*. München: Copress, 1992.

Weber, Cynthia. "Performative States." *Millennium-Journal of International Studies* 27, no. 1 (1998): 77–95.

Whannel, Garry. *Media Sport Stars: Masculinities and Moralities*. London: Routledge, 2001.

Whitehead, Stephen. *Men and Masculinities: Key Themes and New Directions*. Cambridge: Polity Press, 2002.

Whitehead, Stephen, and Frank J. Barrett. *The Masculinities Reader*. Cambridge: Blackwell, 2001.

Whitson, David. "The Embodiment of Gender: Discipline, Domination, and Empowerment." In *Gender and Sport: A Reader*, edited by Sheila Scraton and Anne Flintoff, 227–40. London: Routledge, 2002.

Williams, Bob. *Hoosier Hysteria! Indiana High School Basketball*. South Bend IN: Hardwood Press, 1997.

Williams, Linda. "Film Bodies: Gender, Genre, and Excess." *Film Quarterly* 44, no. 4 (1991): 2–13.

Williams, Tony. "'I Could've Been a Contender': The Boxing Movie's Generic Instability." *Quarterly Review of Film and Video* 18, no. 3 (2001): 305–19.

Winn, J. Emmett. "Every Dream Has Its Price: Personal Failure and the American Dream in *Wall Street* and *The Firm*." *Southern Communication Journal* 68, no. 4 (2003): 307–18.

Wollen, Tana. "Over Our Shoulders: Nostalgic Screen Fictions for the 1980s." In *Enterprise and Heritage: Crosscurrents of National Culture*, edited by John Corner and Sylvia Harvey, 178–93. London: Routledge, 1991.

Wood, Robin. *Hollywood from Vietnam to Reagan*. New York: Columbia University Press, 1986.

Wood, Stephen C., and J. David Pincus, eds. *Reel Baseball: Essays and Interviews on the National Pastime, Hollywood, and American Culture*. Jefferson NC: McFarland, 2003.

World Urbanization Prospects: The 2007 Revision. New York: United Nations, Department of Economic and Social Affairs, Population Division, 2008.

Wright, Will H. *Six Guns and Society*. Berkeley: University of California Press, 1975.

Yuval-Davis, Nira. "Belongings: In between the Indigene and the Diasporic." In *Nationalism and Its Futures*, edited by Umut Özkirimli, 127–44. Basingstoke: Palgrave Macmillan, 2003.

Zucker, Harvey Marc, and Lawrence J. Babich. *Sports Films: A Complete Reference*. Jefferson NC: McFarland, 1987.

INDEX

American dream (*continued*)
95–96; *Rocky IV* depicting, 96–98,
102; *Rocky V* depicting, 103; *Rocky
Balboa* depicting, 106–10; *Rocky* series
depicting, 13, 20, 79–80, 112–14;
small-town settings for, 20–21, 115–16,
118, 124, 126, 128–30; sports films and,
190n50; urban settings for, 21, 118,
137–38, 144, 146; validity of, 184
American exceptionalism, 81
"And Did Those Feet in Ancient Time"
(Blake), 36, 192n25
Anderson, Benedict, 10, 11, 58, 59, 181
Anglican Church, 42, 192n22, 193n42
Anglo-Saxon heritage, 36–37, 43, 167,
193n42
anti-Semitism, 26, 27, 32–33
Ardolino, Frank, 99, 103, 110, 112
aristocracy, 44–45, 46, 47, 49
Ashby, Justine, 174, 176
Asians, British, 153, 167, 168, 170–71, 174, 176
audiences: contemporary, 29–30, 31;
emotional authenticity and, 15, 17–18,
68, 75, 184–85; familiarity level of,
27–28, 67; male, 165–66; post-German
reunification, 20, 77
authenticity, emotional. *See* emotional
authenticity

Babich, Lawrence J., 4, 187n2
Babington, Bruce, 5, 7, 18, 189n50
Baker, Aaron, 5, 18, 83, 136
Balboa, Adrian (fictional): character of,
110; death of, 104; health problems
of, 89–90, 92; marriage of, 91–92;
supporting Rocky Balboa, 84, 88–90,
92, 96, 97, 100; working outside
home, 102
Balboa, Rocky (fictional), *94, 101, 105*;
aging of, 106, 108–9; American dream
and, 79–80, 92–93, 95–96, 103, 106–7,

109–10, 112; Apollo Creed and, 89–90;
character of, 89, 90–91; Clubber
Lang and, 93, 95; as coach, 97; as
father, 102, 104, 110; illness of, 110–11;
marriage of, 91–92, 97; masculinity
and, 86–87, 88, 95–96, 103, 108–9;
publicity on, 191n14; race issues and,
92, 110–11; as self-made man, 84,
86–87, 99; technology and, 99–101; in
training, 86–87, 93, 95, 99–100; wife's
death and, 104
Bale, John, 119, 121, 199n6
banal nationalism, 10, 116–17
Barnes, John, 170
baseball, 129, 154–55, 157–58
Baseball Hall of Fame, 157–58
basketball, 123–24, 126, 129, 137, 188n46
Bavaria, Germany, 59, 178, 179–80
BBC, 169, 191n12
Beckham, David, 169
Bellew, Anthony, 188n33
Benavides, O. Hugo, 131–32
Bend It Like Beckham: Bollywood compared to, 168; continued popularity
of, 3; cultural conflict in, 167, 168–69,
170, 171–73; female athletes in, 169,
170–71; femininities in, 171, 174–75;
gender issues in, 21; inclusiveness in,
169–70, 185; lesbianism in, 175–76;
male validation in, 176–77; mothers
in, 173–74; national identity in,
153, 169–70; nationalism in, 11–12;
significance of, 181
Berlin Wall, 52, 68, 70
Bertier, Gerry (fictional), 131, 135
Bhamra, Jesminder "Jess" (fictional): in
conflict with heritage, 167, 168–69,
170, 171–72, 176; daydream of, 169–70;
as Other, 173, 177; as possible lesbian,
174–76; support for, 202n38
Bible, 32, 192n22, 192n25

Billig, Michael, 10, 12, 116–17
Bill of Rights, 104, 106–7
blacks: American dream and, 82, 111–12, 144; in biographical films, 111; as fathers, 200n46; percentage jailed, 200n45; in school integration, 131, 132–34, 135–36; stereotypes of, 88, 93, 95, 111; upwardly mobile, 85, 88, 92; in urban communities, 126, 137–38, 139, 144
Blair, Tony, and Blairite politics, 172–73, 185
Blake, William, 36, 192n25
The Blind Side, 11
Bollywood and Bollylite, 168
Boone, Herman (fictional), 131, 133, 134–35, 136–37
boxers, 13, 95, 108, 110, 188n33, 197n37
boxing commission, 106–7
boxing training, *94, 101*
Brass, Tom, 121–22, 127
Breitmeier, Florian, 57, 63, 64–65, 195n36
British Film Institute, 24
British Heritage Films, 19, 30
British Olympic Committee, 27, 33, 46
Brooks, Herb, 1–2
Brown vs. the Board of Education of Topeka (1954), 131
Bush, George W., 107, 110, 113
Butler, Judith, 42–43, 116–17

Cahn, Susan K., 151, 152–53
Caius College, 26, 33–34
Caldwell, Wilbur W., 82, 96, 129–30, 152–53
Cambridge University, 43–44. See also Caius College
Campbell, Julius (fictional), 131, 135–36
Capital in the Twenty-First Century (Piketty), 196n14
Carter, Ken, 138–39, 140, 141–44, 200n46
Catholicism, 179, 192n22, 193n42
Chacko, Mary Ann, 171

Chak De! India, 168, 202n37
Chare, Nicholas, 5, 18, 148
"Chariot of Fire" (phrase), 192n25
Chariots of Fire: accuracy in, 28; continued popularity of, 3, 23–24; criticism of, 45; emotional authenticity in, 25, 27–30, 49–50, 185, 191n9; English identity in, 43–46; as heritage film, 19, 25, 30; inaccuracies in, 25, 28, 191n9, 193n42; issues covered in, 27; Jewishness in, 191n9; movement-image in, 24, 35–37, 38, 40–41; muscular Christianity in, 194n54; musical score of, 23, 29, 31, 32, 43; mythmaking in, 30–35; narrative in, 27–28, 32–35, 37; national identity in, 24–26, 35–37, 38–40, 49–50; nationalism in, 11–12; Scottish identity in, 46–47; shared identities in, 42–49; time-image in, 24, 35–37, 38–39, 40–42; timeline of, 26, 29, 37, 41–42; visual style of, 30–32
Chariots of Fire (stage adaptation), 23–24
Christianity, 27, 32–33, 37, 42, 47, 193n42, 194n54
Cinema I: The Movement-Image (Deleuze), 37
Cinema II: The Time-Image (Deleuze), 37
civil rights movement, 84–85, 88
Civil War, 134–35
Clinton, Bill, 80, 113
Coach Carter, 145; academics in, 138–39, 142–44; on African American males, 200n45; authenticity in, 13; compared to *Hoosiers*, 140–41; sense of community in, 141, 146; sense of place in, 139–40, 145; small-town aspects of, 140–41; urban setting of, 21, 137; women in, 142
coaches, female, 190n60, 201n2
Cold War, 2, 53, 70, 97–98
collectivity, sense of, 42, 58, 61–62, 65

"Lebanese" mixed up with, 175; men and, 166; as Other, 149; potential, 157, 164, 169, 175–76; as threat, 148, 152–53

Liddell, Eric: background of, 26; falling in race, 47–48; Harold Abrahams and, 33–35, 46–48; legacy of, 24, 191n3; life of, 19, 27–28, 191n10; as mythic hero, 35, 49; religion and, 24, 26–27, 32–33, 46, 48; Scottish identity of, 33, 36, 46–47

Liebe im Ring, 13

Lieberman, Viridiana, 148

Life, 165

Lincoln, Abraham, 135

Lindner, Katharina, 148, 175, 202n40

Lindsay, Lord (fictional), 26–27, 28, 32, 41, 45–46, 47, 48, 49

Lineker, Gary, 169–70

Little Nikita, 98

London, England, 39–40, 167

"Lord Randall" (song), 200n35

Lowenstein, Ira (fictional), 151, 165, 166

Lubanski, Bruno (fictional), 55, 69, 71, 73–75, 74

Lubanski, Matthias (fictional), 52, 54–55, 59, 68, 69, 71, 76

Lubanski, Richard (fictional), 54, 55, 58–59, 69–73

Major League Baseball. *See* MLB (Major League Baseball)

male athletes, 21, 42, 108–9, 148–49, 151–52, 160, 181. *See also* homosexuals and homosexuality

Manchester United, 169, 170

Manhood in America (Kimmel), 83–84

manliness. *See* masculinity

man versus machine, 99–100

Marla (fictional), 161–62, 164–65

marriage, 158, 164, 166, 167

The Marriage of Maria Braun, 52, 53

Marshall, Penny, 147

Martin-Jones, David, 19, 24, 38–40, 42–43, 193n40

masculinity: aging and, 108–9; American dream and, 83–84, 103; in blacks, 88, 112; hypermasculinity as, 107–8; ideal, 150; of muscular body, 101; pioneer, 83, 98; primitive, 87; Puritanism and, 83; reclaimed, 162; remasculinization and, 83, 85–86, 96, 107–8; traditional, 85–86, 91–92, 111, 141, 148–49; versions of, 93, 95–96, 150; in whites, 126, 137; women and, 151–52, 160, 177–78

Match of the Day, 169–70, 176

materialism, 82–83, 88–89, 90–91, 103, 113

May, Claudia, 173–74

McFarland, USA, 11, 13, 20–21, 115

Mean Machine, 13

Memento, 38

memory, prosthetic. *See* prosthetic memory

meritocracy, 134, 154, 172–73, 183

Mickey (fictional), 89–90, 95, 102

The Mighty Macs, 13

Million Dollar Baby, 13

Miracle (film), 1–2

The Miracle of Bern, 60, 66, 74; accuracy in, 65, 67; characters in, 67–70, 71–75; continued popularity of, 3; criticism of, 61; East Germany and, 73–74; emotional authenticity in, 77, 185; as heritage film, 52–53, 58; inaccuracy in, 62–63; national identity in, 191n10; nationalism in, 11–12, 58–59; production of, 59–60; as prosthetic memory, 53, 56–57; purposes served by, 70–71; reunification and, 19–20, 53–54, 70–71, 183–84; significance of, 7, 52; storylines in, 54–55, 75

Miracle of Bern (event). *See* Wunder von Bern (event)

The Miracle of Bern (musical), 52

"Miracle on Ice," 1–2

MLB (Major League Baseball), 155
modernity, 21, 115, 122, 150
montages, 43, 61–62, 73–74, 93, 165
Montague, Aubrey (fictional), 26, 29–30, 41, 43
Mosse, George L., 22, 149–50, 152
mothers and motherhood, 142, 149, 166, 173–74
Motson, John, 169
movement-image: definition of, 37–38; disruption and, 19, 24, 44, 47; flashbacks and, 41–42; reterritorializing of, 46, 48, 49; time-image and, 37–40, 192n28
muscular Christianity, 27, 47, 194n54
muscularity, 151–52
"musculinity," 109, 151–52
Mussabini, Sam (fictional), 26, 32, 46–47, 47–48
mythology: of agrarian communities, 115–16, 121–22; of American dream, 80, 82–83, 89, 98, 112–13, 190n50; baseball and, 154–55; British national identity and, 19, 24, 25–26, 27, 35, 50; gender issues and, 148, 180; German national identity and, 19–20, 51, 53–54, 55–56, 60–61, 63, 64, 75, 76–77; narrative creating, 32–35; nostalgic past and, 126–27, 129–30; reconfiguration making, 53; sports films and, 2–3, 9; visual style creating, 30–32

narrative: American dream and, 130; disruption in, 37–39, 41–42; muscularity and, 152; myth and, 32–35, 63–64; national identity and, 40, 48; place and, 120, 129, 137; of sports, 8, 16
narrative arcs, 8, 16, 89, 93, 122, 135
nation (concept): changing ideals of, 11–12; definition of, 58; everyday life and, 72; gender and, 21–22, 149–50,

186; globalization and, 8, 178; sexuality and, 149–50, 178; sports and, 1; sports films and, 2–3, 9–10, 12, 18–19, 185–86
national anthem, banned, 62
national identity: in agrarian settings, 121, 127; American, 1, 83–84, 89, 97, 106–7, 113, 114, 135; baseball and, 155; basketball and, 116; British, competing, 37; British, constructed, 24; British, contemporary, 26, 27, 36, 42, 185; British, historical, 35, 42; British, inclusive, 169, 176–77; British, Margaret Thatcher influencing, 25, 44–45, 47; British, unified, 24, 34, 48–50; constructed, 11, 12, 24, 37, 116–17; emotional authenticity and, 15–18; English, 45, 48, 169; essentialist, 36–37; ethnicity issues in, 153, 169; football and, 116; gender issues in, 148–49, 153, 155, 159, 169, 175–76, 178, 180; German, 51–52, 58, 61, 64, 77; intercultural context for, 172; movement-image and, 37–40; physical boundaries and, 117; Scottish, 46, 48; small town-ness and, 116; sports films and, 2–4, 9–12, 18–19, 183, 184, 185, 186; time-image and, 37–40
nationalism, 8–9, 10, 36, 57, 116–17, 149–50, 183. *See also* national identity
Nationalism and Sexuality (Mosse), 149–50
Nationalisms and Sexualities (Parker et al.), 149
National Socialism. *See* Nazism
nation-states, 9, 10, 11, 58–59, 81, 117, 150
Nazism, 58–59, 62, 63, 71–73, 150
NCAA championship game (1966), 14
neoconservatism, 84–85, 110, 113
Newspaper Proprietors' Association, 191n12
Newsweek, 191n14
New York Times, 1

normativity, 148, 153, 158, 163, 174, 178, 185

nostalgia: for American golden age, 116, 118, 119, 120; aristocracy and, 46; in heritage films, 25, 45; for imagined past, 125–27; individualism and, 114; masculinity and, 84; purpose of, 32, 56, 62, 70; small-town culture and, 128–30, 132; uncritical nature of, 58, 62

Olympia, 63

Olympic Games, 1, 23–24, 26–27, 48, 191n3, 192n25

ordinary people, 54, 58, 64–65, 67–68, 71, 75–77

Ostalgie (nostalgia for East Germany), 70, 74

Other: as abnormality, 157, 162, 167; attitudes toward, 181; ethnicity and, 168–69; homosexuals as, 148–49, 150, 169, 178; lesbians as, 148–49, 169; male hegemony challenged by, 151; as non-threat, 176–77; place and, 119; as positive agents of change, 185–86; possibilities for, 179–80; United States as, 48–49; women as, 148, 150, 153, 155. *See also* hero Others

Palmer, William J., 97–98

parallel universes, 38–39, 40

Parry, Hubert, 192n25

pastoralism, 98–100, 102, 115–16, 133

Pat and Mike, 180–81

Paulie (fictional), 87, 100, 104

Paxton, Juliette "Jules" (fictional), 167, 170–71, 172–73, 174–75

Paxton, Mrs. (fictional), 170–71, 173–75

Peasants, Population, and Postmodernism (Brass), 121–22

performativity, 42–43, 44, 46, 48, 116–17

Perinbanayagam, Robert, 8, 9, 16

Personal Best, 153, 166, 177–78, 180–81

Philadelphia Boxing Commission, 106–7

Philadelphia Museum of Art, 3, 79

Photographic Journal, 4

Piketty, Thomas, 196n14

place, sense of, 115, 119–21, 128, 130, 136–37, 139–40, 146, 185

prisoners of war, returning, 57

professionalization, 26–27, 45, 46

prosthetic memory: emotional authenticity and, 19–20, 67–68, 77; *The Miracle of Bern* as, 53; ordinary people and, 68, 75; small-town sports films and, 130; theory of, 55–56, 127

Prosthetic Memory (Landsberg), 55–56

Pumping Iron, 152

Puritans and Puritanism: in American dream, 81, 98–99, 119, 124, 129, 199n18; masculinity and, 83, 86, 96; work ethic of, 81, 83, 96, 114

Pyta, Wolfram, 57, 63–64

QueerStrokes (rowing team), 179

race issues: after 9/11, 107–8; American dream and, 82, 111–12; anti-Semitism in, 26, 33; and in celebration of whiteness, 123, 129; civil rights movement and, 88; portrayal of blacks, 125–26; in *Rocky* series, 92; in sports films, 21; stereotypes in, 93, 95; in team integration, 130–31, 132–33, 135–36

Racine Belles, 157

radio, 51–52, 61, 62, 64–65, 74, 160, 163, 191n12, 194n2

rags-to-riches concept, 95, 103, 106, 113

Rahn, Helmut (fictional), 55, 61, *66*, 76–77

Reagan, Ronald, 97–98, 99, 100, 103, 107, 110, 113, 126

realism, 13–14, 29–30, 31–32, 76, 129

Red Dawn, 98

34–35, 61; in urban settings, 137–39; with women coaches, 201n2

Sports Films (Babich and Zucker), 4, 187n2

Stallard, Henry (fictional), 26

Stallone, Sylvester, 79–80, 97, 99, 107, 111, 198n64

success, 33, 46, 81–84, 87, 89, 143–44, *145*

Summer Storm, 153, 178–80, 181

The Sunday I Became World Champion (Delius), 52

symbols, 44–45, 58, 63–64, 72, 87, 95, 128, 135, 147, 153

Tasker, Yvonne, 108–9, 151–52

Taxi Driver, 197n42

technology, 100–102

television, 17, 28, 61–62, 65, 67, 74, 181, 191n14, 195n36

Texas, 120–21

Thatcher, Margaret, and Thatcherism, 19, 24, 25, 44–45, 46, 47, 49–50

time, labyrinthine, 37, 38, 40, 44

time-image: definition of, 37; deterritorializing by, 42, 47, 49; disruption and, 19, 24, 50; movement-image and, 38–40, 192n28; subtypes of, 192n28

Times (London), 191n3

Titans (football team), 133

Tocqueville, Alexis de, 82, 83

Top Gun, 98

topophilia, 119–21, 140

topophobia, 119

Trump, Donald, 8–9

truth, 9, 29, 184–85

Tudor, Deborah V., 5, 18, 148, 200n30

Union Jack, 24, 30, 32, 34

unity: British, 24, 35, 38, 50; German, 20, 53, 56, 70–71; inner, 20, 70, 71; small-town,

125, 127, 133, 137; sports films and, 2–3, 11–12, 19–20, 183; team, 131

urban settings, 21, 115–16, 118, 126, 133, 137–38, 142, 144, 184

Vangelis, 23, 29, 31, 32

Varsity Blues, 116, 117, 120–21, 129

verisimilitude, 17–18, 27, 31, 49

Vietnam War soldiers, 197n42

Wallenfeldt, Jeffrey H., 5, 7–8

"We are somebody again," 7, 62, 195n26

weddings, 170, 175

Welland, Colin, 24, 29

Westalgie (nostalgia for West Germany), 70

West Germany: East Germany and, 57, 70, 73–75; postwar, 51–52, 57, 58, 63; prosthetic memory and, 56, 75; reunification and, 54, 70, 77; socioeconomic contrast within, 59, 69; World Cup and, 51–52, 56–57, 60–64, 76–77

Whip It, 185–86

White Nights, 98

whites: American dream and, 82, 129, 144; as athletic stereotype, 18, 21, 149, 185; globalization and, 9; masculinity and, 85–86, 107–8, 137, 141; in rural communities, 123, 125, 126, 137, 141, 144; in school integration, 131, 132–34, 135–36; upwardly mobile blacks and, 84–85, 88, 92

winning (concept), 89, 128

Wir sind wieder wer, 7, 62, 195n26

women: agency of, 155, 164–67; as athletes, 147; attitudes toward, 31, 110, 140, 157–58; backlash to feminism and, 91–92; as coaches, 190n60, 201n2; postwar, 156; sexuality of, 149; traditional role of, 109, 125, 147–48, 171–72, 173–74; during war, 68, 159–61. *See also* female athletes

To order or obtain more information on these or other
University of Nebraska Press titles, visit nebraskapress.unl.edu.

www.ingramcontent.com/pod-product-compliance
Lightning Source LLC
Chambersburg PA
CBHW021542260326
41914CB00001B/133